JAPANESE

GARDENS

DEC 21

SECRET TEACHINGS

IN THE ART OF

JAPANESE GARDENS

*You must never
show this writing
to outsiders.
You must
keep it secret.*

*Kono sho yumeyume soto miseru bekarazu.
Kore hisu beshi.*
—concluding line of the *Illustrations*

SECRET TEACHINGS

IN THE ART OF

JAPANESE
GARDENS

DESIGN PRINCIPLES

AESTHETIC VALUES

DAVID A. SLAWSON

Kodansha International
Tokyo • New York • London

Book design by Steve Renick.

Composition by Harrington-Young, Albany, California.

Distributed in the United States by Kodansha America, Inc., 114 Fifth Avenue, New York, N.Y. 10011, and in the United Kingdom and continental Europe by Kodansha Europe, Ltd., 95 Aldwych, London WC2B 4JF. Published by Kodansha International Ltd., 17-14 Otowa 1-chome, Bunkyo-ku, Tokyo 112, and Kodansha America, Inc.

Copyright © 1987 by Kodansha International Ltd. All rights reserved.
First edition, 1987. Printed in the United States of America.
First paperback edition, 1991. Printed in Japan.
 95 96 97 98 5 4

Library of Congress Cataloging-in-Publication Data

Slawson, David A., 1941–
  Secret teachings in the art of Japanese gardens.
  Bibliography: p.
  Includes index.
  Contents: The art of Japaanese gardens—Translation: Il-lustrations for designing mountain, water, and hillside field landscapes/by Zōen.
  1. Gardens, Japanese. I. Myer, Mary Eugenia. II. Zōen. Senzui narabini yagyō no zu. English. 1987. III. Title.
SB458.S66   1987   712'.0952   86-45723
ISBN 4-7700-1541-0

To my parents,
and to the woods of my childhood
                    beyond our house

All black-and-white photographs by Mary Eugenia Myer
except plates 1 and 27, by Kiichi Asano; plates 3, 4, 8, and
21, by the author; plate 5, courtesy Ritsurin Park; plate 12,
by Manshichi Sakamoto; plate 15, courtesy Shibundo; plate
29; plate 31, by Hiromichi Inoue.

Line drawings by Donald Dean based on author's sketches.

The poem "Dimly, dimly . . ." is reprinted from *Japanese
Court Poetry* by Robert H. Brower and Earl Miner, with the
permission of the publishers, Stanford University Press.
© 1961 by the Board of Trustees of the Leland Stanford
Junior University.

CONTENTS

ACKNOWLEDGMENTS

This book first appeared as my doctoral dissertation, and has been newly revised and expanded to better serve not only those with a special interest in landscape design or the Japanese arts, but potentially anyone—from photographer to philosopher—who is fascinated by an art that seeks to capture our deepest experiences of nature. Many people have contributed to its realization. My thanks go all the way back to 1969 when, as a graduate student in East Asian philosophy at the University of Hawaii's East-West Center, I had the good fortune of studying under Professor Chang Chung-yuan. Professor Chang instilled in me a deep appreciation for the aesthetic values nurtured by Chinese Ch'an Buddhism and Taoism. This was to prove an invaluable resource during my succeeding Japanese garden internship. It was under Professor Kinsaku Nakane, in Kyoto, that I began my practical training in the art of Japanese garden design. To Professor Nakane I owe a special debt of gratitude, not only for his kind and generous guidance during my apprenticeship in 1971–72, but also for the time and expertise he gave so willingly during my Fulbright year in Kyoto in 1980–81. Professor Kenneth Yasuda honored me by sharing his insights and guiding my study of Japanese garden aesthetics at Indiana University. As a mentor and the chairman of my dissertation committee, Professor Yasuda constantly challenged and encouraged me to strive for a deeper understanding of the art of Japanese gardens. To Professor George Elison, who gave generously of his enormous critical skills in matters of rhetoric and historical documentation, I would also like to extend my gratitude. Three other members of my dissertation committee, Professors Judith Berling, Yoshio Iwamoto, and Susan Nelson, contributed many useful suggestions.

A number of individuals and institutions gave me invaluable assistance during my research. I am indebted to Makoto Nakamura, chairman of the Department of

Landscape Architecture at Kyoto University, for permission to use the resources of the Library of the Faculty of Agriculture. Thanks are also due to the Garden Research section of the Nara National Research Institute of Cultural Properties for allowing me to use their facilities in 1979 and 1981, and for the assistance that members of the research staff so generously provided. I would also like to express my appreciation to Yasushi Egami of the Tokyo National Research Institute of Cultural Properties for devoting two hours of his afternoon one day to sharing his insights on the fifteenth-century garden manual, *Senzui narabi ni yagyō no zu*, and for giving me copies of the five issues of *Bijutsu kenkyū* in which his research on that manual originally appeared. For material support, I am indebted to the Fulbright Commission, whose grant made it possible for me to spend an uninterrupted year studying garden design in Japan.

Many others have made valuable contributions. I owe a large measure of gratitude to Janice Morgan, who has been a devoted listener and critic throughout this project. My thanks also go to Julie Moir Messervy, for the many hours she spent with me discussing Japanese garden aesthetics in Kyoto coffee houses during the winter of 1980–81, and for her continuing support. It would be remiss of me to leave out the Runcible Spoon coffee house in Bloomington, Indiana, which never failed to provide the nourishment of its cozy atmosphere and fresh-roasted coffee. I am indebted to Al Scaccia of Cleveland, whose keen sense of the expressive possibilities of local materials and uncanny knack for improvising ways to move them into the desired position confirm my belief in the universal applicability of sound design principles. Mary Eugenia Myer very generously gave of her time during her travels in Japan to take some of the photographs in this book. Yoko Takaya of Kodansha International was instrumental in coordinating details in Japan. Thanks also to my editor, Peter Goodman, who first saw the potential of this study and then persistently challenged me to amplify and more fully articulate its basic assumptions.

One of the most important lessons I learned in the course of my apprenticeship in the art of Japanese gardens took place during year-end cleaning of the Yabunouchi tea garden in Kyoto. I had been squatting for some time with both feet flat on the ground in Japanese fashion, sweeping between the aspidistra (*haran*) with the customary bamboo whisk broom. It was an awkward position—I had to be constantly on guard so as not to plant one of my feet on a *haran* clump—and I was tired. To relieve the tension (so I thought), I shifted my weight forward onto the ball of my left foot, leaving my right foot flat on the ground with little weight on it. To my surprise, the crew chief immediately and sharply reprimanded me. Then he told me what I had done wrong. His explanation took the form of a parable. Imagine, he said, that the master of this garden were a blind person. Close to the garden every day, he would constantly breathe its air and become sensitive to its every mood. The uneven distribution of my weight in cleaning the garden would produce a disturbance in the atmosphere of the garden, an uneasiness that the blind master would sense. Hence even in the simplest act of garden maintenance I must conduct myself in the spirit of harmony the garden is intended to convey.

This story-lesson was indelibly impressed upon my mind, and I have never ceased to appreciate the crew chief's kindness in telling it to me. The lesson that the spirit with which one performs any task, no matter how "menial," is more important than getting it done cannot be ignored by any serious student of the art of Japanese gardens. The essence of that spirit is to be "centered." My body position indicated I was not. Perhaps in the early years of the crew chief's own apprenticeship his superior had kindly communicated the same message to him. In any event, I had been initiated into one of the traditional secrets of the art through the time-honored technique of oral transmission.

The beauty of classical Japanese gardens and the perhaps naive belief that I could uncover the secrets of their design have led me to seek both the skills required to create such gardens myself and an understanding of their underlying principles. The degree to which these two things are interdependent cannot be overstated.

This is a lesson I learned from my apprenticeship in Kyoto under Kinsaku Nakane in 1971–72. Professor Nakane is well known in Japan as a restorer of classical Japanese gardens and as a creator of new gardens in the classical tradition.[1] My time as an apprentice with him was one of the most arduous and exacting of my life. I would usually awaken at six o'clock, travel to the job site, work hard all day while trying to understand explanations in colloquial Japanese, and often (when the site was out of town) not return until eight or nine at night. I learned as I performed a variety of tasks—everything from the demanding physical labor of fastening the cable and tamping the earth for rocks being set to planting delicate ferns and laying moss; from charring fenceposts to tying decorative knots with the black-dyed rope (*shuronawa*) used in fencemaking; from pinching back new pine candles to smoothing the gravel with a wooden rake as part of regular garden maintenance.

Garden design, however, was entirely the province of the *sensei*. I often wanted to ask Nakane why he did things as he did on the job site. But there was no time, for my teacher was completely focused on the job at hand. Just like a calligrapher or brush-and-ink painter, he worked quickly, spontaneously, and with complete confidence. When Nakane held informal teaching sessions with students from abroad, I would often act as interpreter and sometimes I could use this as an opportunity to ask my own questions. Some of Nakane's answers I understood. Some I did not. But by the time I left to return to America to begin making my own gardens, I felt I knew enough to begin drawing on some of the many good solutions to design problems I had internalized during my study.

I soon realized, however, that I wanted a firmer grasp of the basic principles that informed Japanese garden design. And so in 1975 I returned to the university to pursue doctoral studies in Japanese aesthetics. This book is the result of the questions I have asked my teachers and myself while seeking a deeper understanding of the art.

What makes a Japanese garden a Japanese garden? What criteria does one apply in judging the quality of a Japanese garden?

The answer to the first question may appear simple: Why, of course, any garden made in Japan in the native tradition. But when and where does one begin? Is the essential feature to look for an island fashioned in a manmade pond—an innovation by the powerful court dignitary Soga no Umako in about A.D. 620? Or is it a landscape in which water is intentionally absent, its presence suggested instead through the artful use of rocks, plants, and raked gravel, as in the "dry landscape" garden of the Zen Buddhist temple Daisen'in, created in 1513? Or perhaps the essential features are the familiar stepping-stone path, the stone lanterns and basins, and the rustic hut of the tea garden, which flourished in the sixteenth and seventeenth centuries in response to the ideals of the tea ceremony. Or again, perhaps they are found in the "stroll garden" type, with its winding path leading the viewer to an ever-changing sequence of scenic effects, an example of this being the garden of the Katsura villa in Kyoto, built in the seventeenth century.

From our vantage point, the historical development of the Japanese art of garden making presents an overwhelming complexity of garden types. It is all too easy to forget that each of these types was at first an innovation—a creative response to changing needs, tastes, economic conditions, and social values within Japanese culture. Copying imported styles rather than responding to native locales and materials may explain why so many Japanese gardens made in the United States have an almost museum-piece quality. There is a catchy allure in the familiar exotic of imported stone lanterns and pagodas, arched half-moon bridges, and torii gates. In fact, the finest traditional gardens in Japan rarely exhibit the stereotypical trademarks Westerners often associate with Japanese-style gardens.

Gardens that rely too heavily on such motifs for their charm begin to take on a Disneyland quality. The theme-park approach is fine as far as it goes, with its prettied-up storybook conventions and clean, well-tended look. But a Japanese garden is after something else. If we can understand what that something is, we will see the connection between the various garden types that have developed in Japan since the early seventh century; and we will know in our imagination that new types may yet be created in response to changing conditions and the values of our own culture.

Josiah Conder, writing twenty-five years after Japan opened its doors to the West in the Meiji Restoration of 1868, was one of the first to tell Westerners that the aesthetics of Japanese gardens might have application beyond the shores of Japan.[2]

> Robbed of its local garb and mannerisms, the Japanese method reveals aesthetic principles applicable to the gardens of any country, teaching, as it does, how to convert into a poem or picture a composition, which, with all its variety of detail, otherwise lacks unity and intent.

Following in Conder's footsteps was another Westerner, Samuel Newsom. While praising Conder's book, *Landscape Gardening in Japan*, as being among the best written in English on Japanese gardens, Newsom sought to remedy what he saw as its failure to "connect the theoretical and practical aspects." In the preface to his own 1939 book, *Japanese Garden Construction*, Newsom goes on to say:[3]

> It is hoped that anyone, by means of this guide, will be able to design a scene with something of the feeling of far mountains and distant lakes, in a comparatively limited area. It should be especially useful to those interested in Rock Gardens, as the laws of Japanese stonework are international in application.

What emerges from the words of these two Westerners is a picture of the Japanese garden as a landscape art raised to the level of painting or poetry. As with painting, the feeling of far mountains and distant lakes may be conveyed in a limited area. Undoubtedly it is this aesthetic exploitation of a small space that so fascinates Americans accustomed to the wasteful land practices of suburban sprawl. And from this fascination comes the common misconception that Japanese gardens are characteristically made on tiny plots of land. In fact, one can find scenic effects of great beauty in Japanese gardens designed on sites ranging in size from that of a small room or corridor up to ten or thirty acres. The only restrictions on size come from the particular site, the budget, and the limitations of the human senses.

Nor are mountains and distant lakes necessarily preferred over other types of scenery. That motif may at times have held a special charm for Japanese who could afford to build gardens, but so did the scenery of marsh, meadow, and hillside fields. If it is true, as a fifteenth-century Japanese garden manual says, that "the landscape garden mirrors nature," then landscape designers are indeed blessed with an infinitely varied palette of scenic effects from which to choose.

The central message at the heart of Japanese garden aesthetics is that the designer should not copy existing gardens, but rather that a garden should reflect selected qualities of the natural environment so as to nurture the hopes and needs of the client. And since it is true that the landscape in America (from Northeastern to Southwestern, from mountain to prairie) differs in type and tone from that in Japan, it follows that landscape gardens created here will draw upon the unique qualities of native scenery and materials. In so doing they will differ subtly but substantially from gardens in Japan. When Americans begin studying the art of Japanese classical gardens the way they have studied European classical music, America will begin producing its own George Gershwins and Aaron Coplands in landscape design, and a powerful new American idiom growing out of the land and the people will be born, just as the Japanese converted what they learned from Chinese gardens into an art reflecting their own land and culture.

Unfortunately, the Conder-Newsom approach has not occupied so much as a tributary, much less the main current, in the stream of books on Japanese gardens in English published during the four decades since World War II. This mainstream approach may be characterized as follows: Japanese gardens are classified according to historical periods or generic types, not unlike the way an archaeologist views the remains of cultures of the past. These types include the ones we have already mentioned: the pond-and-island garden, the dry landscape garden, the tea garden, the stroll garden. The result is that these gardens are "quaintified," divorced from the human purpose and values that brought them into existence and that still link them to the important issues of our own time. Such quaintification may serve the purpose of keeping the art of Japanese gardens a "purely Japanese" phenomenon to be held up to the world as a mark of Japanese uniqueness or as something exotic. But this narrow view does a disservice to the art of Japanese gardens and to the capabilities of the Japanese people, for, to the extent that the art of Japanese gardens entertains universal and therefore cross-cultural principles, it is an art of which the Japanese can justly be proud.

The central argument of this book is that these principles of Japanese garden design can indeed be shared with the West. My approach differs from the usual treatment of Japanese gardens in that its organization is not based on a cataloging of selected Japanese gardens, or the various types of Japanese gardens, or the historical periods in which those types first appeared. Such studies of the Japanese garden are readily available in both Japanese and English. Instead, the organization used here is based on the aesthetic principles governing the art.

These principles have been grouped according to natural categories of human perception. Chapter 1 of part 1 is called "Transmission of the Art" and discusses how the art of Japanese gardens has been handed down through the ages. Chapters 2, 3, and 4 form a group called "The Art We See" and embark upon an investigation into the aesthetic principles that underlie classical Japanese garden design. The subjects of these chapters—"scenic effects," "sensory effects," and "cultural values"—denote three basic areas of human experience within which the diverse aspects of garden design kept recurring in my study. Reflecting as they do the natural world that is our home, the senses through which we perceive that world, and the human values by which we establish our personal relationship to that world, it is no wonder that a deep awareness of these three areas is essential to the creative process of garden design. The chapter on sensory effects is much longer than the other chapters because I believe that this area, which has constantly been neglected in the study of Japanese gardens, is in fact central to our understanding of the art.

Important to any study of Japanese garden aesthetics are the two oldest extant Japanese garden manuals: Tachibana no Toshitsuna's eleventh-century manuscript, *Sakuteiki*, or *Notes on Garden Making*, and a fifteenth-century manuscript first compiled by the priest Zōen, *Senzui narabi ni yagyō no zu*, or *Illustrations for Designing Mountain, Water, and Hillside Field Landscapes* (hereafter called simply the *Illustrations*). These so-called secret texts confirm many of the aesthetic principles that are traditionally employed in Japanese garden design, and references to them occur frequently in the pages that follow.

The principles in both *Sakuteiki* and the *Illustrations* were intended for gardens viewed from a fixed or slowly changing vantage point along the buildings that faced the garden. Tea and stroll gardens, which readers are perhaps more familiar with (and which may be of more immediate interest to modern landscape designers), are a later development in the art and—because observers physically penetrate their spaces—are logistically more complex. These newer garden types, however, were created by extending and reinterpreting the principles used in fixed vantage point gardens. This is a similar adjustment to the one landscape architects had to make when they began designing the landscaped strips along superhighways, where the vantage point is that of an automobile traveling at speeds of fifty-five miles per hour or more. New variables may complicate the design process, but the same basic principles of perception still apply. To understand these principles, it is best to go back to the earlier and less complex model provided by gardens viewed from a fixed or slowly changing vantage point—the type of design, in short, that the two earliest manuals were devoted to.

Of the two, *Sakuteiki* has been given far more attention than the *Illustrations* in English-language books on Japanese gardens. An English translation of *Sakuteiki*, by Shigemaru Shimoyama, was first published as a book in 1976, albeit in a limited edition that is not readily available.[4] The other text, which is at least as important, has until now only been available in Japanese. To restore the balance, I have included my translation of the *Illustrations* as part 2 of this book.

The two oldest Japanese garden manuals complement one another far more than they overlap. In *Sakuteiki,* for example, there is an important section on making various types of waterfalls that does not occur in the *Illustrations*. The *Illustrations* boasts an extensive vocabulary of named rocks and plants that are nowhere mentioned in *Sakuteiki*. The *Illustrations* is also unique in that it has sections dealing with such practical matters as the proper pruning and transplanting of trees, not to mention the concoction of a curious growth retardant! It is my hope that the translation of the *Illustrations* will stimulate further studies of Japanese garden aesthetics and provide a new source of ideas for designers.

In the course of my discussion I sometimes refer to existing gardens in Japan as examples of particular points. These gardens are drawn from the corpus of classical gardens preserved from past ages, mostly in Kyoto, and include some twentieth-century gardens designed in the classical tradition. By the corpus of "classical" Japanese gardens I mean simply those that Japanese garden specialists refer to repeatedly as the finest works of Japanese garden art—the *meien*, or "renowned gardens"—each of which incorporates in its design creative applications of the abiding principles of the art. Descriptions of *meien* mentioned in the text appear in appendix 1.

Appendixes 2, 3, and 4 provide additional information that may be of use to modern-day garden designers seeking to improve their understanding of Japanese landscape garden techniques. Appendixes 2 and 3 are tabular analyses of rocks and plants mentioned in the *Illustrations*—they leave no doubt about the extent to which the aesthetic of using rocks and plants in the Japanese landscape garden is rooted in the observation of nature's geological features and habitats. Appendix 4 is an informal discussion, based on my own experience, of some practical techniques for interiorizing insights into the qualities—scenic, sensory, and cultural—of nature and art so that they may find expression in the garden: only by absorbing many forms of knowledge and experience can a designer imbue the garden space with the beauty of landscape so that it speaks to the viewer's innermost heart.

PLATES

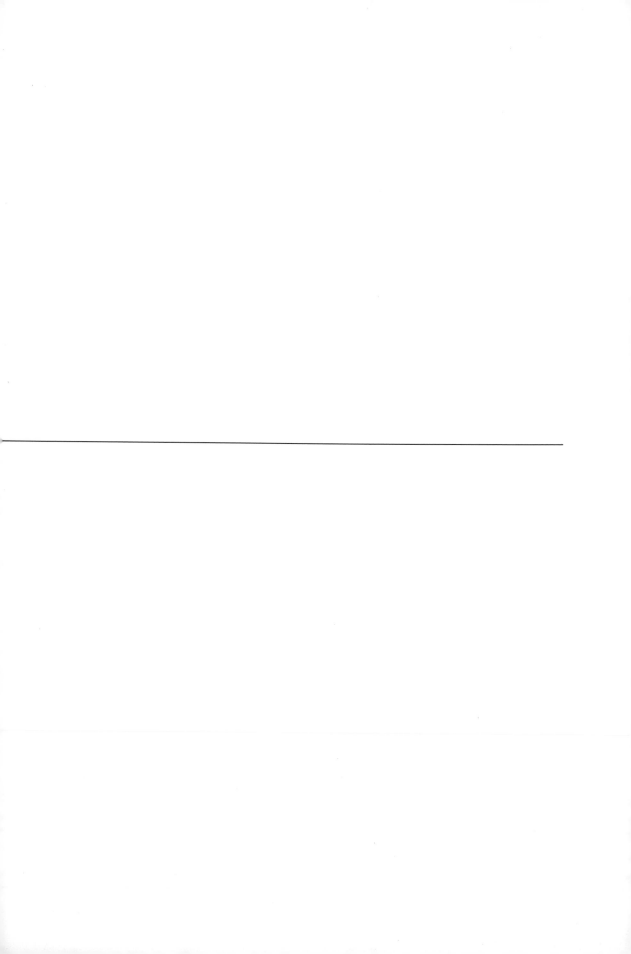

1.   The baymouth sandbar Amanohashidate near Tango Peninsula on the Japan Sea.

2.   Island re-creating the scenery of Amanohashidate in the garden of the Katsura
      imperial villa, Kyoto.

3.   Pines growing on the craggy coast of the Japan Sea at Takasu.

4.   Gardener pruning a Japanese black pine transplanted from the mountains to a dry landscape garden at the Adachi Art Museum, Yonago.

5.   Composition of rocks simulating an ocean beach on the shore of the pond, viewed from the pavilion Kikugetsu-tei at Ritsurin Park, Takamatsu.

6.   Rocks placed to create the effect of a winding stream in the Heian-style garden at Rakusuien, Jōnangū, southern Kyoto.

7.   *Haboku Landscape*
by Bokusai (?–1492).
Shinjuan, Daitokuji, Kyoto.

8.   Photographic sequence of waterfall composition in the northeast corner of the dry landscape garden at Daisen'in, Daitokuji, Kyoto.

9.   Pine islet near the north wall, Daisen'in.

10.   Rocks at the south end of the crane island, Daisen'in.

11.   Rock shaped like a cargo junk, Daisen'in.

12. Dry waterfall composition in the rear corner counterbalanced by the rock island in the foreground across a gravel "sea" at Daitokuji Honbō, Kyoto.

13. *Portrait of Musō Soseki* by Mutō Shūi. Ca. 1350. Myōchi'in, Kyoto.

14. Peninsula jutting from the right across the pond at Tenryūji, Kyoto.

15.   Sculptural rock composition in the Tsuki no Katsura dry landscape at the
        Katsura residence, Hōfu.

16.   The leftmost group of five rocks in the dry landscape garden at Ryōanji, Kyoto.

17.   Rock triad west of the abbot's
quarters at Kōrin'in, Daitokuji,
Kyoto. Composition by Kinsaku
Nakane.

18.   Rock triad located beyond Momoyama (sixteenth century) style garden designed by
Kinsaku Nakane at Rakusuien, Jōnangū.

19.   Arrow effect at Ryōanji produced by rock groups 3, 4, and 5 pointing back at group 2.

20.   Turtle island in Tiger Gorge Garden at Nishi Honganji, Kyoto.

21.   Photographic sequence of Tiger Gorge Garden.

22.　*Landscape* by Sesshū. Ōhara Collection, Kyoto.

23.　The cascade and pond as seen from the principal viewing position of the lower garden at Taizōin, Myōshinji, Kyoto.

24. Stepping-stone path leading to the *nobedan* (formal stone-paved walk), viewed from the shelter opposite Sago Palm Hill in the garden of the Katsura villa.

25. View from the north end of the pond at Tenryūji, with the Reclining Moon Rock in the foreground and the mountain Arashiyama in the distance.

26.   A large foreground rock sets off the view of the pond from the veranda of the teahouse at Isuien, Nara.

27.   The water basin Furisode (Hanging Sleeves) set next to the veranda overlooking the pond garden at Jōjuin, Kiyomizudera, Kyoto.

28. Crouching Tiger Rock composition with striped bamboo grass, in the northeast corner of the pond garden at Tenryūji.

29. Dry landscape west of the Bōsen tearoom at Kohōan, Daitokuji.

30. Rock of the Spirit Kings on P'eng-lai island in the Ninomaru garden of Nijō Castle, Kyoto.

31. Example of the Boat-concealing Rocks at Tenryūji, viewed from the southwest corner of the pond.

SECRET TEACHINGS

IN THE ART OF

JAPANESE
GARDENS

ONE

THE ART OF

JAPANESE GARDENS

TRANSMISSION

OF THE ART

1

Go to the pine if you want to learn about the pine, or to the bamboo if you want to learn about the bamboo. And in doing so, you must leave your subjective preoccupation with yourself. Otherwise you impose yourself on the object and do not learn.

—Matsuo Bashō

How is the classical art of Japanese gardens learned? The answer to this question is important, not only for what it tells us about the art, but also for what it reveals about an approach to learning that has almost totally disappeared in the West. This learning process has five different stages or aspects, and setting them forth right at the beginning will give us a clear picture of the direction we are headed:

1. Viewing the works of past masters

2. Learning from nature

3. Apprenticeship

4. Oral transmission

5. Secret texts

The list above might give the impression that the designer has very little latitude for creativity or self-expression in the traditional design process. But this is far from the truth. The traditional methods of learning the art were intended, above all, to assure that the student gained the tools and sensitivity needed to create highly satisfying solutions for the gardens he was charged to design. When Michelangelo was asked by the Church to do the fresco on the Sistine Chapel ceiling, he sought with fervor to express the spiritual qualities of his subject in forms humans would understand. We know he drew upon the methods of past masters, just as he studied human anatomy and so learned from nature. His greatness as an artist, we might say, results from the way he reached deep down inside himself to create something beyond himself, something powerful for all people to experience.

Japanese garden design aims at the same thing. The traditional learning methods seek to develop in the designer a sensitivity to the qualities of materials, to the potentialities of the garden site, and to the needs of the client. To bring these three into a mutually productive relationship requires the utmost creativity and expressiveness.

Viewing the Works of Past Masters

All the texts written about traditional Japanese garden aesthetics, including the invaluable secret texts, do not contain as much information on the subject as the gardens that have been preserved in Japan over the last six centuries. Each of these gardens represents a particular design solution to a distinct set of constraints involving the owner-client and his reasons for having the garden, the site (including the surrounding environment), and the materials available. Some gardens occupy only a small courtyard; others cover a whole hillside. They may be filled with rocks and plantings, or be almost empty of them. Certain common design principles have been used in their construction, but how or why they work as they do can never be fully conveyed in words, just as one would never confuse a painting with an observer's description of it. The Japanese have long believed that going to gardens and quietly observing them—letting their special qualities sink in—is one of the most effective ways of learning the art. Indeed, the second of the three general guidelines at the beginning of the eleventh-century garden manual *Sakuteiki* reminds the designer to "study the examples of works left by the past masters."[1]

When I began my apprenticeship under Kinsaku Nakane in 1971, the first assignment I was given was to view thirty or so of the finest gardens in and around Kyoto. To my question, "Is there anything special I should keep in mind as I view them?" he replied, "No, just view them *bon'yari shite*"—in other words "with a detached gaze," without preconceptions, in a state of total receptivity (fig. 1).

This manner of looking is not unknown to artists working in other visual media. The filmmaker Akira Kurosawa, for example, explains that the director shooting a scene "has to catch even the minutest detail. But this does not mean glaring concentratedly at the set. . . . Watching something does not mean fixing your gaze on it, but being aware of it in a natural way. I believe this is what the medieval Noh playwright and theorist Zeami meant by 'watching with a detached gaze.'"[2]

Viewing the works of past landscape garden masters is the most natural and effective stage at which to begin studying the art of Japanese gardens. And like the other stages, it is never left behind but is continued as part of a lifelong learning process.

Fig. 1.   Author's study of the waterfall rock composition at the garden of Kinkakuji, Kyoto. The arrows indicate force vectors. The center rock at bottom is a powerful sensory form representing, in the wriggling movement of a leaping carp, the struggle for spiritual attainment.

Learning from Nature

Japanese landscape garden design is an art that, like landscape painting, is rooted in the beauty of natural scenery. The third general guideline given at the beginning of *Sakuteiki* pays homage to these roots when it says, "Think over the famous places of scenic beauty throughout the land."[3] But the message that is transmitted orally to apprentice garden designers goes much further. The designer is to roam the countryside—from the highlands to the fields and plains, from the mountains to the sea—like the Japanese poet Bashō in his journey along the "Narrow Road to the Deep North" or the American folksinger Woody Guthrie on his "Nine Hundred Miles." Armed with sketchpad and notebook, he might devote as many as three years to such travels, drawing, jotting down his impressions, living close to the natural forces of the earth.

Making sketches of striking aspects of natural landscape is an invaluable exercise. It takes the act of seeing and converts it into a form of learning that actively engages the kinesthetics of the body, programming the mind and nervous system in a way that seeing alone cannot. Examples of what can be learned, firsthand, on such a journey to the mountains or the seashore are found in the fifteenth-century garden manual, the *Illustrations*. Presented in items 6 through 8 and in figures K and L are several types of natural phenomena the designer must be well acquainted with. Whether it is "craggy mountains with gnarled trees" (item 6) or "flowing water, constantly obstructed as it seeks the sea" (item 8), there is no better way for the designer to experience these phenomena than to learn them directly from nature (fig. 2).[4]

Learning from nature also means learning from oneself about the human organism and how it responds to a sensory environment. Each person apprehends a work of art through one or more of the five senses, hence the designer must have practical knowledge of how the human senses respond to varied stimuli in the physical world. Only by understanding the limitations or "defects" of the senses can the landscape artist create a world of intense beauty for the viewer.

Apprenticeship

Traditionally, a student of landscape garden design in Japan serves an apprenticeship to an acknowledged master of the art. During my apprenticeship in Kyoto there were about ten other young men like me, who had come to live in Kyoto and work under Kinsaku Nakane (unlike me, usually for three to five years) before opening up their own design office or returning to their family nursery business.

Much of the apprenticeship is hard work, requiring both physical endurance and mental concentration. For the student, for whom most of the techniques are learned by watching and doing, and not by asking questions—it represents another level of

Fig. 2.   A depiction of "craggy mountains with gnarled trees," here the setting for a hermit's hut. From the *Mustard Seed Garden Manual of Painting*, a sourcebook of Chinese painting techniques compiled in the seventeenth century.

initiation into the art. This is the stage of most direct involvement, of truly learning by doing, or "body learning." In the previous two stages, the senses have been in a receptive mode, but now the whole body is actively involved. "You must learn with your body, not your head," a senior apprentice explained to me. This may not come easy to people who have become comfortable with a style of formal education heavily weighted in favor of theory and conceptually oriented design.

The work of the apprentice can be divided into two categories, garden construction and garden maintenance. During the construction of a new garden designed by the master-designer or teacher (*sensei*), apprentices perform every phase of the labor, from moving rocks into the proper position to planting trees and building fences (fig. 3). Since what is taking shape is like a landscape painting—albeit in three dimensions—every aspect of construction is closely supervised by the *sensei*. Particularly during the initial phase of setting the rocks in a composition, the master-designer's supervision fairly resembles that of an orchestra director, with

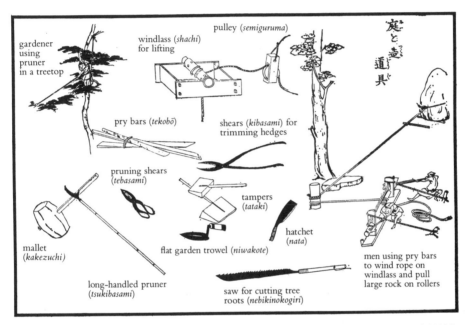

gardener
using
pruner
in a treetop

pulley (*semiguruma*)

windlass (*shachi*)
for lifting

pry bars (*tekobō*)

shears (*kibasami*) for
trimming hedges

pruning shears
(*tebasami*)

tampers
(*tataki*)

mallet
(*kakezuchi*)

flat garden trowel (*niwakote*)

hatchet
(*nata*)

men using pry bars
to wind rope on
windlass and pull
large rock on rollers

long-handled pruner
(*tsukibasami*)

saw for cutting tree
roots (*nebikinokogiri*)

Fig. 3.   Tools used in making gardens. From *Tsukiyama teizōden*, an Edo-period (1615–
1868) gardening manual.

apprentices responding automatically to deft hand signals indicating which way the
rock should be moved and how far. The apprentices learn to follow these signals
with complete trust so that there is an untrammeled flow of the teacher's intentions
from signal to final execution.

During the summer growing season, garden maintenance—centered around the
very important task of pruning—occupies most of the apprentice's time. A traditional apprenticeship, the aspirant is apt to be told more than once, was supposed to
last for fifteen years—long enough to make even the most patient Westerner give up
in despair. Until the 1960s, beginning apprentices were for the first three years
confined to menial chores and not even allowed to pick up a pair of pruning shears.
Today, young apprentices no longer have to serve this three-year initiation but
instead are allowed—in fact, expected—to do pruning from the very first day on the
job. This change is no doubt a sign of the times, an instance of a traditional art
striving to keep pace with the pressures of modern life in Japan. But were

apprenticeship to disappear entirely, the art of the Japanese garden would likely die with it.

Oral Transmission

The term "oral transmission," *or kuden*, in its most general sense refers to any verbally transmitted insight or technique. All builders and designers have sources of oral transmission, and most of the time take them for granted. Information about materials and techniques freely given by local contractors, nurserymen, and craftsmen regarding their areas of expertise, for example, can be not merely instructive but indispensable to the success of a particular project.

Within the esoteric tradition of the Japanese arts, however, "oral transmission" refers to a body of "secret knowledge of technique" passed on from master to disciple. Swordmaking, pottery, tea, flower composition—and landscape garden design—all share this method of transmitting their techniques. Ideally, such verbal communications—whether oral or written—are initiated by the teacher only when the disciple is ready to receive them.

It is through experience gained in the above-mentioned three stages of learning that the disciple reaches a state of readiness. The process is largely one of personal growth. Just as Zen Buddhists believe the initiate is already enlightened but must find that out for himself, the "secret knowledge" of an art is regarded as a potential in human nature, as part of the structure of the senses linking heart and mind with the physical world. A person can actualize this knowledge—make it his own—through the proper combination of personal experience and conceptual learning. The oral or written communication, therefore, does not carry "truth," but acts as a fixative on the heightened awareness the student has already gained for himself. Performance and knowledge are, in the Japanese tradition at least, inseparable.

When the transmission is presented at the right psychological moment, the student grasps the significance of the *kuden* in an "aha" ("aha, *now* I understand") experience. If the student is not yet ready, even though he may think he understands, the level of understanding remains superficial. The term "oral transmission" (*kuden*) as it is used here contains within it the sense of knowledge *realized*, simultaneously, within the teacher and pupil.

In reality, oral transmissions often do reach the student before he is ready. When this happens, the verbal message can be stored away, to await an experience that will make it meaningful, as happened to me once while hiking along a mountain stream in the Maroon Bells near Aspen, Colorado, several years after completing my initial studies in Japan. As I descended the valley path, I was suddenly struck by how the rushing water was being deflected around a turn in the stream by a large rock on the opposite bank. This was exciting, for I knew instantly that what I was seeing was the natural basis for a landscaping technique I had learned in Japan. Called the River Style (*ōkawa no yō*), it is a way of composing rocks along the bend of a garden stream (fig. 4). Its description in *Sakuteiki* is an example of an oral transmission that has been committed to writing in a "secret" text:[5]

Fig. 4.   Rocks at the bend of a stream. From *Yokei-zukuri niwa no zu*, an Edo-period gardening manual.

> The placing of stones for the garden stream should start at a place where it makes a turn and flows along. This turn is supposed to have been caused by the presence of this rock which the stream could not demolish. The stream after the turn flows with added momentum and hits hard against the object it encounters. . . .

Oral transmissions may be of a higher or a lower order. Higher-order transmissions generally consist of an insight that comes close to establishing a universal design principle, like the River Style. A lower-order transmission, however, is limited in its scope and aesthetic power, and is likely to be culture-specific, like this *kuden* recorded in item 23 of the *Illustrations*:

> Have ready about 1 *shō* of rice (depending upon the size of the garden) and when you set the named rock [the Happiness & Prosperity Rock for the master of the house], with the rice still in the measuring box put it into the hole. . . . So that people will not know it is the named rock, after you have had the hole dug for the nameless rock, put the rice while still in the measuring box into it too, then remove the measure and put a little rice

into each hole. This is done so that people will not be able to distinguish
between the named rock and the nameless rock. This is a secret matter!
(—oral transmission)

Such ritualistic gestures no doubt served an important cultural function at the time
the *Illustrations* was written down. Putting rice into the hole for the Happiness &
Prosperity Rock was probably a Shinto-derived folk ritual intended to guarantee the
efficacy of the rock, while confusing people as to which was the named rock was
similarly a way of protecting its power, this time through secrecy. Sacralizing one
rock in the garden was thus a way of propitiating forces beyond human control: the
rock became a talisman for the owner's happiness. The labels "secret matter" and
"oral transmission" in this case have a pre-aesthetic function. They should not be
discounted, however, for such communications may have helped guarantee that
designers maintain the proper attitude of reverence when practicing their art.

This book is another kind of oral transmission, one that takes the form of a
commentary seeking to amplify the more universal principles of Japanese gardens.
In Japan, receiving the oral transmissions was regarded as a kind of diploma, or
certification, without which one was not allowed to practice the art. The injunction
at the very beginning of the *Illustrations* makes this clear: "If you have not received the
oral transmissions, you must not make gardens" (fig. 5). In the following section, we
will look further at the relationship between oral transmissions and the "secret
texts."

Secret Texts

Classical Japanese garden manuals like *Sakuteiki* and the *Illustrations* were esoteric;
that is, they were written for and understood by the specially initiated alone. They
were not available to the general public, nor would they have been readily compre-
hended by anyone aside from a select few even at the time they were written. With
our present-day emphasis on disseminating information to as wide an audience as
possible, "secret texts" seem a fascinating and curious phenomenon. What role did
these texts play in transmitting the art through the ages, and why were they confined
to just a small circle of initiates?

Secret texts, called *hidensho*, are found in all of the traditional arts of Japan. They
represent a compilation of the master-designer's experience and knowledge, written
in a concise, often pithy form. One of the master's primary motivations for writing
such a text was to insure that his art would be handed down to posterity within his
own lineage. He would bequeath it to a trusted disciple or other worthy initiate who
had attained an appropriate level of mastery of the art. The text was not a "how to"

不受口傳不可作庭

Fig. 5.   *Kuden ukezareba, niwa tsukuru bekarazu*: "If you have not received the oral transmissions, you must not make gardens." From an Edo-period version of the *Illustrations*.

book of the sort found in bookstores today. It was open-ended, incomplete without the initiate's tacit knowledge of the art. It could not be followed literally, nor could gardens be built in strict accordance with its prescriptions. Item 32 of the *Illustrations* says as much when it cautions even the initiated against a too-rigid interpretation:

> Even if it means the dimensions of the rocks will differ somewhat from what is prescribed, set them in accordance with their assets and faults. If you do not grasp this, you will not be able to set them in a composition.

The text served instead as a mnemonic device to assure that the most important tenets were complied with. It also challenged the designer-heir to continually deepen his understanding and aim for the highest standards of the art.

The latter was apparently one of the motives of Tachibana no Toshitsuna (1028–94) for writing *Sakuteiki*, for in the process of reflecting upon his own study of the art of garden making, he laments what he sees as a lapsing of the standards:[6]

> The priest-gardener En-en Ajari was a person who inherited the secret documents of the art of garden making. I also have inherited the documents. Although I have thus studied and understood the main principles, the import and the fascination of this art are so inexhaustible that there are many things that are beyond my comprehension. In recent years, however, there is no one who has a thorough knowledge about this matter. One simply observes nature and then dares to make the garden without even knowing about the matters of taboo.

To support his point, he cites the difficulty his father, the imperial regent Fujiwara no Yorimichi (the Lord of Uji), had in recruiting capable garden makers during the restoration of the Kayanoin Palace:

> At the time of the restoration of the Kayanoin Palace [begun in 1021] it was found that the artisans of garden making had completely disappeared by then. Persons around that time who were expected to know the art were summoned but were rejected because they were far from meeting the approval of the lord. Under such circumstances, the Lord Uji himself came to take command of the work of garden construction. At that time I had the opportunity of visiting the site of construction, carefully watching and listening to the art of placing stones and making the garden.

Toshitsuna's comments reveal a great deal about how the art of garden making was transmitted in the mid-eleventh century. It had long been a tradition for members of the educated class—the court aristocracy and the Buddhist priesthood—to devote themselves wholeheartedly to the study and practice of such arts as poetry, painting, and landscape gardening. What Toshitsuna says and the candor with which he says it show that that tradition was still firmly in place when he wrote *Sakuteiki*. He learned the art from "documents" that were handed down to him and by carefully observing garden construction, in particular that directed by his father at the Kayanoin Palace.

At this time the secrets of garden making were not guarded jealously from outside eyes by closed circles with a vested interest in keeping the art to themselves. As long as the court aristocracy had political power and economic security—which it did until the end of the Heian period in the late twelfth century—the arts were pastimes and had no perceived economic value. Teachings, including those in written form, could be shared openly within the educated class, even if it was through the traditional master-disciple relationship. This was still a matter of pedagogy and not economics.

The translation of Toshitsuna's comments quoted above is somewhat misleading as regards the instruction materials that he says were handed down to him. The word *sōden* has there been translated as "secret documents," but the word "secret" is neither present nor implied in the original Japanese. *Sōden* literally means "mutual transmission," suggesting a communication of knowledge where there is a bond of respect and affinity between the two parties involved (the teacher and the pupil). The whole tone of *Sakuteiki*, one of genuine respect and candor with regard to what is being transmitted, bears out the thesis that it was not intended as a secret text.

Furthermore, the word "secret" never occurs in the text proper, but is only found in the final colophon—"You must keep it secret!"—that was added by a much later heir (it is dated the summer of 1289).[7] By that time the court aristocracy in Japan had lost most of its power to the warrior class, and with it, much of its economic security. In order to maintain their accustomed standard of living, aristocrats fell back on the one thing they practically monopolized—knowledge of the arts. They used this knowledge for profit by becoming tutors to the more aspiring members of the warrior class who wanted to add polish to political power by acquiring the high culture the court aristocracy had created. It was out of economic need, then, that in the thirteenth and fourteenth centuries aristocrats developed a system of guarding their knowledge and passing it on secretly. The secret texts were the offspring of this system.

By the year 1466, when the *Illustrations* was handed down to the priest Hōin Shingen, several of the Japanese art forms—the short poetic form known as *tanka* and the Noh drama, for example—had a well-established system of secret transmission including secret texts written by learned masters. In some of the arts, different schools vied for the patronage of prominent members of the military class or of economically powerful institutions. Secret texts, artists believed, would give their art the competitive advantage it needed to survive in succeeding generations. This is what prompted the playwright Zeami in the early fifteenth century to write his now highly respected treatises on acting and the Noh theater (these remained secret until the early twentieth century).

The art of Japanese gardens was not in this medieval period (1185–1573) or any time thereafter blessed with a theorist of such high caliber. Since landscape garden design is a nonrepetitive art with a continually changing clientele and a heavy investment in materials and labor, it was difficult for dynamic, highly cohesive schools of gardening to develop in Japan as they did for more formally structured arts like Noh, the tea ceremony, and flower composition. At least, however, there were scribes who were conscientious enough to write down what they learned about contemporary gardening practices as well as transmit the writings that had been handed down to them. For this we must be grateful, even if they did not offer their own reflections or commentary on the teachings.

Among the works they gave us is *Illustrations for Designing Mountain, Water, and Hillside Field Landscapes*, a translation of which constitutes part 2 of this book. The *Illustrations* was the principal gardening manual of its time. The version I used is in the form of a scroll approximately eleven inches high and thirty-three feet long, and contains over a dozen sketchy brush-and-ink drawings. Dated 1466 by its transmitter, the priest Shingen, it is written in the language of the fifteenth century but contains instructions from earlier periods as well. It would appear that the priest Zōen—credited as its original compiler—lived before the eleventh century and thus predates Toshitsuna, the author of *Sakuteiki*, but exactly who he was is by no means clear.

Like other contemporary esoteric manuals, the *Illustrations* was intended to be treated as a secret text. This is made abundantly clear by the final sentences (prior to the colophons) of the actual text, "You must never show this writing to outsiders. You must keep it secret," and by the occurrence of the term "secret matter" (*hiji*) no less than seven times in the text proper.[8] The injunction to secrecy applies not only to the manual, but to the very principles of the art: "The illustrations concerning rocks, the locations for setting rocks, and the locations for planting herbs and trees must be kept absolutely secret."[9]

If the *Illustrations* was so secret, who had access to the text, and how much impact could it have had on the design of classical Japanese gardens? This is not so easily answered, for there are no written records—at least none to my knowledge—revealing who used the text and how. Since the scroll bears the seal of Shinren'in, a subtemple of Ninnaji, a major Shingon-sect temple in Kyoto, it was probably compiled with the approval of the so-called rock-setting priests, or *ishitate-sō*, who were attached to that temple and responsible for much of the garden building in Kyoto at the time.

At the end of the text of the *Illustrations* are the Chart of the Transmission and two colophons containing a total of forty-seven names of Buddhist priests and aristocrats—some famous and others unknown—through whose hand the *Illustrations* supposedly passed. Almost certainly some of these names were added without substantiation to lend authority to the text. Still, even if the lineage set forth is more ideal than real, the list tells us who would have been expected to study and transmit the text—namely, the masters of garden design throughout Japanese history. Among the more famous garden makers whose names occur here is Toshitsuna (the author of *Sakuteiki*), En'en Ajari (the priest mentioned by Toshitsuna in *Sakuteiki* as having inherited the documents of garden making), and Ryūmon Oshō (or Musō Soseki), a fourteenth-century priest known for his gardens at Saihōji and Tenryūji in Kyoto (pl. 13).

These gardens by Musō, along with the garden at Kinkakuji built by the shogun Ashikaga Yoshimitsu in the late 1300s, are three of the earliest Japanese gardens that remain today. As they were built in the century prior to the Ninnaji copy of the *Illustrations*, they may well have been designed in accordance with its precepts and so contain living examples of some of the rock compositions presented there (allowance must of course be made for the fact that certain aspects of these gardens have been altered over the years). A garden built by Ashikaga Yoshimasa in the 1480s, much closer to the time of the *Illustrations*, can be seen at Ginkakuji in eastern Kyoto. The buildings here look out on a pond like its fourteenth-century predecessors. But the compressed scale and stark dignity of this garden are a fair summary of the qualities of the age: the Ashikaga's central authority was on the wane, resources were shrinking, and the mainstream aesthetic was more and more reflective of a restrained and lofty style of Chinese painting favored by Zen priests for its economy of expression.

The existence of four Edo-period copies of the *Illustrations* is evidence of the esteem in which it was held by subsequent generations of garden specialists. Modern-day Japanese garden historians and designers still consider the *Illustrations* one of the earliest and most important compilations of garden principles and techniques. They refer to it both for their own edification and when they are seeking to understand extant gardens from past ages in places like Kyoto today.

Probably one of the original motives for writing an esoteric manual was to have an indelible record of the teachings that in the past had been transmitted orally. Examples of oral transmission that have been written down and still are referred to as *kuden* can be found in both *Sakuteiki* and the *Illustrations*. *Sakuteiki* in particular has a section containing fourteen "Oral Transmissions on Setting Rocks," of which the following is an example:[10]

> The stones should be placed firmly, which means the bottom of the stone should be buried deep into the ground. However, even when the bottom is deeply buried the stone might still appear weak unless it is associated with the front stone. On the other hand, a shallowly placed stone might give a firm appearance because of the front stone attached to it. This is an oral instruction.

Oral transmissions like the above generally contain an insight, and provide some explanation or reason for doing what is suggested.

Sometimes, however, oral transmissions are referred to in the esoteric manuals without actually being set forth in the text. The phrase usually goes, "There is an oral transmission." The implication is that the disciple-heir either knows the instruction or must inquire into it himself. In this case, the relationship between the oral transmission and the secret text is complementary: a *kuden* acquired apart from the text provides a valuable key to understanding the written instruction. There is even a reference in item 87 of the *Illustrations* to *kudensho*—separate documents in which oral transmissions have been written down. Designers and garden historians wanting to know just what these transmissions are and where they can be found might begin their search with the *Dōji kudensho*, a compilation of oral transmissions that is appended to Edo-period variants of the *Illustrations* and that also excerpts a substantial portion of *Sakuteiki*.

Some instructions in the garden manuals take the form of prohibitions, or taboos. Educated Japanese of the Heian period placed a great deal of importance on taboos in the conduct of their daily lives. Some taboos warned against travel in a given direction at certain times of year. Other taboos prohibited certain activities, like house repairs, on specified days. Our own "blue laws" limiting certain activities on Sundays serve as a contemporary reminder of such prohibitions.

It is too easy to see the taboos that governed Japanese life at this time as mere superstitions. When Toshitsuna, author of *Sakuteiki*, criticizes the level of knowledge among the garden makers of his day by saying, "One simply observes nature and then dares to make the garden without even knowing about the matters of taboo," he is not decrying the breakdown of religion in Heian society but the carelessness of contemporary garden design. For taboos were intended to help produce better gardens. They may not have communicated in todays "scientific" language of cause and effect, but within the context of their culture their meaning was perfectly clear. In *Sakuteiki* is the following taboo:[11]

> The pond should be shallow. If the pond is deep the fish that live therein will become large. If the fish become large, they will turn into noxious worms and thereby harm the people.

Shimoyama, in the preface to his translation of *Sakuteiki*, interprets this taboo as follows:[12]

> That a pond should not be built deeper than necessary is a universal truth of present day engineering science. The rest of the explanatory words must have been unimportant to the author. (The growing fish might imply the growing cost of construction and maintenance, and the worms to harm the people could mean the resulting safety hazard!)

The section of *Sakuteiki* with the heading "Oral Transmissions on Setting Rocks" (cited above) is immediately followed by a substantially longer section listing some thirty-one taboos, most of which have to do with setting rocks. A brief introduction sets the tone for this section. Who would doubt the power of such taboos to guarantee observance of their instructions?[13]

> There are many taboos concerning the placing of stones. It is said that if even one of them is violated, the master of the house would constantly suffer from illness to the ultimate loss of his life, and that the place would be deserted to become an abode of demons.

Both taboos and oral transmissions are meant to assist the garden maker in producing an effective design. Oral transmissions are frequently presented with brief, common-sense explanations to support what is suggested. Taboo-type transmissions are presented as "don'ts." For taboos, the rationale comes in the form of harmful consequences that will befall the client if the instructions are not followed by the designer. In fact, for most of these rationale there is a corresponding aesthetic gain.

The Learning Process

The first three stages of learning the art of the Japanese garden are all forms of "body learning," rooted in sensory experience. They are—to use a term that reflects the

West's dominant bias favoring verbal learning—"non-verbal." The final two stages are verbal. However, the traditional form of verbal communication in Japan has not been the explicit, exoteric style we value so much in the United States, but rather has tended toward the esoteric—meaning that in order for the transmission to be completed, the student's mind must be ready to receive it. This can only come with a sufficient level of experience. The Japanese expression "make it your own" conveys the importance of deep internalization of knowledge when a student is seeking to master one of the traditional Japanese arts. The three experiential stages and the two verbal stages are thus interdependent in the learning process:

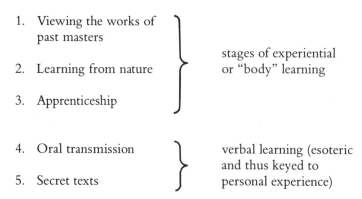

1. Viewing the works of past masters

2. Learning from nature   stages of experiential or "body" learning

3. Apprenticeship

4. Oral transmission   verbal learning (esoteric and thus keyed to

5. Secret texts   personal experience)

While today's students in the fine or practicing arts may spend more of their classroom time in the experiential than the verbal mode, students entering the professional design disciplines of architecture and landscape architecture will still find in our American universities the traditional academic balance weighted in favor of verbal learning. They will also spend far more time at the drawing board than at the construction site. Anything resembling the apprenticeship experience must be gained by students away from the university, during summer vacation or after graduation. Figure 6 graphically illustrates the relative weights given verbal and experiential learning in our own Western system of formal education and in the art of Japanese gardens.

Edward T. Hall states in *Beyond Culture* that two very different types of communication characterize various cultures to a greater or lesser degree. He calls them "high-context" and "low-context" communication.[14]

> A high-context (HC) communication or message is one in which most of the information is either in the physical context or internalized in the person, while very little is in the coded, explicit, transmitted part of the message. A low-context (LC) communication is just the opposite; i.e., the mass of the information is vested in the explicit code.

Hall's definition of a high-context communication is a perfectly succinct description of how information about the art of Japanese gardens was traditionally stored away and handed down through the ages. Such "high-context" learning requires that the student be immersed in the art and its culture, so that learning takes place by an osmosis-like process, through the senses, with little theorizing into the underlying principles. Kinsaku Nakane continually emphasizes that students must expose

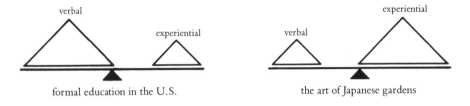

Fig. 6. Learning: Western and Japanese models.

themselves to as wide as possible a spectrum of Japanese arts and culture—from tea ceremony to kimono design—if they are to grasp the aesthetic principles and expression of Japanese gardens. He also recommends television (everything from traditional dramas to the latest in pop culture) as a medium for developing the student's awareness of visual styles—colors, rhythms, textures, and moods.

The experiential "learn by doing" approach is certainly appropriate for anyone who wants to practice an art. As Rudolf Arnheim observes,[15]

> A person made aware of the principle underlying his action may find himself hampered in his performance. This happens in the learning of almost any skill and can become an invincible disturbance. In the arts, for example, to learn a generic formula for which one is not ready intuitively can be harmful. . . .
>
> However, it is also true that superior performance may be attained if the principles inherent in it have been identified and then absorbed again in intuitive application.

Extracting the principles of an art and making them explicit is not easy to do. Yet it is one of the most important tasks for the art theorist, and for the artist can in fact lead to the highest level of mastery. It first requires that we abandon the traditional dichotomy between intuition and intellection—between what it means to be an artist on the one hand and an art historian or theorist on the other.

So often is it said that artists don't analyze and critics don't practice their art that we have come to accept this as the natural order of things. In fact, the process of first sensing our environment, then standing back from our sensory experience to reflect on it, and then returning once again to the world of experience is one of the basic rhythms of human life. It is this natural cycle that has guided me in the examination of classical Japanese garden aesthetics that follows.

THE ART WE SEE:

SCENIC EFFECTS

2

The grandeur of the scene was softened by the haze that hung over the valley—light as gossamer—and by the clouds which partially dimmed the higher cliffs and mountains. This obscurity of vision but increased the awe with which I beheld it, and as I looked, a peculiar exalted sensation seemed to fill my whole being, and I found my eyes in tears with emotion.

—Lafayette Bunnell

It is no secret, the power that natural scenery has to move us. From majestic mountains to peaceful valleys, nature provides an endless variety of scenic effects that stimulate our senses and often touch our feelings in peculiar ways. It would appear that Lafayette Bunnell's emotions upon viewing Yosemite are shared in East Asia, for there they have been expressed and idealized in a long tradition of nature-oriented poetry and painting.

Just as much of that tradition was imported from China and Korea and found fertile soil in Japan, so did the related art of landscape gardening reach the shores of Japan from the mainland.[1] Archaeology has revealed Korean influences on Japanese gardens from as early as the seventh century. Throughout the eighth century, the Japanese fell firmly under the cultural sway of China's flourishing T'ang dynasty, and developed a great interest in all manner of things Chinese. Their new capital, Heiankyō (present-day Kyoto), built in A.D. 794, was laid out in a grid just like the T'ang capital of Ch'ang-an, and the gardens of the court nobility who established their new residences in the hills surrounding the city combined water and land features in a pond-and-island arrangement, imitative of the vast naturalistic parks built by the Chinese. The purpose of these gardens also bore a similarity to that of Chinese gardens—for entertainment, boating, and genteel sports, to provide aesthetic pleasure, and to display the owner's wealth and culture—not so unlike the goals of many gardens and parks we see today (fig. 7).

The Japanese priests and aristocrats who set forth to bring the fruits of Chinese culture and religion to their own land faced a harrowing journey by sea. En route they doubtless heard of the fabled Isles of the Immortals, swathed in clouds, inhabited by Taoist sages, unapproachable by men. In and around the T'ang capital they saw examples of China's own landscapes and gardens. What a thrill it must have been, too, to set sail for home and catch a glimpse of the crags and pineclad islands along the Japanese coast coming into view on the horizon after so long and terrible an absence. It is easy to understand why such travelers might have wished to re-create faraway scenes and recall powerful emotions in gardens, where they could share them with others or reflect on them at their leisure.

Helping these foreign influences to take root in the Japanese garden was Shinto, an indigenous system of folk myths and customs centering on ritual purity and the immanence of divine spirit in trees, mountains, rocks, and other natural phenomena. Early Shinto worship rites were conducted in roped-off forest clearings. These clearings, it is thought, were the prototype of the open sites attached to religious and secular buildings that subsequently evolved into landscaped gardens. The sacred roots of these early gardens made them perfect receptacles for the foreign religious symbology—such as Buddhist and Taoist images of paradise—that the Japanese were increasingly importing from the mainland. They also infused the garden in Japan, from earliest times, with the power to profoundly touch the spirits of those who viewed them.[2]

From these powerful experiences did the landscape of the classical Japanese garden emerge. As the task of garden building passed from Chinese and Korean to Japanese hands, and as the Japanese withdrew from further contact with the mainland, a true, native gardening style began to develop, one that would thrive in the temperate climate of Japan, as well as exploit the natural resources and the superb physical setting of the Kyoto basin, abundant in water and surrounded by gentle, verdant hillsides. By the middle of the Heian period (794–1185), when the earliest extant Japanese garden manual, *Sakuteiki*, was written, continental ideas had been sorted out and assimilated according to the dictates of Japanese taste, and the art of gardening had reached a high level of sophistication in Japanese hands. The general guidelines presented in the very first lines of *Sakuteiki* clearly establish that at this time one of the most important ideals of the classical Japanese garden was to re-create the effects of natural scenery:[3]

> You should design each part of the garden tastefully, recalling your memories of how nature presented itself for each feature. . . . Think over the famous places of scenic beauty throughout the land, and . . . design your garden with the mood of harmony, modelling after the general air of such places.

Fig. 7.   A Heian-period garden with musicians in "dragon boats" accompanying a performance on shore. From a seventeenth-century edition of the historical tale *Eiga
monogatari*. Collection of East Asiatic Library, University of California, Berkeley.

Feature-Oriented Landscape

The emphasis on natural features and scenic places reveals a "feature-oriented"
approach to landscape design. Chosen features of natural scenery were re-created in
the garden so that they were convincingly present and evoked some of the same
feelings one had when actually viewing them in nature. This is a goal we can
understand, even if it is not within the mainstream of our own American landscape
architecture. Why it is not is unclear. Perhaps it has something to do with the
American notion that nature must either be totally controlled or totally left alone—a
polarity that denies us the deep and satisfying relationship with nature that we yearn

for. The irresistible charm of such scenic effects is evident when we read in *The Tale of Genji*, a fictional work written in the Heian period only a half century before *Sakuteiki*, of courtiers viewing the garden's pond landscape from Chinese-style pleasure boats:[4]

> The lake, as they now put out toward the middle of it, seemed immensely large, and those on board . . . could hardly believe that they were not heading for some undiscovered land. At last however the rowers brought them close in under the rocky bank of the channel between the two large islands, and on closer examination they discovered to their delight that the shape of every little ledge and crag of stone had been as carefully devised as if a painter had traced them with his brush.

The enjoyment of ocean scenery reminiscent of that seen on an excursion along the coast of Japan must have been what the military ruler Ashikaga Yoshimitsu had in mind when he created his garden of the Golden Pavilion (Kinkaku) in Kyoto in the final decade of the fourteenth century. Not only are there records of extravagant boating parties here, but there is a boat landing alongside the Golden Pavilion and "some of the finest rock arrangements [are located] at places where they can only be seen from a boat—that is, on the far side of a large island."[5]

Later, in the seventeenth century, when nostalgia for the Golden Age of Heian culture was in vogue, Prince Toshihito created a garden to revive the artistic sentiments of that age as he understood and imagined them. On a shore of the pond in the garden of his villa on the Katsura River in southwest Kyoto, he (or his son, who carried on the construction of the garden) made an island in the form of the pineclad sandbar Amanohashidate, or "Bridge of Heaven," a famous natural landscape located on the Japan Sea in his wife's home province of Tango (pls. 1, 2). In seeking to re-create the aesthetic qualities of a famous place of scenic beauty, the garden at Katsura was addressing the spirit of those general guidelines laid down at the beginning of *Sakuteiki*.

Much of *Sakuteiki* is given to an encyclopedic listing of landscape types, mostly water-related, with perceptive comments on essential features to bear in mind when creating each one in the garden. It describes, for example, eight types of waterfalls, and presents some seventeen waterscapes, from the Ocean Style to the Mountain Rapids Style.

The fifteenth-century Japanese garden manual, the *Illustrations*, contains no such listing of specific landscape types. Still, the feature-oriented approach is evident at the very beginning of its text, too: "First, when laying out the plains, the mountains and peaks, and the waterfalls and rivers of a garden, . . ." The clause that completes this sentence, "you must regard rocks and trees as the structural elements," is the first clue offered as to how such scenic effects are created.

Like its close relatives *ikebana* (flower composition) and *bonsai* (dwarfed-tree cultivation), the art of Japanese gardens may be unique for its use of natural objects in a relatively unaltered state—the rocks not at all, the trees in keeping with their inherent growth pattern—to effect selected impressions of the natural environment where they originated. Perennial herbs and ground covers provide the finishing touches, contributing to the atmosphere but not to the enduring form. A gnarled pine from the mountains (or a similar one from the nursery) serves in the garden not merely as a weathered tree but also, by virtue of the way it is planted in a composition of rocks, as a powerful agent for evoking the atmosphere of craggy mountains far from civilization.

Given the expressive possibilities and the availability of rocks and trees,[6] it is no wonder that these natural "found objects" were the preferred materials of classical landscape designers. In addition to their role in the creation of scenic effects, rocks and trees also served as screens and framing devices, and could lend the garden specific sensory qualities such as color and luminescence, sound (a waterfall, wind soughing through the trees), shape (shrubs or trees massed to represent a mountain), fragrance (osmanthus or lilac), and rhythm (the special capacity of rocks).

Manmade found objects have also played an important role in garden design, particularly with the advent of the tea garden in the sixteenth century. Most of these objects were made of stone, and were used as much for their aesthetic qualities as for their original function. A discarded pillar foundation stone, designers were quick to discover, made an attractive and functional joint at the intersection of two paths. Millstones could be used as stepping stones. Stone lanterns, formerly serving as votive lights in front of temple sanctuaries, found their way into the tea garden, where they were used to light the path at night and provide a visual accent. More recently, quarried stone has been used instead of naturally weathered rock, both to evoke a desired landscape experience and to modulate between the qualities of a traditional garden and the stark lines and planes of modern architecture (see chart).

Natural and Manmade Materials Often Used in Japanese Gardens

material	how used
	NATURAL
ROCKS:	serve as the "bone" structure of the garden; used to create effects of mountains, outcroppings, waterfalls, stream beds, natural bridges, etc.
PLANTS:	to create scenic effects of source habitats of trees, shrubs, herbs in nature; to soften and hide defects of rocks; massed, to create effect of a hillside or mountainside; like rocks, to fill out structure of landscape
WATER:	for "water effects": ocean, lake, pond, marsh, waterfall, stream; trickling from spout into water basin (for sound as well as sight)
EARTH:	as "flesh" for skeletal rock structure; to create artificial hills or mounds (*tsukiyama*) on which rocks can be set; as planting medium; sometimes as a bare earth ground cover
BAMBOO:	for making fences, water spouts for basins, or pipes to convey water to a waterfall or stream (saplings and natural logs can be used in the same ways)
	MANMADE
STONE WATER BASINS:	(originally from temples or shrines, first introduced into landscape gardens for use in the tea garden) as water basins for ritual purification, when rinsing hands and mouth before tea ceremony; as decorative focal points in garden
STONE (OR WOOD) LANTERNS:	(originally votive lights from temples or shrines) for lighting tea garden path; as decorative focal points in garden
PILLAR FOUNDA-TION STONES:	cast-off stone was borrowed for use as pivotal stepping stone at intersection of two paths
MILLSTONES:	for stepping stones
QUARRIED GRANITE:	for stone bridges; to form paving blocks for formal stone-paved walk (*nobedan*); as curbing along edge of rain gutter at drip line of eaves
ROOF TILES:	set on edge in ground, as decorative edging to separate gravel area from moss, etc.

Two other materials were essential in the creation of classical Japanese gardens. Earth gained in excavating the pond and stream was used to form the *tsukiyama*, or artificial hills, on which rocks were positioned and trees planted. And water, brought in by conduit from a nearby river or spring, served as the medium for producing the water-related scenic effects—waterfalls, mountain rapids, seashore, and marsh—that figured so prominently in these gardens. The *Illustrations*, in item 1, leaves no room for doubt about the importance of water: "Mountains, water, and rocks are like the three legs of a tripod—if even one is missing, there can be no garden."

Plants and the Principle of Natural Habitat

How are rocks and trees and earth and water used to achieve the desired scenic effects? The most explicit answer to this question in either of the two classical garden manuals is a statement in item 10 of the *Illustrations* that, confining itself to the use of plants, establishes a correspondence between a plant's habitat or home in nature and its most appropriate setting in the garden:

> In the planting of trees and herbs, you make their natural habitats your model. You will not go astray so long as you bear in mind the principle of planting trees from deep mountains in the deep mountains of the garden, trees from hills and fields in the hills and fields, herbs and trees from freshwater shores on the freshwater shores, and herbs from the seashore on the seashore. For the landscape garden mirrors nature. And thus it is said that in each and all we must return to the two words, natural habitat.

This we will call the principle of natural habitat. It corresponds to what *Sakuteiki* calls *yō*, meaning a "type" or "style" of landscape. Interestingly, there is a shift of emphasis from *yō* or types of landscape in *Sakuteiki* to the designer's materials—in this case plants—in the *Illustrations*. *Sakuteiki* mentions only sixteen varieties of plants and has little to say about how they are used to re-create the scenic effects of their habitats. Item 63 of the *Illustrations* treats this same topic as a matter of great importance: "The placement of herbs and trees may appear simple, but there is not one person in a thousand who knows how to do it." Accordingly, the *Illustrations* offers pertinent information on some forty-three varieties of plants, their natural habitats, and their placement in the garden (a summary of which appears in appendix 3). These habitats range from mountain peaks and "deep mountains" down to lowland marshes and ocean shores. In between are hills and fields, valleys, and the cultivated land of farming villages. This is a picture that makes visual sense to us today. Missing, to be sure, are the prairies, plateaus, canyons, and mesas of the American West—habitats that do not exist in the landscape vocabulary of Japan, particularly not in that of the Kyoto basin where most of the classical gardens were being built.

The marsh-pond is one habitat that occurs both in *Sakuteiki* and the *Illustrations* (fig. 8). It is especially interesting because it contains a number of the smaller flowering plants whose beauty had long been admired by the cultured Japanese

Fig. 8. A marsh-pond scene (with rocks "visible only here and there"). From *Tsukiyama sansui ishigumi sonoo no yaegaki, shinsen teisaku den*, an 1894 version of an Edo-period gardening manual.

aristocracy, particularly when viewed in proximity to water.[7] The marsh-pond has obvious merit for exploiting such beauty. And the geographical conditions of the Kyoto basin, with its myriad springs and wealth of water, would have made this scenic effect all the more desirable. Probably such plants were discovered growing there in the wild when the city was established in 794 as the new "Capital of Peace and Tranquillity." So great was the aristocrats' fondness for these natives of fresh-water shores that few could resist the temptation to plant them wherever there was water, even on the garden seashore, a practice that clearly violated the principle of natural habitat, as the author of the *Illustrations* points out in item 19:

> On the seashore, one should not find such plants as sweet flag, rabbit-ear iris, and kerria. It is common practice nowadays to use such plants when creating the scenic effects of the seashore, but this matter should be taken more seriously. People who are discerning with regard to this type of scenery are rare. It is all the more important, therefore, that you view the garden with a discerning eye, always bearing in mind that a mountain is a mountain, an ocean is an ocean, and a stream is a stream.

Curiously, while the *Illustrations* tells us to plant "herbs from the seashore on the seashore," we are given no specific information as to what those herbs might be. As for trees, only one variety, the pine, is mentioned in regard to a type of seashore scenery, the ebb-tide beach. [8]

HABITATS IN THE GARDEN

The two habitats having the most plants associated with them in the *Illustrations* are deep mountains and villages. [9] No doubt these both had a special significance and charm for the aristocrats living in the capital, many of whom had never experienced such scenery other than in literature and paintings. These habitats may also have been attractive for their contrasts: one rugged and remote, the other pastoral and domesticated.

In the deep mountains of Japan, cypress and cryptomeria grow in stands, not unlike our American redwood. Aromatic trees such as camphor scent the air, contributing to the dark, mysterious quality and to the sense of lofty remoteness these uninhabited areas possess. Beneath the canopy of trees, there is wild sumac and bamboo grass. In contrast, on the open fields of agrarian villages, near farmhouse fences, one finds such fruit-bearing trees as mandarin orange and pomegranate. In the landscape garden, such trees were often planted in association with a wooden fence in order to bring out this domestic quality. At ground level useful herbs like calanthe and horseradish were planted.

There is a great physical and psychological distance that separates the habitats of cypress and mandarin orange. The first is remote, secluded, dark, and cool. The second is close to human habitation, open, bright, and warm. So in a garden where scenic effects are consciously taken into account, planting a cypress and a mandarin orange side by side in an undifferentiated landscape (without providing significant visual cues to a change in geological terrain and thus habitat) would be stretching credulity to the limit, and the effect would be lacking in meaning and beauty. At the same time, it should be borne in mind that in an art seeking to convey the experiential quality of natural landscape, the designer, like the painter, may compress a great distance into a relatively short interval of time or space. For example, in the left rear corner of a site no more than thirty feet square, the designer might plant several cypress on an artificial hill to create the effect of a deep mountain, with a retaining wall of boulders to simulate a rocky cliff. The mandarin orange could then be planted in the right front corner near the residence, in a sun-filled meadowy space that extends out to the front bank of a stream bed (wet or dry) running along the base of the retaining wall. The stream bed thus serves as the primary demarcation between the two habitats and their corresponding geological zones.

Just as the principle of natural habitat implies that plants from distinctly different habitats do not belong together, it suggests that plants from the same habitat have an affinity for each other. The members of a plant community share a given habitat because they have similar or symbiotic needs for light and nourishment. One such example is a pair so inextricably linked in the Japanese mind that item 40 of the *Illustrations* maintains, "It is unthinkable to plant wisteria without pines." This combination, striking in its natural setting because of the way the lavender-pink wisteria clusters are set off by the deep green of the pines on which they twine, was regularly depicted in Chinese and Japanese painting. Our own version of this scenic effect may be found along the coastal plain of the Southeast, where a wisteria can grow as high as seventy-five feet up a hundred-foot Loblolly pine. "Nevertheless," the text goes on to say, attaching less importance to the conventional pairing than to the beautiful color contrast, "because of the fascinating effect, it is fine to plant [wisteria] in the umbrage of other trees such as hinoki cypress."

Merely installing a plant in the appropriate setting in a landscape garden is not enough. In nature, not only do environmental factors such as orientation to the sun, soil type, and weather impose limits on the types of plants that will survive in a given habitat, but they shape these plant materials as they grow. By comparison, conditions in the landscape garden are generally milder and more conducive to rapid growth.[10]

Pruning is a natural solution to this problem. As an ancillary art pruning was highly developed in Japan and to this day constitutes an important part of the traditional garden designer's apprenticeship. Basic principles of pruning are presented in the *Illustrations* in item 56, one of six dealing with the care and planting of trees and herbs.

The essential message here is that each type of tree should be pruned to bring out its inherent qualities. Trees are divided into three categories, depending on whether their habit is upright, oblique, or spreading (vertical, diagonal, or horizontal—the three basic shapes or forces that occur prominently throughout the text; fig. 9). A fourth category includes those trees whose main interest lies in their foliage and whose branches are left hidden by the outer leaves as they would be in nature. You must never cut the central leader of an upright tree (if you cut it, you will destroy the tree's natural form, and you will be kept busy in succeeding years pruning the new vertical shoots that will compete to replace it). Similarly, the habit of an oblique or horizontally branched tree must be respected.

There are other qualities of trees that would affect pruning: Is the branching pattern of the tree opposite or alternate? Is it a pine tree (whose new candles can be pinched back each spring)? Do the flower buds form on last year's or the current year's growth? Generally, Japanese pruning techniques tend to accentuate, at a much earlier age than would normally be possible, the beautiful lines of the trunk and branching structure and spreading crown that a tree takes on as it reaches maturity.

The Japanese black pine provides a striking example of the application of such techniques. Like our Monterey pine of the West Coast, it thrives on rocky cliffs subject to harsh seacoast conditions. In the garden it is planted in coarse sandy soil and then pruned to suggest the irregular branching pattern and gnarled, windswept effect of its counterparts growing in the wild (pls. 3, 4). The philosophy of garden design expressed in the principle of natural habitat has a kindred spirit in the Prairie school, a regional movement that grew up around Chicago in the late nineteenth and early twentieth centuries. It was Frank Lloyd Wright, the best-known architect of this school, who once called the movement's lesser-known crusader in the field of

Fig. 9.   Illustration of sinuous pines embodying all three forces: vertical, diagonal, and horizontal. From the *Mustard Seed Garden Manual of Painting*.

landscape architecture, Jens Jensen, a "nature poet." The principle of natural habitat set forth in the *Illustrations* has an uncannily similar modern correspondent in Jensen's musing on the roles that plants play in the landscape garden:[11]

> Some plants express their beauty in a lowland landscape and some on the rocky cliffs. Some fulfill their mission in the rolling hilly country, and some belong to the vast prairies of Mid-America. Others sing the song of sand dunes, still others of rocky lands. A grove of crab-apple trees on the edge of the open prairie landscape gives a distinct note to the plains.

With the ecology movement of the 1970s, there has been a rebirth of interest on the part of landscape architects in "the re-establishment of prairie-like plantings as a viable alternative to the standard lawns and woody ornamental plantings seen throughout most of the country's cities and suburbs."[12] While the prairie restoration movement has a number of objectives, including ecological, functional, and educational concerns, "some may be aesthetically-oriented, with a primary goal of recreating the 'visual essence' of prairie. . . ."[13] This notion, it will be seen, comes closest to the classical Japanese garden ideal we have been discussing.

Rocks and the Principle of Geological Zones

The prairie restorationist most likely begins by considering how a disturbed site must once have looked. He then determines what varieties and arrangement of plants would be most suitable in restoring the appearance of its original habitats. The Danish immigrant Jens Jensen chose for his palette the native plants he found growing in their habitats around Chicago, where rolling, wooded hills gave way to the prairie. He worked these plants into the existing terrain by applying them in softly sweeping masses of texture and color along prairielike clearings of grass and water. Though he spoke of such geological features as rocky cliffs, rolling hills, and sand dunes, it seems he did not venture very far to create in a landscape garden geological effects not already on the site.

The classical Japanese garden designer was in this regard more adventurous. While he was expected to fully exploit existing features on the site, the designer could also manipulate the terrain and position rocks and plants to create effects that differed markedly from the surrounding landscape. Even a plot of land that had originally been level, such as that of the Katsura villa, could be transformed into an ever-changing montage of scenic effects ranging from those of the deep mountains to the seashore. Such manipulations meant that the designer had to devote as much attention to the geological formation of the landscape as Jens Jensen devoted to plants and their respective habitats. For the Japanese garden designer was, in effect, creating the various habitats from the ground up.

In nature, geological forces literally lay the groundwork for habitats to evolve. After that, the forces of erosion gradually help shape the land. Finally, climate plays a major role in determining the plant communities characteristic of each habitat. It is rock that, through igneous, sedimentary, and metamorphic processes, functions as the skeletal "bone" that shapes the earth's topographical features.

In the Japanese garden, compositions of natural rocks play a comparable role. As in nature, the relationship of exposed rock—whether in concentrated formations or loosely scattered—to the landforms in the garden provides visual cues regarding the geological forces that have shaped the landscape. So one may expect to find in a classical Japanese garden anything from the dramatic scenery associated with exposed vertical rock formations (if water is available, there is apt to be a towering waterfall and a rushing mountain stream) to the more gentle scenery of rolling hills and fields and marsh, where rocks only occasionally dot the landscape.[14]

Any number of classical garden examples bear witness to the primacy of rocks in the traditional Japanese landscape garden. The two earliest extant garden manuals confirm this: the proportion of text devoted to rocks compared to that devoted to plants is 25 : 10 percent for *Sakuteiki* and 50 : 35 percent for the *Illustrations*.[15] *Sakuteiki*'s very first words, *ishi o taten koto*, are used in the sense of "In making gardens, . . ." but literally mean "In setting rocks. . . ."

But if rocks play such an important role in classical Japanese gardens, how is it that neither in *Sakuteiki* nor in the *Illustrations* do we find a statement of a principle governing the use of rocks—a principle of geological zones—comparable to the principle of natural habitat for plants? We do find statements that implicitly point to such a principle. For example, *Sakuteiki* maintains:[16]

> Placing sideways a rock which originally stood upright, or setting upright a rock which originally lay sideways is taboo. If this taboo is violated, the rock will most assuredly turn into a "rock of revengeful spirits," and will bring a curse.

And the *Illustrations* likewise notes in item 12:

> There is an instruction that says you are not to change the position of a rock from what it was in the mountains. Placing a rock so that the part which was underneath in the mountains is on top is called "reversing the rock," and is to be avoided. To do this would anger the spirit of the rock and would bring bad luck.

mountain

river

ocean

Fig. 10. Examples of mountain, river, and ocean rocks.

In both passages, the designer is exhorted to respect the original position of the rock in nature. But nowhere is he given a general principle stating that rocks are to be positioned in the garden as befits the geological zones where they were first formed and found.

It may be that designers, who already had a rich vocabulary of named rocks available to them, felt no need to stand far enough back from the specific rules governing their use to formulate such a principle. In any case evidence from the oral tradition as it has come down to us today indicates that rocks were indeed classified and used in accordance with the geological zones where they were originally found. On more than one occasion during my apprenticeship, Kinsaku Nakane noted that there were "mountain rocks," "river rocks," and "ocean rocks" (that is, rocks from each of these geological zones in nature), sometimes implying and sometimes actually pointing out examples of how they were used to create the impression of comparable scenery in the garden (fig. 10). At Ritsurin Park, in Shikoku, he directed my attention to a composition of convoluted, whitish rocks seen from the pavilion Kikugetsu-tei (pl. 5), explaining that they had originally been found on the seashore. Here, on a sandy "beach" along the shore of the pond, they re-created the impression of that scenery, though no ocean wave would ever strike their smoothly worn contours again. That work had already been accomplished by the sea, and now, thanks to the designer's successful composition, was there for us to see and sense.

This is an application of what can now be called the principle of geological zones (or the "principle of geological formation," to use an expression that reflects the actual forces and processes involved). Because it so closely parallels the principle of natural habitat, it can be formulated by substituting the word "rocks" for "plants" and the term "geological zones" for "natural habitat" in the statement of the principle of natural habitat in the *Illustrations*. It would then read as follows:

> In the setting of rocks, you make their geological zones your model. You will not go astray so long as you bear in mind the principle of setting rocks from deep mountains in the deep mountains of the garden, rocks from hills and fields in the hills and fields, rocks from freshwater shores on the freshwater shores, and rocks from the seashore on the seashore.

Fig. 11. Offshore composition of Frolicking Birds Rocks, at Yōsuien garden in Wakayama Prefecture, showing the characteristic horizontal and diagonal lines.

It is assumed that the designer possesses keen powers of observation and the creative ability to translate his insights and images into effective perceptual forms. Several such observations of natural phenomena, most often accompanied by terse comments on how to re-create their effects in the garden, may be found in both classical manuals. In *Sakuteiki*, for example, the rationale for setting rocks at a turn in the garden stream is that "this turn is supposed to have been caused by the presence of this rock which the stream could not demolish."[17] Similarly, item 7 of the *Illustrations* tells us that "the phenomenon of 'rocks at the bend of a twisting river' . . . means that you set rocks at eccentric angles where the water flows turbulently as it makes a turn" (pl. 6).

One named rock in the *Illustrations* indicates that meteorological effects were also a part of the working vocabulary of the Japanese garden designer. Item 68 reminds him that the Hovering Mist Rock is a vertical rock set "at a point close to the pond where one might find the trailing ridge of a lower peak. This is because the mist always rises from a point close to the pond." Without a thorough understanding of this phenomenon, we are told, it will be impossible to set this rock properly. Whatever knowledge the designer had of it—and other atmospheric conditions— presumably had to be gained firsthand, through observation.

NAMES OF ROCKS AND THEIR SCENIC EFFECTS

The naming of rock compositions used in Japanese gardens is a fascinating topic, the more so for the lack of such a convention among Western designers. Of the fifty- seven named rocks mentioned in the *Illustrations*, twenty-three (40 percent) refer directly to scenic effects (see appendix 2). No less than twenty of these represent water-related effects, while only three refer to mountain scenery. We should not conclude from this that the scenic effects of mountains were considered less important in the design of classical Japanese gardens. In fact, the rocks that play key roles in the composition, such as the Rock of the Spirit Kings or the Taboo Rock, are mostly "mountain" rocks. Their names, however, have been borrowed from the prevailing social and religious philosophies and allude to rather than directly reveal how they were used. This metaphorical use of names is discussed again in chapter 4.

Several of the names for scenic effects are used figuratively to refer to qualities like those that may be sensed in the movement of birds or fish or in the slanting lines of wind-driven rain. For example, the endearing quality of the fluttering wings of birds at play is captured in a composition of rocks called the Frolicking Birds Rocks (item 88) whose forms produce an interplay of horizontal and diagonal lines (fig. 11). The uses of rocks to re-create impressions other than those derived from the earth's geophysical features might be called imagistic. These two types of visual effects can be compatible—like cumulus clouds, rock formations in nature often do suggest such images as a human face or the figure of an animal.

Given the relatively softer, more densely forested mountains of Japan, where rock formations appear only sporadically through the greenery—as compared with the dramatic uprising rock formations that stretch for miles in the mountains of northern China and the American Southwest—it is not surprising that geological effects such as exposed rock strata, folding, and faulting are not fully exploited in classical Japanese gardens. Were they to be, such natural geological phenomena could have important scenic value, as well as serve as a device for unifying the entire composition. The longitudinal axis and grain of rocks could be set parallel to an imaginary axial line running through the garden, for example. There is no statement of a general principle to this effect in either of the classical garden manuals. But it could rightly be inferred by an American designer who would draw inspiration from the surrounding landscape when making a garden in Phoenix, Arizona.

Fuzei *and the Shift to Quality-Oriented Landscape*

The principles of natural habitat and geological zones serve as keynotes in the broad philosophical framework of classical landscape garden design, and root it firmly in the world of nature that is our home. Especially in *Sakuteiki* do we find an emphasis on re-creating selected natural features and scenic places. While this same feature-oriented approach can be found in the *Illustrations*, it is not there to the same degree. Instead, in the *Illustrations* we find an emphasis on the designer's materials and how they are used.[18]

This is important, for by paying more attention to these perceptual qualities— size, shape, texture, configuration—of materials, the fifteenth-century manual roots the garden not so much in the natural world as in the functioning of the human senses that perceive it. This shift in emphasis is signaled as well by the relative occurrence in *Sakuteiki* and the *Illustrations* of the aesthetic concept *fuzei*. The word *fuzei* is written with the Chinese characters for "breeze" and "feeling" and conveys the sense of "atmosphere" or "mood" (fig. 12). I have translated it here as "scenic effect," and sometimes as "scenic ambience" or "scenic quality," when the atmosphere referred to in the *Illustrations* is that of a particular landscape scene, such as pines clustered along the flanks of a waterfall or isles in a bay viewed on a misty morning. *Fuzei* implies a poetic, quality-oriented approach to design. It describes the effect upon the viewer of those emanations that the design produces by virtue of its peculiar configuration of perceptual qualities. No doubt because these emana-

Fig. 12.   The word *fuzei* is written with the characters for "breeze" and "feeling."

tions seem to pervade the space between the art object and the viewer, charging it with their special quality, the word *fuzei* and several of our own English terms for it contain the element "air" or something similarly ethereal.[19]

Fuzei occurs fifty-nine times in the *Illustrations*, and only four times in *Sakuteiki*. This and the emphasis of the *Illustrations* on the perceptual qualities of materials used in the design would appear to reflect a nascent awareness of the tremendous power that such qualities have to evoke a mood or an atmosphere. Once the awareness becomes fully conscious, the garden designer no longer has to faithfully reproduce features of the natural landscape in order to re-create the moods associated with them. Initially, it must have appeared that such moods belonged to the landscapes in which they were sensed, just as the indigenous Shinto *kami* (spirits) were believed to reside in specially designated rocks and trees and in aspects of flowing water. With the *Illustrations*, we witness the beginning of an awareness of the extent to which such feelings could be generated within the human heart through the pathways of the senses.

REPRESENTATION AND EXPERIENCE IN THE GARDEN

This brings us to an important juncture: What exactly is the relationship between natural scenery and the scenery created in gardens? Many of us Westerners have been taught from early childhood to accept unquestioningly the validity of a way of seeing and establishing our relationship to nature known as "naturalism" or "realism." As a mode of representation, says Carol Donnell-Kotrozo, "naturalism is commonly associated with a certain traditional method of rendering objects through the use of perspective, modeling, and an emphasis on visual description, [and] any deviation from this norm is labeled antinaturalistic and becomes confused with a rejection of nature itself."[20]

Perhaps this explains the almost schizophrenic tendency in the West to regard the "objective" imitation of nature and the "subjective" expression of emotive qualities in art as mutually exclusive, and to value first one and then the other in the pendulum swing of history. Aristotle, in *The Poetics*, finds in human nature two comparable instincts that together gave birth to Poetry (or, we might say, art that has reached the level of poetry)—the instinct to imitate, to create a likeness that can be contemplated and enjoyed, and the instinct for harmony and rhythm, the "poetic instinct." There is no reason to conclude that these two instincts are mutually exclusive. In art, as with human life, there is much more to be gained from regarding them as inseparable aspects of a whole.

feature-oriented ◄─────────────────────────────► quality-oriented

Fig. 13.   The design continuum.

This is the direction that the French impressionist, and even more so the postimpressionist painters were moving. Albert Chatelet describes how Monet and Renoir, for example, in 1869 "were faced with a new problem: that of translating into paint the reflections on the water and the sparkling of the sun on the moving surface [at a tea garden along the Seine]. For unquestionably the first time the painters used juxtaposed touches of paint, unconnected by half tones or moderated passages of color. Through the contrast of these tones, they created a many-hued vibration which becomes a pictorial equivalent of the scintillating quality of the river."[21] It was their poetic instinct for movement and rhythm that enabled these painters to successfully re-create—or imitate—a visual experience of nature.

In landscape design as well, the imitative and poetic instincts can be likened to "feature-oriented" and "quality-oriented" approaches that lie at two ends of a continuum (fig. 13). In the Japanese context, at the feature-oriented end such motifs as the pine tree, a mountain, an island, or a turtle are used for their associative and recognizable narrative value. They are symbols that stand for ideas or emotions. At the quality-oriented end, shapes, colors, textures (formal qualities, or what I call "sensory effects") engage the senses and convey ideas and emotions directly. Yet, while this process of communication may be direct, the interpretation varies according to what Dewey in *Art and Experience* calls the viewer's "funded experience"—the prior experience that colors each individual's perceptions.

In this frame of reference, we need not assume that the closer a work of art or a garden gets to the quality-oriented end of the continuum, the further it is from human experience of the world. The rock garden of the temple Ryōanji in Kyoto has gained fame in the West, largely because of its presumed similarity to nonrepresentational minimalist or abstract art. Yet, in light of the Japanese aesthetic that produced this garden, it would be more accurate to recognize its quality-oriented design as having been inspired by a direct encounter with the powerful forms and kinetic energies actually present in the natural environment. By the same token, more "representational" gardens that lie at the feature-oriented end of the spectrum succeed because they rely on quality-oriented design techniques. In human perception, as in nature, features and qualities interact to form a vibrant, living whole. Similarly, the garden and the observer interact to produce an experience of nature.

CHANGING DEPICTIONS OF NATURE

The shift in emphasis from a feature-oriented to a quality-oriented aesthetic in garden making has a parallel in the approach to depicting nature developed in two successive periods of Chinese landscape painting, the Northern Sung (960–1126) and the Southern Sung (1127–1279). While not entirely true, it is generally agreed that Northern Sung painting is more concerned with representative likeness, clear delineation of nature in its multiplicity based on objective observation, and carefully balanced structure. The result tends to produce monumental and "realistic" works. Southern Sung painting, by contrast, tends to be lyrical, impressionistic, and suggestive. By depicting less, more was left to the imagination. Through light ink washes and simply leaving the paper or silk blank, the effects of mist or haze could be produced and limitless expanses suggested. Fewer brushstrokes were used, but in a highly expressive manner to convey the desired nuances. Southern Sung painters thus found in the quality-oriented approach and the limited materials of India ink, brush, and silk or paper a wide range of expressive possibilities.

Many such works were brought to Japan; by the middle of the fourteenth century there was, for instance, a sizable collection at the Zen Buddhist temple Engakuji in Kamakura.[22] As early as the beginning of the fifteenth century, a number of Japanese painters had already mastered the highly suggestive techniques of this genre, including the use of light washes, coarse brush, and the so-called *haboku* or "broken ink" style (pl. 7). By the late 1400s, many more works of Chinese art had been brought to Japan to become part of the shogunal collection, and a catalog, the *Kundaikan sayū chōki*, was compiled by experts in the employ of the shogun Ashikaga Yoshimasa.

There had been in Japan from at least as early as the Heian period a very close connection between the aesthetic ideals and practices of landscape painting and garden design (many aristocrats and priests did both). We should expect, therefore, that the *Illustrations*, dated 1466,[23] should dwell substantially more on atmospheres and the materials with which these effects were created than did *Sakuteiki*, a much earlier work. Had the fifteenth-century transmitters of the *Illustrations* been as forthcoming with their own reflections and commentary as was the author of *Sakuteiki*, we would likely have a far more explicit statement about the power of certain garden materials, skillfully employed, to produce subtle moods and atmospheric effects of the kind seen in the ink painting of the period.

Such a quality-oriented approach is prefigured in the Frolicking Birds Rocks, a composition in which the horizontal and diagonal lines of rocks evoke an image of birds at play. But such images, once labeled, can easily degenerate into sterile clichés. This is less a problem when the desired effect is diffuse, atmospheric, and therefore not so dependent upon specific forms. In such cases, the word "image" is no longer applicable. Our attention, rather than being attracted to distinctive features, is gently pulled away from the forms by the intangible forces that enliven the entire composition. In an intriguing passage in item 18 of the *Illustrations*, the creation of one such scenic effect, the ebb-tide beach, becomes the ultimate test of the designer's mastery of the art:

> Another type of shoreline scenery is the ebb-tide beach, which has no striking features but simply creates the impression of the tide constantly ebbing and flowing. Here, if just by spreading fine and coarse grades of sand and without setting any rocks you can visually re-create a single scenic ambience . . . you have nothing more to learn. The visual impression of an ebb-tide beach is produced simply by the way the tree is planted and the way the fine and coarse grades of sand are spread.

The emphasis here is not on the materials, tree and sand; these are downplayed. It is the way these commonplace materials are used that is of utmost importance in achieving the effect. Outside of "fine and coarse grades of sand," no specifications are given for the perceptual qualities—size, shape, texture, color—of the materials. The final test is the only test: Does it work? It all hinges on "the way the tree is planted, and the way the sand is spread."

Perhaps the closest that the *Illustrations* comes to articulating such an approach to design is the following sentence in item 32: "Recollecting the subtle seasonal moods of *waka* poetry from ancient times up to the present, you must re-create with a quiet, graceful charm those moods that speak to you in your innermost heart." This passage occurs in the context of important directions on how rocks are to be set in a composition. Notable here is that the "subtle seasonal moods" are not those seen in nature, but those discovered in poetry, and it is these moods, not features of nature, that the designer is to re-create in the garden. As one soon learns in the course of his apprenticeship, the designer must not only be acquainted with nature in all its manifestations, he must also be well versed in the sensitive responses to nature that his cultural forebears have made, whether in painting or poetry or other art forms.

TWO GARDENS AT DAITOKUJI

The experimentation with the expressive possibilities of limited materials that took place in the painting of Sung China and fifteenth-century Muromachi Japan found its way into landscape design with the dry landscape garden (*karesansui*) of the subtemple Daisen'in at the Zen monastery Daitokuji in Kyoto, created in 1513 by the retired head abbot Kogaku Sōkō.[24] Here the palette was close to being monochromatic, limited as it was to the green shades of plants, the off-white gravel and plaster wall, and the muted blue-gray and taupe of rocks, with flowers present only for a time in a restrained way. The design of Daisen'in, as might be expected of such a prototype, is transitional, somewhere between the representational, feature-oriented landscape gardens of the past and the more quality-oriented dry landscape gardens that flourished in the seventeenth century in the early Edo period. In its composition it is modeled on the finely executed vertical scroll paintings of the Northern Sung period, while in its atmospheric qualities it owes much to the more mood-oriented Southern Sung landscapes favored in Japan. The design has been attributed to the great landscape painter Sōami (1485?–1525). It is more likely the result of a collaboration between Sōami and Kogaku Sōkō.

In an L-shaped space barely nine feet wide along the north and east veranda of the abbot's quarters of Daisen'in, a multifaceted landscape has been "painted" in three dimensions with more than one hundred rocks, a few select plantings, and gravel (pls. 8–11). From a background of distant mountains (the dark green, glossy foliage of camellia) and translucent mists (white plaster walls), the landscape moves forward and down, first in a torrential waterfall (vertical white marbling in a jade-green rock) and then in a series of rapids, until the water (now white gravel) rushes beneath a stone bridge and flows out into a river. Gradually the banks widen and steep cliffs (angular rocks) are replaced by more placid, rounded forms. A cargo junk (an unusually shaped rock) floats downstream, as if to carry us out to sea (the gravel-covered courtyard located to the south of the abbot's quarters).

Here no actual water has been used, for, in the words of art historian Yoshinobu Yoshinaga, "The [*karesansui*] garden is an attempt to represent the innermost essence of water, without actually using water, and to represent it at that even more profoundly than would be possible with real water."[25] That the artist, highly attuned to the qualities of a limited range of materials, could provide sensory cues that would so trigger the imagination was the stunning culmination of a wave of culture which broke first over China and then Japan, a wave that has been linked to Ch'an (Zen) Buddhism's emphasis upon radically nondualistic, intuitive knowing.

In creating the dry landscape garden of the Daisen'in, Kogaku Sōkō is said to have had his pick of some of the finest rocks left behind on Kyoto estates after the devastation of the Ōnin War (1467–77).[26] A look at the angular rock of the pine islet and the rocks on the southern end of the crane island with their sharp zigzag lines reminiscent of Sesshū's bold brushstrokes, or the saddle-shaped rock with its chalky white organic form ribbed by taupe extrusions, or the boat stone with its cargo-junk-shaped prow attests to this better than any words could. This is a garden of extraordinary rocks, all interrelated in a masterful composition to produce a sequence of scenic effects like that of a Northern Sung landscape painting.

The courtyard customarily found south of the abbot's quarters in a Zen monastery, which at Daisen'in is simply a gravel expanse with a double-stepped hedge wrapping around the rear and right side, was in the early Edo period quite often used as the site for making a dry landscape garden. One such garden, probably created in the second quarter of the seventeenth century, is located at the Honbō, headquarters of the Daitokuji's monastic complex. A gravel expanse covers more than 60 percent of the area. To the far left, three brooding rocks nestled deep in the shadow of clipped camellia "mountains" serve as a furtive focal point (pl. 12). Two of these rocks are tall, close to seven feet in height, while the third, at the left, stands less than half as high. In texture these rocks are smooth and hard; only a few wrinkles and fissures break the solidity of their surfaces. In color they are dark, appearing almost black in their shadowed enclave.

This composition is said to represent a waterfall. But what kind of water surges from such heights in so somber a manner, not whitened by its fall? Clearly, the designer was more interested in conveying a grave, mysterious mood than he was in faithfully reproducing the features of some waterfall he had seen.

In the foreground at the far right, two low-lying rocks have been set side by side to form a kind of offshore island surrounded by an immense "sea." The rock on the left has a broad, slightly undulating upper surface that rises barely two inches above the ground. It has a smooth, solid texture and a deep taupe color, like the rocks of the waterfall composition. Twice as long as it is wide, its manta-ray-like form points ever so slightly, but unmistakably, to the left. This pointing is echoed by the more upright bump of a rock to the right, which, with its compact form, may in terms of visual dynamics be likened to a tugboat pushing a barge. Its power is concentrated, assertive, while that of the broad rock is amorphous, ponderous.

These two, the waterfall composition at the left rear and the island at the right front, are diagonally counterpoised across an immense gravel sea. A taut stillness reigns, through which a sustained force is about to, or has just broken forth from the silence into sound. It is the compact rock to the right which punctures this silence like a sharp drum beat. Now we sense its lingering reverberations, and involuntarily almost hold our breath until it once again beats inside us like the pounding of our heart. What we are experiencing here is not so much a scenic effect as a purely sensory one of rhythm and stillness.

THE ART WE SEE:

SENSORY EFFECTS

3

In looking at an object we reach out for it. With an invisible finger we move through the space around us, go out to the distant places where things are found, touch them, catch them, scan their surfaces, trace their borders, explore their texture. It is an eminently active occupation.

Impressed by this experience, early thinkers described the physical process of vision correspondingly. For example, Plato, in his Timaeus, *asserts that the gentle fire that warms the human body flows out through the eyes in a smooth and dense stream of light. Thus a tangible bridge is established between the observer and the observed thing, and over this bridge the impulses of light that emanate from the object travel to the eyes and thereby to the soul.*

—Rudolf Arnheim

Physiologically, the human body is tailored to the earth's physical environment. Our bodies are the media by which we know ourselves and the world: our sensations of pleasure and pain tell us whether our inner needs are being met or deprived, and whether we are safe in our surroundings or in some way threatened by them. From earliest childhood, we learn the powers and limitations of our bodies, not by rational observation but in a highly immediate, sensory way. We do not have to understand the principle of gravitational attraction in order to recognize and respond to it. The forces of nature—such as heat and gravity—are real to us only to the extent we experience them. We *embody* them, which is to say that we interiorize them through our sensations so that they become our own, highly personal and absolute. When we stumble on a staircase what we feel is not an invisible force pulling us toward the center of the earth but a sudden loss of balance coupled with a sensation of falling. There are hundreds of such physiological responses that we all learn through firsthand experiences in childhood.

People who choose to be visual artists tend to be acutely attuned to sensory experience; they also must have the capacity to shape materials to express their vision in a concrete form that others may enjoy. When producing sensory effects for others to experience, designers rely on intuition, for their own bodily responses are part and parcel of the human condition. Without the landscape designer's sensitivity to the effects of the forms, textures, and colors relative to one another in the spatial composition, the created object would lack the concentrated power of art. Effects of scale, such as immensity and intimacy; effects of spacing and shape, such as rhythm and movement; effects of texture and color intensity, such as an enhanced sense of depth and luminescence—all these and more play an especially vital role in the art of the Japanese garden. They are at the heart of its power to create an illusion of physical reality by teasing our perceptual systems into belief.

The garden is, of course, primarily a visual art, but it can also directly engage our sense of hearing (a waterfall, leaves rustling in the wind) and our sense of smell (fragrant wisteria, pine needles). The sense of touch—including both the tactile sensations received through the skin and the kinesthetic sensations resulting from the interaction of muscle groups—is directly addressed as one moves physically through a garden designed for strolling in, but it is more often engaged indirectly, through visual cues such as those of texture, shape, and line. The sense of taste is even less directly involved (unless, of course, one actually indulges in a persimmon); yet we do speak of certain gardens as having an "astringent" or "dry" flavor.

Garden Scale: Unity of Site and Situation

Just as an oil painting requires a canvas, a landscape garden requires a site. The analogy is revealing, the more so for the disparity that arises upon closer examination. The canvas stretched over a frame is a cheap, portable, flat surface on which the oil painter can lay his oils. Only in relatively recent times has the Western artist chosen to respect the two-dimensional surface of the canvas by allowing the weave to show through and by rejecting the use of three-dimensional perspective techniques.

But for economic if not ecological reasons, the landscape garden designer has always had to come to terms with the nature of the site; each site is different and will impose its own peculiar qualities on the design at least as much as the designer imposes his imagination on it. What is the topography? Does the site slope up away from the primary vantage point, making it easy to create a sense of enclosure, or is the reverse true? Are there undesirable features, such as a neighbor's garage, which must be screened out? The old brick wall of a commercial building on an adjacent lot may provide an attractive backdrop. And one must have a very good reason for not incorporating a distant mountain peak into the composition.

The designer's other master is the "client." For a residential garden and far more so for a public garden, the client translates into a complex set of demands that may be called the "situation." What does the client want? One person may prefer the elaborate scheme of a pond with a waterfall and a stream. Another may prefer the more suggestive qualities of a dry landscape. What can the client afford? How is the garden to be used? Design constraints will differ depending on whether the area is to be reserved for contemplation or used for activities like children's play or picnicking.

There is ample evidence, in the *Illustrations* as well as in *Sakuteiki*, that classical Japanese garden designers were well aware of how important the site and the situation are in the design process. Figure H of the *Illustrations* puts it this way: "If you are to make an attractive garden, the design must be a highly sensitive response to both the site and the situation, with nothing clumsy or coarse about it."

The choice of a site is, of course, inextricably tied to the client's situation. Will the scale of the garden be large or small? Item 23 of the *Illustrations* cautions the designer to keep an eye on the budget:

> The size of the garden must be determined on the basis of the master's financial situation. If the master lacks the financial means, he may be defeated by the garden. Such matters are of great importance. Keep them firmly in mind.

No experienced designer would deny either the wisdom of this warning or its relevance today.

A high-ranking aristocrat of the Heian period when *Sakuteiki* was written, or of the later age when the *Illustrations* was drawn up, like a wealthy person in modern America, was expected to play host to various social activities that simultaneously advanced cultural and political ends. The garden as well as the architecture provided the proper space and setting for such functions, and served as a visual symbol of the owner's power and position. *Sakuteiki* makes it clear that the size of the garden was primarily a function of the social activities to be carried out there—based, of course, on the wealth and status of the owner—when it specifies that, for a large-scale estate,[1]

> the distance of sixty to seventy feet will be required from the outer pillars supporting the roof of the staircase (*kaiin*) southward to the shoreline of the pond. For the Imperial Palace (*dairi*), the distance should extend even to eighty or ninety feet in order to provide for the imperial ceremonies.

Next we are told that the island in such a garden should be large enough to accommodate the Musicians' Stage (*gakuya*), which was seventy to eighty feet across. Such size requirements had no aesthetic function in themselves, but were the dimensions of a style of life and architecture established by court nobles in the Heian period. Garden estates at this time, around the eleventh century, were built in what is called the *shinden* style, with residential buildings facing the garden to the south, and corridors extending southward from either end of the residence to pavilions overlooking the water (fig. 14). Here courtiers would engage in boating excursions and leisurely view garden landscapes representing famous scenic sites in China or coastal Japan. In subsequent generations, the heirs to power and culture continued to look to the Heian period as a Golden Age. Clues in the *Illustrations* suggest that the *shinden* style of the Heian period still served as the model for the layout of the larger gardens referred to in item 32 of its text—those "estates of between 4 and 8 *chō*" (about 12–25 acres).

Fig. 14. Idealized version of a *shinden*-style residence and garden. From *Kaoku zakkō*, an Edo-period architectural miscellany.

But, as suggested earlier, the aesthetic quality of a garden is not dependent on its size. The same may be said of a skillfully rendered landscape painting or photograph, which has the power to move us in ways the original scenery might. This effect upon the senses is largely due to the fact that our eyes attach far more importance to cues about proportionate relationships, including relative size, that hold among objects in the field of view than they attach to cues—meager at best—about the absolute size of those objects. What this means, and what the artist intuitively knows, is that[2]

> looking from its fixed viewpoint, there is nothing to indicate to the eye
> (apart from the purely physical difficulty of focusing very close objects)
> whether it is looking at a miniature perspective picture 1 in. away, or one
> ten times as high and wide but 10 ins. away, or one 100 times bigger but 100
> ins. away. Neither the scale nor the perspective nor the area enclosed by the
> frame are changed by making the same proportionate change in both
> viewing distance and frame dimensions. So the artist can please himself
> whether he paints a miniature portrait to be looked at one foot away or a
> larger picture to be looked at from a proportionately greater distance.

Similarly, a client of limited financial means can enjoy a vast and aesthetically composed landscape garden even if he has only a modest courtyard site to create it in.

The rocks he uses will be relatively small, depending, of course, on the scenic effect being created. It follows that a more spacious site, such as that of a *shinden*-style garden, will need rocks proportionately larger.

Practical examples of this principle are not hard to find. On the bank of a river running through the spacious grounds of the park-style garden Kōrakuen in Okayama, west of Osaka, is a rock so large—it would appear to be at least fifteen feet high, and even wider—that it was necessary to split it into several smaller units just to get it to the site, where it was then reassembled. Yet a rock no more than six inches high plays a very important aesthetic role in the famous dry landscape at Ryōanji, in Kyoto, where the site dimensions are greatly reduced.

Framing: The Site and the Visual Field

A landscape painter or photographer viewing classical Japanese gardens for the first time would very likely be struck by the similarity of the framing techniques used there to those of his own art. Mass plantings of small-leafed azaleas broken by a massive, flat-topped viewing rock at the water's edge may frame the scene from below; the irregular trunk of a maple or pine may frame it from the left; the horizontally spreading branches of the same tree or the undulating foliage of forested hills in the distance may frame it from above; and forming a crisp frame around the whole picture may be the horizontal and vertical lines of the veranda, posts, and eaves of the owner's residence. Exactly how the garden is enjoyed and how its views are framed will be greatly influenced by the configuration (shape and topography) of the site and the position of the adjacent buildings and surrounding features.

A classical Japanese garden—at least until the advent of the tea garden and its offspring, the stroll garden, in the sixteenth and seventeenth centuries—was primarily viewed like a painting, from the shelter of the residential quarters. To be sure, Heian courtiers did penetrate the space of those three-dimensional landscape pictures when they took their pleasure boats out onto the pond or sat along the banks of the *yarimizu* stream course and engaged in poetry competitions. And by the mid-fourteenth century, when Musō Soseki in Kyoto directed the construction of the temple Tenryūji's hill-and-pond garden, a viewer might even circumambulate the landscape on a path along the shore. Yet it is the buildings that provided the key vantage points for viewing these gardens: first and foremost, from the center of the veranda in front of the main hall; then from peripheral positions along the adjoining living quarters, corridors, and pavilions overlooking the pond.

Such gardens may be compared to a landscape scroll being unrolled horizontally before the eyes of a seated observer, most likely the master of the house or some other important personage. This mode of viewing suited both the genteel tastes of the aristocracy and the more contemplative spirit of the clergy. One need not physically enter the garden in order to partake of its pleasures. When viewers did penetrate the garden space, whether on a pleasure boat or on foot, it was as if they were entering the magical realm of a scroll painting to get a closer look, still within the context of the larger landscape.

These landscapes may have developed partly because Japanese traditional architecture was so well suited to the contemplative enjoyment of them. Wooden post-
and-beam construction (because the walls are not load-bearing) means that large
expanses between posts can be opened to the outdoors from floor to ceiling.
Typically, a roofed veranda runs along the southern exposure of the residence. Each
morning, sliding wooden panels (called *amado*, or "rain doors") are pushed back and
stored in special shutter compartments at either end of the veranda, providing an
uninterrupted view of the garden from inside. Thus does one wall of each south-
facing room become a landscape, just as the garden becomes an extension of the
living space and plays an important role in the well-being of the occupants. (Even in
many modern Japanese residences, privacy is achieved not by exterior walls and
window coverings but instead is a secondary function of the landscape; a wall, a
hedge, informal plantings, alone or in combination, may be designed to serve double
duty as a backdrop and a privacy screen.)

Gardens that are viewed primarily in this way, like a painting seen from several
vantage points centering around a principal one, may perhaps be called "scroll"
gardens to distinguish them from the stroll gardens and tea gardens of later times.
Viewing a "scroll" garden from a fixed position is similar to Japanese filmmaker
Yasujirō Ozu's long takes from a camera mounted at what would be eye level for a
person seated on the tatami-matted floor of a Japanese house. The composition of
each frame has been well thought out, and invites the viewer's lingering contemplation. Viewing a stroll garden while moving through it, on the other hand, is
comparable to the film technique known as montage, in which a succession of
different images is presented to the viewer.

What does the manner in which the garden is viewed have to do with the shape of
the site? To reiterate: a scroll garden is revealed all at once in a single frame, whereas a
stroll garden unfolds in a sequence of many frames. Since a stroll garden is laid out
along a path that may penetrate or wind through the space in any configuration, the
shape of the site is not crucial—an accommodation can be found to practically any
shape. But the proximity of the site to an established or potential observation area
makes the choice of a stroll garden less appropriate. When a site is fully open to view
from a gallery, a wall of windows, or other extensive viewing area, the scroll garden
naturally takes precedence, for the designer would seldom deny viewers the pleasure
of seeing a landscape panorama spread before them. And it is as unpleasant for
viewers to have the landscape they are contemplating marred by strollers as it is for
strollers to feel they are on display before a gallery of viewers. (Yet the two garden
types may be combined to fascinating effect, as may be seen in many Japanese
gardens dating from the seventeenth century on.)

Now, when a garden is viewed in scroll-garden fashion, all in a single frame, the
shape of the site and the way it is framed—two factors that are intimately related—
become much more important. Because so much attention is riveted on a single
frame, as it is with Ozu's long takes, the artist—whether filmmaker, photographer,
or landscape garden designer—naturally lavishes great care on the way the composition is framed. For the landscape designer, this means finding the frame that will
expose (or obscure) just the right amount of the site when viewed from the vantage
point. This may involve designing an entirely new architectural frame to take full

advantage of the assets of the site, as is possible when building a new structure or remodeling an existing one. Most often the landscape designer works within the constraints offered by an existing building, and adjusts the garden frame by manipulating screening devices (trees, bushes, fences) in the foreground and background.

The *Illustrations* has much to say on this important subject. In item 17, it is the trees that serve to illustrate a fundamental rule of "single frame" composition:

> There is an expression, "ten thousand trees in a single glance." If asked what this means, I would reply that you must plant the trees in a garden so that all are visible without exception in just one glimpse. No matter how fine a tree you plant up close to the eaves, it must not conceal the smaller trees in the distance.

Like a painting in which every brushstroke and every patch of color contributes to the overall effect (which is grasped immediately, "in a single glance"), a scroll garden should have no tree—in other words, no element—that is superfluous to the desired effect.

We know that the *Illustrations* must be a manual devoted primarily to landscape gardens viewed in scroll-garden fashion, for only in that context do the above and other statements in the text make any sense. The following passages, for example, appear in connection with figures G and H, illustrating difficult and ideal sites for landscape gardens.

> It is invariably difficult to design a garden for a site that is narrow and runs deep such as the one illustrated [fig. G]. You should leave it open at the back.

> A garden site that is wide across the front such as the one illustrated [in H] is easy to work with and pleasing to look at. If the garden site is square, make it a little wider at the eaves.

Neither a narrow, deep site nor a square site would present any problems to the designer of a stroll garden, so these prescriptions for a less than ideal site can mean only one thing: the garden is to be viewed primarily from one side in scroll-garden fashion.

But why should the ideal site for a scroll garden be wide and not too deep? Film again provides a useful parallel. The movie screen, due to practical necessity, has a fixed shape and size. In the 1950s wide-screen projection techniques were developed to increase the sense of realism. The "aspect ratio"—the proportion of width to height of the image projected on the screen—was raised from 1.33 : 1 to its present range of between 1.65 : 1 and 1.85 : 1, and as high as 2.35 : 1 for CinemaScope.[3] The normal binocular visual field for humans is 214° from side to side (including peripheral vision) and 135° high (60° up and 75° down), a width-to-height ratio of 1.6 : 1.[4] Such wide-screen techniques worked because they accommodated the human visual field. Experiments like Cinerama were attempts to increase the sense of realism even further by "increasing the size of the projected picture so that it dominates the vision of the observer completely by filling the whole visual field and removing the frame of reference of the edges of the screen."[5]

EXTENDING THE FRAME OUT INTO THE GARDEN

The landscape garden centered around a pond west of the main hall of the temple Tenryūji in Kyoto is a mid-fourteenth-century example of a scroll garden.[6] With thirty feet between the veranda and its near shore, the pond spreads out approximately one hundred and seventy feet in width and one hundred feet in depth from the front shore to the stone bridge at the back. Just six feet beyond the bridge stand two massive vertical rocks that form the base of the waterfall composition; from here rises the steep wooded hill that serves as backdrop for the garden. For a viewer seated in the middle of the veranda opposite the waterfall composition, the landscape spreads out in a 180° panorama. We cannot really focus on more than about one-third of the scene at once. Yet, as with Cinerama, "we may not be conscious of what exactly is there, but we are marginally aware of the objects and the space on either side. It is this peripheral vision which orients us and makes the experience so vivid."[7]

In a classical Japanese scroll garden, there is more than accommodation to the visual field to orient the viewer. The very architecture that so often establishes the essential condition for this type of garden—an extended viewing area opening out onto a veranda along one side—is employed as an aesthetic framing device. The clean, uncluttered lines of traditional Japanese architecture are perfectly suited to that role. When the sliding wooden doors are removed and the rooms are completely opened to the garden, the horizontal plane of the veranda, accompanied by the sheltering eaves and supporting posts, offers a stable and secure frame of reference, thereby freeing the viewer's senses to move out into the garden space and explore the composition. Receding to left and right into the observer's peripheral vision, the line of the veranda promotes the "wide screen" effect preferred in scroll gardens. At Tenryūji, the line of the veranda is repeated in the lines of the railing and eaves. And we can find echoes of this horizontal line in the garden composition itself: Tenryūji's stone bridge is a stable horizontal that cuts across the base of the waterfall composition, and the peninsula jutting into the pond from right to left in the center foreground similarly moves across the observer's visual field (pl. 14). The very surface of the pond is a visible manifestation of the horizontal plane, and helps anchor the viewer visually and kinesthetically.

The use of framing devices may be extended to include techniques of modulation, to make a transition not only from architecture to the garden, but also from the garden to features beyond the site that are intentionally incorporated into the design. At the Old Shoin residential quarters of the Katsura villa in Kyoto, a tile-roofed wall of peach brown stucco extends out into the garden from the main entry. The wall steps down to assume a low horizontal as it penetrates the garden space, and is itself penetrated by a door-sized passageway through which the garden path leads. Several feet beyond this opening, the base of the wall begins to disappear into a moss-covered slope, and then the wall is replaced by a clipped hedge that encloses this corner of the courtyard garden in an L-shape. The transition from architecture to garden is complete. At the temple Entsūji, also in Kyoto, a low hedge and tree trunks just beyond it echo the horizontal and vertical lines of the temple building to form a transitional foil linking the courtyard garden with the "borrowed" landscape of Mount Hiei in the distance.

Let us return now to the less-than-ideal sites and methods for improving them introduced in the *Illustrations*. The solution for a site that is narrow and runs deep is to "leave it open at the back." This is simply a way of reducing the effective depth of a scroll-garden site, thereby increasing its width-to-depth ratio. The space at the back, as far as its potential for allowing a deeper penetration of the view is concerned, is discarded just as a painter might reject the use of three-dimensional perspective techniques. Real estate being more expensive than canvas, the portion of the site that has been "discarded" (fig. 15, shaded area) will naturally be put to other uses, such as a storehouse, a garden plot, or a play area, and concealed from view by whatever serves as the garden's backdrop. Kinsaku Nakane was faced with just such a narrow and deep site when he was commissioned to design a combination entry/scroll garden for the Maizuru residence overlooking Lake Biwa in 1972. His solution was to create a natural woodland screen of slender deciduous trees running in a band across the middle portion, as shown (fig. 16). An informal stepping-stone path leads from the formal entry walk across the "wide screen" space in the foreground to the open area at the back. There, hidden behind the lacy screen of trees, a lawn area welcomes informal outdoor activity.

The other less-than-ideal garden site mentioned in the *Illustrations* is square in shape. In order to increase the width-to-depth ratio, the designer is told to "make it a little wider at the eaves." That is, the level area in front of the veranda is kept as open and wide as possible, by using at the front corners only plantings that do not intrude much or by letting the space extend all the way to an attractive wooden fence at the boundaries. Then along the left and right sides of the site, plantings or artificial hills may be worked in so as to encroach more and more upon the view as the eye moves from front to back, and in this way round out and render the rear corners inconspicuous (fig. 17). It would also be wise—and this may be considered a modification of the earlier method of leaving the site open at the back—to bring the rear shoreline forward so that most of the key compositional elements fall within the front two-thirds of the site.

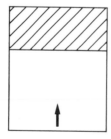

Fig. 15. Plan of a narrow, deep site.

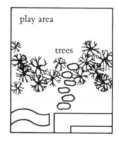

Fig. 16. Nakane's solution to a narrow, deep site at the Maizuru residence.

Fig. 17. How to make a square site appear wider.

In this way is a proper stage created on which the garden elements can be most effectively positioned for the viewer. Just as there is a primary vantage point for viewing the garden, within the garden will usually be a primary focal point around which the entire composition is organized. How this point is chosen, and how the shape of the site is modified to conform to the compositional flow originating in and leading back to the focus are questions that lie at the very heart of the design process. The applicable principles of balance are discussed in the next two sections on rhythm (proportion) and motion (directional forces). As always, such principles never exist in a vacuum, but are applied creatively by the designer according to the constraints of the site, the existing architecture, and the way the garden is to be used.

Rhythm: Proportions of Size and Spacing

Tsuki no Katsura, an early Edo-period dry landscape garden on the outskirts of Hōfu City in Yamaguchi Prefecture, is a study in proportional relationships. Its well-spaced rectangular rocks, some upright and some recumbent, like a modern sculpture invite the eyes to take measure of their relative height, width, and spacing (pl. 15). The stepping of rhythmic units in half- and fifth- and third-notes moves from horizontals to verticals in a clear, monotonous cadence like that of a Gregorian chant. Proportional relationships play an essential role in the composition of all Japanese gardens, but seldom are they so consciously bared as here.

In order to get a clearer picture of how proportional relationships function in the Japanese landscape garden, it is useful to remember that the three-dimensional space of a garden can be resolved into two movable planes that meet at right angles: the horizontal, or ground plane; and the vertical, or elevational plane (fig. 18). These are

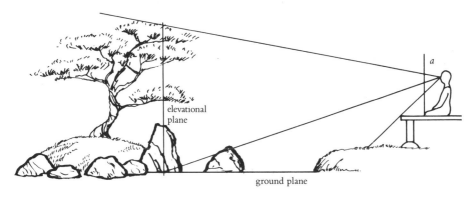

Fig. 18. Resolving the three-dimensional garden space onto a picture plane (*a*).

the same two planes represented in an architect's drawings by "plan" and "elevation" views. For the viewer, the ground plane appears to tilt upward as it recedes toward a vanishing point on the horizon. In human perception, of course, this illusion is corrected by the presence of numerous visual cues in the physical environment—the vertical lines of tree trunks, the horizontal surfaces presented by bodies of water and buildings—and by the kinesthetic sense that our bodies have of being in contact with either a level or a sloping surface.

We have said that landscape design is like painting in three dimensions. To better understand this, assume for the moment that directly in front of the viewer seated in a fixed position on the veranda in figure 18 is a window pane (*a*) that extends out beyond the limits of the visual field. Tracing the image on the glass just as it appears to the viewer would produce a two-dimensional picture of the garden like that recorded on film by a photographer or on canvas by a painter. What the landscape garden designer must now be able to do is project such a two-dimensional image back out onto the three-dimensional environment—in other words, to resolve the picture plane so artfully into the ground and elevational planes that the viewer sees all of its ten thousand trees, rocks, hills, and plains "in a single glance."

The designers of classical Japanese gardens could not have done this successfully without a knowledge of the practical implications of two laws of visual perception that correlate elevational (frontal) and ground (longitudinal) plane dimensions with their projections on the picture plane. (As we shall see, these projections also have a correlate in the two-dimensional plane of the retinal image.) James J. Gibson identifies these two laws as:[8]

> [1.] a frontal dimension (measured along a line parallel to the picture plane) is projected onto the picture plane as a size (S) that is the reciprocal of the distance (D):
> $$S = 1/D$$

> [2.] a longitudinal dimension (measured along a line perpendicular to the picture plane) is projected onto the picture plane as an altitude (A) that is a negatively accelerated function of the distance (D):
> $$A = 1/D^2$$

In other words, with increasing distance from the viewer toward the horizon, a frontal dimension such as the width or height of a rock decreases in a linear fashion as the object moves from the bottom to the top of the picture plane, while a longitudinal dimension of the same size, measured along a horizontal surface from the front to the back of the rock, "is compressed relative to the frontal dimension"—in other words, is foreshortened.[9]

That longitudinal dimensions should decrease—toward the horizon or up the picture plane—at an accelerated rate while frontal dimensions decrease at a constant rate has important implications for the designer, particularly when considering the layout of the garden and the size of key elements. Proportional relationships play a large part in transmitting the experiential quality or scenic effect of a landscape viewed in three dimensions. A rock chosen for its "faraway" qualities must have not only certain attributes of shape, texture, and coloring, but it must be in exactly the right proportion to rocks chosen for their "nearby" qualities. Positioning both rocks so that they successfully interact—with each other and with all the other garden elements—in both the horizontal and vertical garden planes requires a sensitive attunement to balance. So carefully interwoven are all the elements—and their varied spatial effects—that it is no exaggeration to say that moving any one of them is enough to utterly fracture the garden landscape.

TWO DIMENSIONS OF MEANING

The horizontal and vertical dimensions, represented by the ground and elevational planes, also have certain deep-seated meanings for us, a result of the way our senses are structured and of the basic experiences of maneuvering in the environment that we all have from early on in life. The horizontal dimension is the field of human action in which movement is observed with the greatest freedom and ease. Witness the ice skater's effortless glide. Visually, too, a horizontal plane or line tends to have a restful, placid quality. The vertical dimension corresponds to the earth's gravitational field. It requires a great effort to jump up, away from the surface of the earth. When a ballet dancer's body soars up off the stage, we sense visually and kinesthetically the dynamic, forceful nature of the act, and thrill to the momentary overcoming of gravity. The dancer's graceful return to the floor is not unexpected, for we know that what goes up, must come down. It is for the designer to decide, in response to the site and situation, whether the more sedate ground plane or the more vigorous elevational plane will play a larger role in the garden's composition.

Two classical gardens, those of Tenryūji and Daisen'in, illustrate the range of effects made possible by exploiting these two planes while accommodating the nature of the site. Figures 19 and 20 are outline tracings of panoramic photographic sequences taken from each garden's principal viewing position on the veranda. Since the angle of view encompassed from bottom to top is the same for each, we can make an accurate comparison of the relative proportions of the picture plane occupied by such key design elements as water, land, rocks, and trees.

What is surely most striking here is the relative size of the rocks. The two tallest in the Daisen'in outline sketch—*a* and *b* of figure 19 (*b* gains its rank by being closer to the viewer)—occupy a full 53 percent of the picture plane from top to bottom. The two tallest in the Tenryūji sketch—*a* and *b* of figure 20—are the twin upright rocks on the opposite shore of the pond behind the stone bridge. They occupy 7.5 percent of the picture plane, only one-seventh as much as those at Daisen'in. Of course the Daisen'in rocks stand only 10 to 18 feet from the viewer, whereas the Tenryūji rocks are located 140 feet away.

At Daisen'in, horizontal space is constricted between the veranda and the sheer walls of towering rock cliffs to create the impression of a river gorge at the viewer's feet. Vertical space is carved out by the alternating rhythm of pointed upright rocks—some, like *b*, contributing a counterpoint of interlocking planes—rising in a crescendo to the twin peaks at the corner on the left. This predominantly vertical composition is linked with the ground plane by sheer-walled, flat-topped rocks reminiscent of mesas at heights close to that of the veranda. At Tenryūji, although there is a strong vertical emphasis in the rockwork of the waterfall and in the rocky islet serving to counterbalance it from a position out in the pond to the right, these

Fig. 19. Tracing of the Daisen'in dry landscape garden made from a photographic sequence taken with a vertically mounted 50mm lens. The viewing position is the veranda near the wooden bridgeway.

rocks are viewed from some distance and must therefore have a different effect upon the viewer. The landscape experience here is similar to that portrayed in works by the Chinese painter Ni Tsan (1301–74) and certain Japanese painters of the Muromachi period, in which distant peaks are seen from an elevated vantage point across a broad expanse of water.[10] Toward the front shore of the pond, the emphasis is on the horizontal, both in the way rocks are used and in the form of the peninsula that reaches almost to the center line of the pond from the shore at the right.

The important role proportion plays in the creation of scenic effects is well illustrated in *Sakuteiki* by a passage that discusses the width and height of waterfalls, both natural and artificial:[11]

> The width of waterfalls seems to be independent of the height of the falls. When we observe natural waterfalls we notice that tall falls are not necessarily wide, nor low falls always narrow in breadth. They only depend on the breadth of the lip of the stone over which the water falls. However, for a waterfall three or four feet high, its breadth should not exceed two feet. The low waterfall with a broad width has several disadvantages. In the first place, the waterfall itself looks low. Second, it is mistaken for a river dam. Another point is that the crest of the falls is often exposed to full view, making the scene lacking in depth.

While the specific concern here is proportion in the design of waterfalls, a more general point as to the relationship between natural landscape and designed landscape is implied: what works in nature does not necessarily work in a landscape garden. A successful designer must be a keen observer of the natural world, and he must just as keenly observe how the qualities he experiences affect him. Only in this way will he discover how to translate his vision into a sensory form for others to enjoy.

Fig. 20.   Tracing of the Tenryūji garden made from a photographic sequence taken with a vertically mounted 50mm lens. The viewing position is at the center of the veranda.

THE PLACEMENT OF ROCKS

Of the two principal structural elements in the composition of classical Japanese gardens—rocks and trees—rocks are the more important. By analyzing the dimensions of rocks used in proximity to one another we can learn a great deal about the kinds of proportional relationships garden designers customarily used. One good source of this information is existing classical gardens, since the rocks we see here today, unlike the plantings, have not changed much over the centuries. Or, better yet, we can consult the *Illustrations*, where such information has been precisely recorded.

Before looking at rocks in this way, however, we should first establish some ground rules for their placement in a composition. Visualize the rocks in a garden as delineating the garden space, that is, marking it out horizontally from left to right and front to back (in depth) along the ground plane, and vertically from the ground up toward the heavens in the elevational plane. In both cases, the dimensions of the rocks and of the spaces between them translate into proportional increments on the picture plane. Yet the eyes, by means of various cues, can interpret whether the face of an object lies in the ground plane or the elevational plane. The wide, level top of a rock is seen as part of the ground plane, while the steep, vertical surface of a rock is seen as part of the elevational plane.

These two different planes—and their sensory effects in the garden—correspond to two types of rock compositions that both *Sakuteiki* and the *Illustrations* call the Horizontal Triad Rocks (*hinbonseki*) and the Buddhist Triad Rocks (*sanzonseki*). The first is a group of three rocks forming a triangle in the horizontal plane, and shaped

plan view   perspective

Fig. 21. Horizontal Triad Rocks.

like the Chinese character *hin* 品 , meaning "articles" (fig. 21). The second is a group of three rocks forming a triangle in the vertical plane with its base resting on the ground, resembling the way three Buddhist deities are often depicted in statuary with one central deity flanked by two deities of lesser height (fig. 22).

The classical Japanese garden manuals, naturally enough, couch their rules for composing objects in the language and culture of the time. There is no problem translating the character *hin* 品 into present-day language and calling it a Horizontal Triad, for it clearly pictures three objects in a flat, triangular arrangement. The name Buddhist Triad, however, can be misleading if taken literally. *Sanzon* is a common grouping in Buddhist sculpture. Here, it is not primarily the Buddhist signification that is being referred to, but a grouping of three rocks—or other objects with sufficient mass—standing in an upright position, the tallest one in the center. Existing classical gardens provide ample proof that the aesthetic interpretation was intended. In those gardens are dozens of examples of the vertical triad composition called *sanzon*, and each has a unique character that seems to grow out of the design and mood of the garden where it is found.

This is important, for it means that we now have complementary principles of "horizontal" and "vertical" triangulation with which to define the garden space and create a seamless transition between ground and elevational planes. Plate 16, for example, shows how the leftmost group of five rocks in the dry landscape of Ryōanji comprises a cluster of three upright rocks linked with two rocks in the horizontal plane. Spatially, the composition of a Japanese garden may be said to spread out horizontally and vertically by means of an invisible network of triangles. It is not difficult to understand why. Triangles have a stable base and can also imply movement. They are therefore the perfect shapes for creating a garden composition that combines stability and dynamism, with individual elements "looking" toward and "moving" in response to one another.

There is no limit to the different kinds of proportional relationships that can exist among the rocks in a garden composition. An imaginative designer therefore welcomes the constraints imposed by the site and the surrounding locale with its unique material assets. Once the designer has formed his conception, selected the rocks, and had them brought to the site, he proceeds to direct their placement, one by one, in a sequence that facilitates the use of rock-moving equipment and affords him the most efficient use of his intuition. As *Sakuteiki* makes clear, the rocks brought to the site should already have been laid on the ground so that the "heads" of those to be used in an upright position and the upper sides of those to be used in a recumbent position are easily identified.[12]

plan view   perspective

Fig. 22. Buddhist Triad Rocks.

The actual sequence of setting rocks, as item 32 in the *Illustrations* says, is from large to small: "As a rule, first set the largest rock, and then set each succeeding rock in proportion to it. This can only be done intuitively." *Sakuteiki* says the same thing in a different way: "[In setting the rocks] you should first complete the placing of the principal rock having a distinct character, and then proceed to set each succeeding rock in compliance with the 'requesting' mood of the principal rock."[13]

The phrase "in compliance with the 'requesting' mood of the principal rock," here characterizes the dynamic relationship between succeeding rocks and the principal rock in the composition. Grasping this relationship is at the very heart of Japanese garden design. Only by releasing his intuitive faculties and being sensitive to the nature of each rock can the designer unlock the inherent qualities of the rocks and subtly interweave them into a composition of great beauty.

The best way to grasp the process of setting rocks in a composition is to experience it firsthand. Let me describe how the composition unfolded in one courtyard garden that I watched Kinsaku Nakane build. First, a dense composition of mostly upright rocks was set on the farthest mound opposite the principal vantage point. Here Nakane began directing the placement of rocks to simulate a distant range of lofty mountain peaks—his vision of Shumisen (Mount Sumeru, the mythical center of the Buddhist universe) and the eight mountain ranges that surround it. For him, the essential quality of these peaks is one of mystery, and so he would employ the rocks to the best advantage in capturing this quality.[14]

The very first rock was the second tallest in the Shumisen composition (fig. 23). By establishing a middle height, it would control the height of all the rest in relation to the ground plane. The tallest rock was set immediately to its right. Two more rocks, lower and bulkier, were then set to the right and forward of the two tallest rocks. Rocks 5 and 6, rather flat on top and still lower and broader, were stepped down to the left. Of these two, the shape and grain of rock 5 led the eye up toward the tallest peak, while rock 6 established a counterthrust up and to the left, lending the composition variety and a sense of life. The seventh rock, pyramidal in shape, was set off to the right, with a space between it and the tight grouping whose "requesting mood" it was responding to. With this, the focal composition of seven rocks took on the form of a stable triangle, its center of mass slightly left of center. Three more rocks, much smaller, were set just in front to lend the central "peaks" depth and dignity.

Fig. 23. Sequence of placing rocks in a modern-day representation of Mount Sumeru.

HEIGHT AND PROPORTION

In olden times gardens may have been more extravagant, but the fundamental principles governing their construction were much the same as those used by a modern-day designer like Kinsaku Nakane. The late sixteenth-century garden of Sanpōin, located on the southeast outskirts of Kyoto, is known for its sumptuous display of rocks in a composition that is surprisingly well unified for its complexity. A three-tiered waterfall flows into the *shinden*-style pond at the far left. Islands are connected to the shore by wooden and earthen bridges built high enough to allow pleasure boats to pass beneath them.

Occupying a position on the rear shore of the pond about one-third of the way from the left end of this "scroll" composition, and enjoying an unobstructed view from key vantage points along the veranda, is a good example of what *Sakuteiki* refers to as a "principal rock having a distinct character." It is the rock named Fujito, famous throughout Japan for its beauty and for its sixteenth-century owners, the powerful warlords Oda Nobunaga and Toyotomi Hideyoshi.[15]

Flanked on either side by two rocks one-third its height (fig. 24), the Fujito Rock is the central figure in a tight cluster of three rocks with proportions perfectly matching those of the Master Rock and Attendant Rocks described in item 84 of the *Illustrations* (*shaku* is a Japanese measure of about a foot in length):

> The Attendant Rocks are set to either side of the Master Rock. . . . These are flat-topped rocks, resembling persons with their heads lowered, respectfully saying something to the Master Rock. Their height is 1 *shaku* for a 3-*shaku* Master Rock. Adjust their height based on that proportion.

The Attendant Rocks take their compositional cues from the Master Rock. The Master Rock, however, looks not to other rocks but to the entire garden conception:

> [The Master Rock] has an understated elegance that commands people's respect. It should be set at a height of 3 *shaku* or, depending upon the garden and the desired effect, at a height of 2 or even 1 *shaku*.

Smaller rocks are to the large rock as the large rock is to the entire garden. When a rock's height depends not upon the height of other rocks but upon the "garden"—

Fig. 24. Fujito Rock and its attendant rocks in the garden of Sanpōin.

that is, the scale of the garden and the desired effect—we can be sure it is a key rock in the composition, one that sets the tone or "requesting" mood for all the other rocks below it.

There are several other rocks in the *Illustrations* that we can assume are meant to play such key roles in the composition. They too have suitably important-sounding names, like the Rock of the Spirit Kings, a key rock even more venerable than the Master Rock. Nowhere in the *Illustrations* is the variation in the size of the rocks to meet the needs of a wide range of design situations more clearly indicated than in this simple passage in item 87: the Rock of the Spirit Kings "should be set at a height of 3 *shaku* or, depending upon the garden, as little as 1 *shaku*, 0.8 *shaku*, 0.6 *shaku*, 0.7 *shaku*, or even 0.3 *shaku*." In item 27, the Absolute Control Rock, "king among all the rocks," is also assigned a maximum height of 3 *shaku*, "that being to scale for an estate of 8 *chō*."[16]

It is noteworthy that several of the proportions expressing the relationship between principal and subordinate rocks in the *Illustrations* come close to the ratio of the Golden Mean so admired by the ancient Greeks. This ratio results when a line is divided so that the smaller segment is to the larger as the larger is to the whole, or $a : b = b : a + b$. It can also be obtained mathematically by dividing the larger into the smaller of any two consecutive numbers in the Fibonacci series (1, 2, 3, 5, 8, 13, . . .) where each succeeding number is the sum of the two just preceding it. While the relationship between the lowest numbers in the series ($\frac{1}{2} = 0.50$, $\frac{2}{3} = 0.67$) only crudely approximates the Golden Mean, higher and higher consecutive numbers approach the quotient 0.618034 : 1, its perfect expression.

The Fibonacci series, it turns out, is found in nature in many forms: the spiraling placement of leaves on a tree and the equiangular spiral of a seashell are but two examples.[17] In the *Illustrations*, it is found—albeit in its crudest form as represented by the first three numbers of the series—in the 3 : 1 proportions of two very important key rocks and their subordinates, the Master Rock with its Attendant Rocks, and the Absolute Control Rock with its Mirror Rock. In each case, the height of the lower rock (*a*) equals one, the distance between the top of the lower rock and the top of the taller rock (*b*) equals two, and the height of the taller rock (*a* + *b*) equals

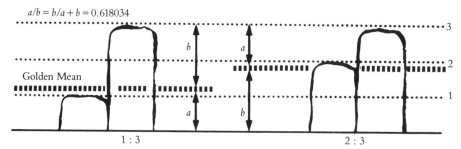

Fig. 25. Comparison of Golden Mean to 1 : 3 and 2 : 3 rock pairs.

three. The same proportions occur, with the positions of the lower rock and the space above it reversed, in the Twofold World Rocks, where the lower rock is 2 *shaku* high. Figure 25 shows just how close the proportions of the 3 : 1 and 3 : 2 rock pairs come to the ratio of the Golden Mean. The variance from the perfect proportion immortalized by the Greeks amounts to about 5 percent of the taller rock ($a + b$). Strictly speaking, the lower rock of the group on the left should be 1.15 *shaku* in height, and the lower rock of the group on the right should be 1.85 *shaku* in height.

We can overlook this minor discrepancy. The *Illustrations* is not a scientific treatise, but a "high context" garden design manual written for the few who have a deep, practical knowledge of the art. For such transmissions, the numbers 1, 2, and 3 in the ratios 3 : 1 and 3 : 2 may well be preferable as mnemonic devices to the more accurate, but more cumbersome, ratios mentioned above. Rocks, after all, are natural materials given to irregularity, not sculpted geometric forms such as those found in the architecture of the Greeks. The variation in their sizes, shapes, textures, and colors required that the classical garden designer with a sensitive eye to their most fitting balance use the specified proportions only as rough guidelines. Perhaps we may see in the more precise proportions of another important pair of rocks mentioned in the *Illustrations*—the 1-*shaku* Status Rock and its 0.62-*shaku* Companion Rock—a more finely tuned statement of the ideal ratio, to be applied as a model in other design situations.

SPACING BETWEEN ROCKS

Proportional relationships of course involve more than the up-and-down rhythm of rocks produced by their height in the vertical plane. The phrase from *Sakuteiki*— "in compliance with the 'requesting' mood of the principal rock"—suggests that the designer consider not only the height but also the width and depth of the rocks and their spacing. Here again applies the notion that space in the Japanese garden is constructed of a network of horizontal and vertical triangles. Such ratios as 1 : 0.62 or 3 : 1 and 3 : 2 and others that produce the desired rhythmic quality are as effectively applied in the horizontal plane as they are in the vertical, and in the relationship between the two as well. A horizontal rock three feet wide and one foot high may be set at the base of an upright rock three feet high and two feet wide (fig. 26). The *Illustrations* leaves the matter of the relative width and spacing of rocks

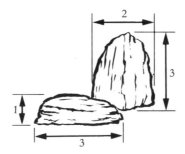

Fig. 26. Horizontal and vertical proportions interact.

almost entirely to the designer, no doubt because these choices are so dependent upon the particular garden, and perhaps also because a catalog of ideal proportions has already been set forth in its sections dealing with the heights of key rocks and their subordinates. The spacing between rocks can nevertheless produce a visual sensation as intriguing and intense as any arising from the character of the rocks themselves. The effect can be further heightened when the rocks also establish a complementary pattern of movement, or thrust. Such is the case at the rock garden of Ryōanji, famous for its stark beauty. Here is a dry landscape composed of five groups of rocks set in a walled gravel courtyard thirty feet deep and seventy-eight feet wide running along the veranda of the abbot's quarters (fig. 27). Viewers enter at the left and move along the gallery-like veranda from left to right, the more serious pausing to contemplate the string of rock "islands" from several seated positions.

The first two groups of rocks are spaced at quite some distance yet form a compositional unit in the left half of the garden's rectangle. Beginning with the most massive group at the extreme left, there is a subtle yet unmistakable rightward thrust whose gliding, effortless quality is given physical form in the recumbent, whale-shaped contours of the second group, close to the rear wall.

The remaining three groups form a tightly spaced compositional unit in the right half of the garden. While several of the rocks are ambiguous as to the sense of lateral movement they exhibit, the smaller whale-shaped rock just to the right of 3a has a leftward thrust which begins to counteract the rightward momentum of groups 1 and 2. That counterthrust is given its most palpable form in the dynamic braking gesture of rock 4a, the flat top of which is tilted ever so slightly to the left.

The sensation of momentum being arrested is particularly intense when the entire composition is viewed with a slight backward glance from a standing position (X) centering on groups 3, 4, and 5. This is because the pattern of thrust and counterthrust described above has been heightened by a visual effect even more powerful in its immediacy: from this vantage point, the relative spacing between the five groups decreases geometrically from left to right. The tightening of space here in negatively accelerated increments is comparable in its visual dynamics to the sensation one experiences when a speeding train is being brought to a halt at a station platform.

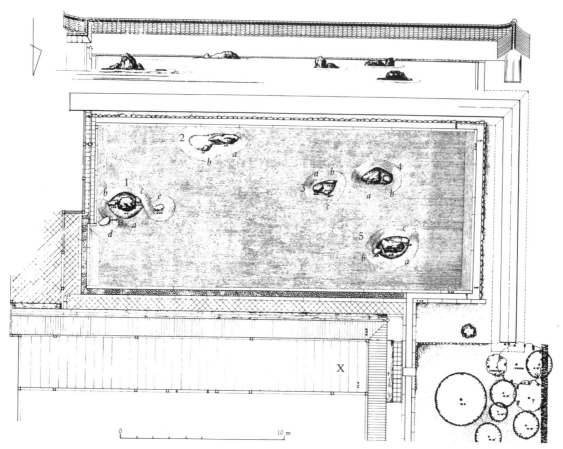

Fig. 27. Plan and elevation of the Ryōanji rock garden. Drawing by Mirei Shigemori.

Motion: Directional Forces
of Shape, Grain, and Juxtaposition

Rocks and trees can move, as well as move the viewer. In the choreography of a modern dance or ballet, it is the specific quality of the feeling or sensation being expressed by the dancers that determines the force and direction of their movement. For example, a broad, upward-sweeping gesture of the arm raised to the oblique, with the dancer's eyes cast in the same direction, can suggest aspiration. The classical Japanese garden designer is in this sense also a choreographer, with rocks and trees as his chosen dancers. The geological and biological growth forces already encapsulated in the shapes and grain of these materials may be directed up and down in the vertical plane or from side to side in the horizontal plane, with the characteristic effect upon the senses that these two planes exhibit, the horizontal suggesting repose and the vertical, stored tension, as discussed in the previous section.

These forces may also be directed along a third axis—the diagonal. The diagonal is characterized by its dynamic quality. In fact, vertical and horizontal forces cannot "move" until they are connected by diagonal forces. The slanted lines forming the tip of an arrow (→) illustrate this quite well. The three Japanese terms for horizontal, diagonal, and vertical (as a group, *ōshakei*) occur prominently in the *Illustrations*, always in connection with the very important matter of selecting rocks and trees and then placing them in a composition. Item 3 in the text sets forth the aesthetic significance and the benefit of combining the three forces in a single composition:

> You should set rocks bearing in mind the three forces—horizontal, diagonal, and vertical—introduced above. These three are equivalent to the triad, Heaven, Earth, and Man. First of all, set these three together at one spot that is to be the focal point. Once you have set the triad—Heaven, Earth, and Man—and then planted an upright tree to complement it, the result is a flawless gem fit for a king. . . . It is said that when you compose the garden next to the residence in this way, the occurrence of misfortune is avoided by virtue of the garden.

Heaven corresponds to the vertical forces that come into play when we lift our heads to look up at the sky or when we move our bodies in opposition to the force of gravity. Earth corresponds to the horizontal forces we observe in objects—carts, boats, birds—moving along the ground plane parallel to the horizon. Man corresponds to the diagonal forces we perceive in dynamic human activity—the slanting lines of legs and arms as a person walks or runs, transmitting the force of gravity from the upright body to the horizontal ground plane. In the above passage from the *Illustrations*, the upright tree is an added element that—like the final stroke in the Chinese character 玉, for "gem"—completes the picture.

The principle of the three forces, *ōshakei*, is one of the most powerful aesthetic tools the *Illustrations* offers the designer. The three may be found counterpoised in one rock of complex shape, such as the Never Aging Rock, which "combines all three forces —horizontal, diagonal, and vertical" (item 85) or the Rock of the Spirit Kings, which is not only flat-topped, with a ledge in front, but "on top it has the shape of a vertical rock, and in front, that of a diagonal rock" (item 87).

Rocks of such complex shape are rare, and so it is fortunate that they serve a limited—albeit special—function in the design. More commonly found, and better suited to the designer's purpose, are rocks (or trees) with shapes distinctly exhibiting just one, or at most two, of the three forces. Also, the Rock of the Spirit Kings, whose sensory significance is that of a great mass in which the three forces are tightly counterpoised, could just as well consist of three closely spaced rocks, each an embodiment of one of the three forces, as shown in figure 28.[18]

In the classical gardens of Japan are numerous variations on the triad theme (pls. 17, 18). The idealized triad illustrates how the three forces can work together in any landscape composition, but it is also a reminder of something even more basic—the importance of the triangle as the module of spatial organization in Japanese gardens. When the rocks and trees of Japanese gardens are joined by imaginary lines, the figure formed is, with few exceptions, not a circle or a square or a rectangle, but a

Fig. 28. A composition of rocks embodying the three forces—horizontal, diagonal, and vertical.

triangle. The triangle, it will be recalled, is the simplest two-dimensional shape in the sense that it is generated with the fewest points (three); it is also the most stable form for transmitting forces from one point to another, which is why it is so often used by structural engineers in the design of bridges.

The most stable form for directing the forces of gravity directly down to the earth is a symmetrical triangle with one side, preferably the widest, resting upon the ground. We are all familiar with the Egyptian pyramids, which use the intrinsic stability of the triangle as a visual manifestation of the concept of immortality. Another example, so close at hand that we probably do not notice it, is the stable triangle formed by the human body when a person sits cross-legged or kneels on the floor (fig. 29). The frontal posture in particular presents a symmetrical triangle where the lateral forces are in a state of equilibrium. No wonder this seated position has been the traditional one for meditation or contemplation—it fosters alertness and at the same time minimizes bodily tension. In the Japanese garden, while the effect of the whole upon the senses is likely to be one of restful equilibrium, there is typically a dynamic, highly engaging interaction of forces among the various elements of the design. The object, after all, is to entice and reinvigorate the viewer, but not to tire or alienate him. To understand how this is achieved, we need to know how the simplest shapes can create a sense of movement.

THE MOVEMENT OF OBJECTS AT REST

An effect called "gamma motion"—experienced, for example, when a flashing traffic light appears to expand and shrink from its center —has led to a better understanding of what Rudolf Arnheim in his classic work *Art and Visual Perception* calls the directed tension of an object or visual pattern:[19]

> Experiments have shown that this motion varies with the shape and orientation of the object. It occurs essentially along the axes of what I have called the structural skeleton of the pattern or, to use Newman's language, along the lines of force. . . . There is . . . a tendency of the motion to be strongest in the horizontal directions, and in the vertical there is more upward than downward push. This appears most clearly in the square [fig. 30]. The lateral motion is most pronounced, the upward one weaker, the downward one almost absent.

  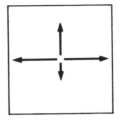

Fig. 29. The human body forms a triangle when in a kneeling or cross-legged position.

Fig. 30. Arnheim's diagram illustrating gamma motion for a square.

The movement of a rectangular object occurs primarily along its major—or longest—axis. A rectangle that is long and narrow therefore behaves much like a line. When the length of the minor axis (perpendicular to the major axis) of a rectangle approaches that of the major axis, the object behaves more like the square in figure 30.

One of the ways to create lateral movement in a classical Japanese garden is to use a horizontal rock "that has its grain running lengthwise along the top when lying in a level position" (item 2). In this case, the lines of force that run horizontally along the major axis are accentuated by the grain of the rock. Yet the movement of this rock, defined by its rectangular shape and its horizontal orientation, is ambiguous: the directed tension pulls equally to the left and to the right like a tug of war that ends in a draw (fig. 31*a*). How can the tension be directed primarily to one side? Arnheim again: "This ambiguity can be eliminated by the context. If an oblong is rooted in a heavy base, the tension will be directed toward the free end. Thus arms and legs and the branches of trees are seen to move outward from the trunk."[20]

This effect is illustrated in figure 31*b*, where the horizontal rock shown in figure 31*a*—now rooted in the mass of the square-shaped rock to its left—appears to move rightward toward its free end. In figure 31*c*, the long horizontal line of the pine tree branch similarly stretches rightward from the trunk to point the eye like a ballet dancer's pose. This is a technique that, with the assistance of proper pruning methods, reaches a high level of refinement in the Japanese garden.

In item 2, the *Illustrations* lets it be known that a rock which qualifies as a horizontal also may be used as a vertical. When a rock, or an upright tree such as a cypress or cryptomeria, is used to produce directed tension in the vertical, "the preference for upward over downward motion, suggested by the gamma phenomenon [fig. 30], helps to define direction."[21] In this case it is the ground—often given additional weight by the placement of subordinate rocks and shrubbery at the base of the vertical element—that provides the heavy base for directing the tension toward the free end. With this in mind, it is possible to regard the Earth and Man rocks in figure 28 not merely as horizontal and diagonal rocks, but as subordinate rocks providing a heavy base for the Heaven rock.

The triangle has already been mentioned in several important respects: for its role in the triad of the three forces, as the module of spatial organization in Japanese

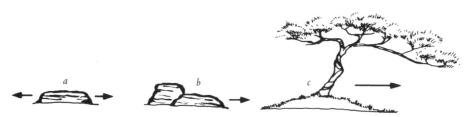

Fig. 31. Directed tension, shown here for objects in the horizontal plane, moves away from the heavy base toward the free end.

gardens, and as the most stable figure. It is time to consider the triangle from the standpoint of movement. Here too, the triangle emerges as a powerful sensory tool, with far more capacity to elicit a sense of movement than a rectangle or a line. Arnheim describes it this way:[22]

> The movement in a rectangle or homogeneous line is not strong, probably because the shape is symmetrical and balanced. No such symmetry exists along the main axis of a wedge or triangle. . . . Dynamically the wedge shape represents a crescendo or decrescendo of breadth—a first illustration of the general rule that all perceptual gradients make for movement.

Movement in a triangle or wedge "is preferably oriented toward the point. It produces the arrow effect. Presumably this is so because the broad end fulfills the function of a heavy base, from which movement issues toward the slim point."[23] The arrow effect can be produced by the shape of a single object or by the juxtaposition of several objects. As with the rectangle, the direction of movement depends on the shape and orientation of the triangular pattern, and also on the context in which it occurs.

MOTION IN THE GROUND AND ELEVATIONAL PLANES

The contexts for a landscape are basically of two types. In the first, the triangular shape is perceived as a figure lying in the ground plane. Such is the case when a single rock or group of rocks exhibiting a triangular or wedge-shaped pattern from above (the Horizontal Triad Rocks, say) is viewed from a position high enough (and the objects are low enough) that the pattern appears in "plan view" perspective against a homogeneous ground plane—be it the surface of a pond, an expanse of gravel, or some other evenly textured ground cover. Slightly elevated vantage points were typical for gardens in Japan, as the floor and veranda of traditional architecture was generally raised two feet or so above ground level to enhance air circulation and protect the wood against decay. Garden designers naturally exploited the aesthetic potential the ground plane offered.

When the triangular pattern lies just in front of (or on top of) and parallel to the background plane, the arrow effect will be as described above, with movement issuing toward the slim point. There is an example of this effect in the rock garden of

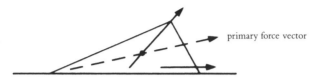
primary force vector

Fig. 32.   Motion for a wedge-shaped triangle resting on the ground is away from the slimmest point and toward the apex side.

Ryōanji (pl. 19). To experience it, one must step down at the far right corner of the veranda, take several steps out along the granite rain gutter, and look back. From here the three groups in the right half of the garden produce an arrow with group 3 at its tip (see fig. 27). The effect—pointing as it does back at group 2—is indeed forceful, as if the energy in groups 4 and 5 was being driven forward and channeled through the sharp focus of group 3. While this view does not lie along the route of modern-day visitors to the temple, it would have been common when, in the Edo period, a covered walkway connected the southwest corner of the abbot's quarters to a building that once stood just beyond the present west wall.[24]

In the second type of landscape context, the triangular shape is perceived as resting upon the ground plane and rising perpendicular to it in the elevational plane. In other words, the composition is viewed more from the side than from the top. As long as the slimmest point is at the apex of the triangle, the arrow effect will work as described above, and in fact will be enhanced by the heavy base the ground provides and by the preference for upward over downward motion in the vertical. However, if the triangle is wedge-shaped, and the longest side rests upon the ground (fig. 32), the effect is reversed: movement is toward the apex side and away from the slimmest point.

The primary directional force of such a triangle appears to follow the longest axis, running from the slimmest point through the center of gravity to exit near the midpoint of the shortest side. This force vector may be visualized as the resolution of a horizontal vector running along the ground plane (the base being the longest side) and a second vector moving up from the base through the center of gravity to exit at the apex. This second vector is of course an instance of the arrow effect, the only one possible when a triangle rests upon the ground and is viewed in the elevational plane.

Another way to picture the movement of a wedge-shaped triangle whose longest side rests upon the ground is to imagine that the arrow effect serves to "pull" the eye up the easy incline of the triangle's longest leg toward its apex. The shortest leg, the one with the steepest incline, then becomes the leading edge in the triangle's movement.

We do not have to search very far in the *Illustrations* for an example of a single rock that has the shape and thrust described here. The Attendant Rock, pictured in the lower left corner of figure D, uses the characteristic movement of the wedge-shaped triangle—away from the slimmest point resting on the ground toward the leading edge just below the apex—to convey the impression that with head "lowered" it is "respectfully saying something to the Master Rock" (item 84).

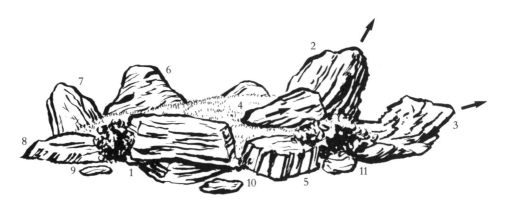

Fig. 33. Turtle island at Nishi Honganji.

Fig. 34. Simplified schematic of turtle island at Nishi Honganji.

Fig. 35. Crane island at Nishi Honganji.

ROCKS THAT MOVE AT NISHI HONGANJI

The dynamics of the wedge-shaped triangle shown in figure 32 work not only with single rocks but with any composition that rests upon the ground plane and rises in the elevational plane. Figure 33 is a sketch of an "island" located left of center in the seventeenth-century dry landscape garden of the temple Nishi Honganji in Kyoto. The viewing position for this garden is the veranda running along the west side. The island is intended to conjure up the image of a giant sea turtle swimming to the right (pl. 20). In fact, the three rocks that supply the three points of the island's wedge-shaped triangle (fig. 34) may be easily imagined as (rock 2) the turtle's left front flipper raised just before taking another stroke, (rock 3) the turtle's head, and (rock 8) the tail. At the apex of the triangle, the dynamic gesture of the flipper rock is accentuated by the rock's diagonal grain to create a powerful force vector moving upward and slightly forward at one o'clock. At the right, the head points forward and is lifted slightly upward to create a force vector at two o'clock. The wedge-shaped rock 4 at the base of the raised flipper echoes the shape of the entire island's wedge and—with prominent grain perfectly aligned to its major axis—provides added forward momentum at the two o'clock position. Together, rocks 2, 3, and 4 produce a combined thrust that is equal to the task of pulling forward the great mass of the horizontal rock 1 that serves as the island's anchor. It is as if the three were stretching at a sturdy cable attached to the massive rock at its center of gravity. In modern terms, the experiential quality of the turtle island's rightward thrust may be likened to a heavy bomber slowly gathering momentum as it takes off.

Our eyes now follow the pointing of the turtle's head, cross the gentle arch of the stone bridge spanning the gravel sea, and come to rest upon a magnificent jade-green mountain, the largest rock on the island located right of center in the garden (fig. 35). This jade Mount Everest (rock 1) and its mirror image, the slightly smaller but more sharply pointed rock 2 to the right of it, lend their island a decidedly vertical

Fig. 36.   Tiger Gorge Garden at Nishi Honganji: complete view showing how the turtle and crane islands form a triangle with the rock composition in the center rear.

emphasis in strong contrast to the low diagonal thrust of the turtle island. The twin peaks are called upon here not only to create compositional variety, but also to represent the wings of a crane, the auspicious bird this island is intended to suggest.

With these two tallest rocks there begins a clockwise movement through the seven most prominent rocks of the island composition, from the highest to the lowest. After rocks 1 and 2, the eyes next alight on rock 3 at the right end of the island—the crane's tail. Its pointed top and wide-spreading base offer the perfect transition between the upright wing rocks and the two horizontal rocks below and to the left of it. Although the tail rock is roughly symmetrical in shape, the slight bulging at its right side provides a heavy base that joins with the pointed tip on the left side to create an arrow effect moving back toward the center of the island.

The tip has deliberately been strengthened for this important task: it stands out against the mossy slope into which it is set, and is further accentuated by arrow-shaped white marbling at the left side of the rock. The leftward movement in turn is given added impetus by the small, two-tiered horizontal rock 4 below it, which also has its heaviest end to the right and white marbling on the left-sloping "arrow" side.

The leftward and clockwise motion established by rocks 3 and 4 is now picked up by the long, sleek, horizontal rock 5. Its force, gathered from its own slightly wider right side and from the combined mass of rocks 2, 3, and 4, is free to move across the open gravel sea to the left, returning our gaze to the base of the jade mountain and the bridge. From here, the force of the clockwise motion; the small, flat-topped rock 6 that suggests the crane's head; and the jade mountain rock's movement—upward and back to the left—all conspire to carry the eyes of the viewer up to the central focal point of the entire composition, a dry waterfall set in lofty peaks at the rear of the garden.

When we return our gaze to the turtle island at the other side of the arched bridge, we see that the turtle's flipper and the top of the turtle's head point not simply to the right but back into the composition, to the triangle of those same lofty peaks.

It is time now to stand back and view the entire scene that is spread before our eyes (pl. 21, fig. 36). From our vantage point midway along the veranda, we cannot fail to notice that the three focal points of the garden—the turtle island on the left, the crane island on the right, and the steep mountains in deep center—together form a stable triangle, full of variety and movement.

Spatial Quality: Depth Cues and Atmospheric Effects

Since the garden space is already three-dimensional, it may sound strange to hear that the garden designer employs visual devices to enhance its sense of depth. The fact is, no matter how many miles of space lie before us, we cannot begin to comprehend it until it is articulated by changes in shape, size, texture, or color along a surface stretching out before us. Recall that disoriented feeling you get when looking out an airplane window into a thick gray fog or total darkness and you will know what a lack of variation in visual surface quality does to depth perception. Our eyes are made to guide us over an earthly terrain composed of varied shapes and textures spreading in an unbroken tapestry from our feet to the horizon and skyward to the tops of buildings and trees and mountains. It is the heterogeneity of the physical environment—and of works of art seeking to portray it—that enables us to see three-dimensionally, and to sense the spatial qualities of "nearby" and "faraway," of intimacy and immensity.

Visual devices that aesthetically reproduce the intriguing spatial qualities so integral to our experience of the natural and manmade environment are no stranger to Japanese landscape design. Auditory effects, such as the muffled and therefore "distant" sound of a waterfall, also may be employed to heighten the sense of near and far. Since every landscape design will have its own spatial effect depending on how the materials are used, lack of attention to this important aspect of design can only lead to results that are nondescript or awkward.

It is not always greater apparent depth that is the goal. Rather, the designer strives to bring each part of the whole garden into the most satisfactory relationship to the viewer. Depending on the nature of the site, delicate adjustments may require shortening the apparent depth in some places, and letting it out in others, as if the designer were tailoring a suit to fit the human senses. When the garden artist's vision is well conceived and well executed, the landscape scene virtually comes to the viewer, wrapping him in a special world that, like a tonic, refreshes and invigorates his entire being.

Over the past hundred years or so, science has come a long way in experimentally isolating the visual cues that give normally sighted people impressions of depth. If such cues work on human visual perception they must also have a bearing on the arts that seek to create a sense of depth. James J. Gibson, in his seminal work, *The Perception of the Visual World,* lists thirteen visual cues[25] for the perception of three-dimensional space. Painters, he notes, have long used the following six in their portrayals of nature:[26]

1. *Overlapping* (completeness or continuity of outline):   "If one object seems to 'cover' another, it must be nearer."

2. *Linear perspective:*   "If edges known to be parallel seem to converge, they must really recede."

3. *Size perspective:*   "If objects known to be of similar size seem progressively smaller, they must really be progressively farther away."

4. *Relative upward location in the visual field:*   "If one thing appears above another it is probably not suspended in the air but merely lying on the ground at a greater distance."

5. *Aerial perspective:*   "If an object seems bluish and blurred [or hazy, with less color saturation] it must be distant like the hills on the horizon."

6. *Transition between light and shade:*   "If an object is partly in light and partly in shadow its surface cannot be flat but must really be curved or bent."

These are all monocular cues, requiring only one eye to perceive three dimensionality. One of the conclusions of Gibson's study is that binocular vision plays a much smaller role in depth perception than had been thought. The belief that "the only important basis for depth perception in the visual world is the stereoscopic effect of binocular vision"[27] has its roots in the eighteenth-century Cartesian geometrical model of space, which has proven useful in the study of physics but has little relevance for understanding visual perception.[28]

> Depth, we have argued, is not built up out of sensation but is simply one of the dimensions of visual experience. The accepted belief is contradicted by the fact that persons having vision in only one eye . . . see the visual world in depth just about as the rest of us do. . . .

Painters—and artists in other two-dimensional media—have naturally seized upon the above-mentioned monocular cues to help them create the impression of three-dimensional space. For the problem they faced was basically the same one nature had already solved with the two-dimensional, light-sensitive surface of the retina. Gibson defines the retinal image as "an arrangement of focused light on a physical surface of two dimensions which is specific to an array of reflected light from physical objects and surfaces in three dimensions."[29] Painters have never been particularly frustrated or handicapped by having to work in two dimensions. Gibson's theory tells us why this is so, by demonstrating that depth perception is in large part the result of cues projected onto, and then "read" from, a two-dimensional surface.

What does all this mean to the landscape artist who works in three dimensions? Simply this: if space perception is so much a matter of cues that can be communicated in two dimensions with or without the presence of actual depth, then a landscape designer seeking to give a limited garden space a sense of depth far beyond its actual size—to create for example the illusion of a vast natural panorama—can do so by selecting and manipulating garden elements with the same techniques used by painters. And this, we find, is exactly what Japanese garden designers did.

The classical art of Japanese gardens developed in close alliance with the art of painting. The historian Teiji Itoh notes that, "in Japanese painting, the techniques of composition, the view of nature, and the manner of achieving harmony often contributed, if only in part, to fundamental concepts of garden design. Moreover, there was a time when the painter himself was both a garden designer and a leader in the construction of gardens."[30]

The time Itoh refers to here is the Heian period, from the ninth to the twelfth century. But the close relationship between painting and garden design lasted long beyond that. We have already discussed the relationship of the Daisen'in garden to Chinese painting styles. Sōami (1485?–1525) was one of Japan's greatest landscape painters and has had more gardens attributed to him than he could possibly have done in his lifetime. But even spurious attributions are evidence of the strong link between painting and landscape gardens. To an extent, the relationship continues to this day. Kinsaku Nakane, for example, demonstrated a remarkable facility at traditional brush-and-ink painting when he took time out to give me a few informal lessons.

THE PRINCIPLE OF "NARROW-AND-WIDEN"

The problem of producing the effect of spaciousness or immensity in the limited space of a garden is addressed early on in the *Illustrations*, with figure D, the first of several that show entire garden compositions. The piece of paper the scene is drawn on illustrates how the impression of a landscape very great in size is to be created within the confines of the garden: "Just as this single piece of paper is titled 'Ten Thousand Leagues,' you must make the stream valley appear to extend on and on, while at the same time you must reduce it to a small size." Figure E continues the theme of capturing an immense landscape—perhaps this time the term should be seascape—in a very small space: "This is titled 'Single Mountain in a Boundless Sea.'

Fig. 37.   Figure D of the *Illustrations*, showing the "narrow-and-widen" principle applied to a watercourse.

In a garden like this, the scenery of an immense ocean stretching out before a single mountain is reduced to a small size." Item 8 of the *Illustrations* is a concise explanation of how the designer can achieve the effects of spaciousness and immensity portrayed in figures D and E:

> We are told of the phenomenon of large rocks scarcely visible above the water, and of flowing water, constantly obstructed as it seeks the sea. This being so, you should narrow the watercourse here and there, and then widen it so it appears like the sea.

The swirling, undulate shorelines in figures D and E give graphic form to this "narrow-and-widen" principle. The great contrast between the narrows, where the water is constricted or enclosed by projecting fingers of land, and the expansive areas, dominated by the level surface of the water, help make us feel we are viewing an immense landscape. There is also implicit in the "narrow-and-widen" principle a zigzag movement along diagonal axes back into depth or, from the standpoint of a two-dimensional surface, up the picture plane. Such a pattern of movement is evident in figure D of the *Illustrations*, reproduced here as figure 37 with arrows drawn in to indicate the two principal axes along which the shorelines are oriented. Here is an instance of Gibson's depth cue "relative upward location in the visual field" given an added dimension, that of recession into space along diagonal axes.

Designers have long known that zigzag movement into space enhances the impression of depth by leading the eye up and into the distance along an extended path many times longer than the shortest route straight up the picture plane. What makes the undulating-shoreline technique so effective is that it allows a double use of diagonals—first, along the main axis of flow; and second, along the S-curve undulations themselves, which provide a kind of musical ornamentation to the main axis. The undulations are for the most part aligned parallel to the horizontal, like an "S" rather than like a "W" whose peaks and valleys are aligned to the vertical.

As the "ins" and "outs" of the S-curve shoreline carry the eyes back and forth up the picture plane and into the deep space of the composition, an additional feature of their horizontal alignment comes into play: the fingerlike projections pointing to left and right lead the eyes beyond the side limits of the composition, further enhancing the impression of unlimited space. Yet another such technique is used to heighten the effect of the zigzag S-curve movement into depth. The curve is obliterated here and there by an object like a rock or a tree or a hill so that its course at that point must be imagined. In this way, while the beauty of the meandering line is maintained, there is the suggestion of magical places that lie hidden from view—secret coves, fishing villages, mountain shrines. Classical Japanese garden design was an art that did not discount the fertile expanses of the imagination.

The double S-curve zigzagging up the picture plane and back into space according to the "narrow-and-widen" principle has applications beyond that of a shoreline where land meets water. It may similarly form the edges of a path which zigzags between hills and trees, or of a sequential composition of stepping stones varying in size and changing direction along diagonal axes. To any of these variations, the dimension of linear perspective may be added: the two zigzagging edges will gradually draw closer as they engage in their undulating dance toward the horizon. Linear perspective used in this way can be called "natural" in contrast to the more scientifically oriented "geometric" type that originated in Europe in the sixteenth century, although that too has been employed architecturally in at least one Japanese garden: the west wall of the courtyard at Ryōanji slopes down more than six inches from the point opposite the veranda to the far corner, creating the impression that the garden is deeper than it actually is.

Linear perspective and zigzag movement into space were frequently used in combination by Chinese and Japanese painters. A striking example—achieved by a path "ricocheting" between steep cliffs and rocky outcroppings from the right foreground to the left middle ground—is the *Landscape* by Sesshū (1420–1506) in plate 22.

Another fine example is a *Landscape* attributed to Kano Masanobu (1434–1530).[31] Characterizing the ground plane, which occupies the lower third of this painting, is a river that diminishes by steps along its zigzag path toward the horizon until the final section before it fades out of sight is no more than one-tenth as wide as it was in the foreground. Portions of the river are concealed by the branches of a large pine that rises in the left foreground, enhancing the impression of depth.

The use of the "narrow-and-widen" principle combined with natural linear perspective may be found in the lower garden of the subtemple Taizōin at Myōshinji in Kyoto, a 1965 design by Kinsaku Nakane in the classical tradition. The main axis is a cascading stream, and while it is straight-on rather than at a diagonal to the principal viewing position, it gradually widens as it swirls down around rocks lodged along the banks until it reaches a pond that spreads out in a wide expanse at the viewer's feet (pl. 23). A famous example of the same technique is provided by the stepping stones of the path leading, this time along a diagonal axis, to the outdoor shelter in front of Sago Palm Hill at the Katsura villa. When viewed from the shelter, the stepping stones diminish dramatically in size from the first and most massive one—nearly eight feet wide—next to the formal stone-paved walkway in the foreground, to the much smaller stones in the distance, some of which are only one foot wide (pl. 24).

RECESSION IN THE ELEVATIONAL PLANE

All these variants of the double S-curve zigzagging up the picture plane lie in the ground plane and therefore are read as receding into depth. Elevational-plane variants of this same design principle play a somewhat different yet equally important role in the composition. Certain varieties of trees are particularly well suited to it, the most obvious choices being evergreens such as pines with their layered, horizontal branching patterns and substantially wider spreads at the bottom than at the top. This is no doubt another reason that pines have always been the mainstay among trees in the classical Japanese garden: "As a rule, it is difficult to imagine a landscape garden, even one in an enclosed courtyard, without a pine tree. Only the pine tree can be planted in so many different ways to interesting effect" (item 35).

As a pine tree matures, the major branches gradually separate into distinct, billowy horizontal bands that seem to dance back and forth as they diminish in size toward the crown of the tree. This is the effect sought after and intensified in the art of *bonsai* and, on a larger scale, in the Japanese garden. Time-consuming pruning methods achieve the desired results in a much shorter time—and in a crisper, more striking form—than occurs in nature. The zigzag dance of the pine tree leads the eye not into depth along the ground plane but upward toward the heavens. At the same time, there is an accord between ground-plane variants of the "narrow-and-widen" principle and elevational-plane variants like the pine: both carry the eye up the picture plane and both point the eye—the pine by virtue of its horizontally spreading branches—to left and right beyond the side limits of the composition. Thus not only do pine trees contribute to the sense of spaciousness in the Japanese garden, but they are instrumental in bringing together the warp and woof of the composition to produce a deep and abiding sense of unity.

THE PRINCIPLE OF THREE DEPTHS

Another important principle of spatial composition found in Japanese gardens is mentioned in neither the *Illustrations* nor *Sakuteiki*. This may be because it would have been well known to anyone familiar with the techniques of Chinese and Japanese landscape painting. Called the "principle of the three depths," it hinges upon the depth cue "relative upward location in the visual field" and, like the above-mentioned method of using pines, relies upon the visual effect of horizontal bands or layers moving up the picture plane. According to George Rowley,[32]

> the Chinese perfected the principle of the three depths, according to which spatial depth was marked by a foreground, middle distance, and far distance, each parallel to the picture plane, so that the eyes leapt from one distance to the next through a void of space. . . . This use of three depths gave the artist an arrangement of motifs and intervals as clear-cut and intelligible as the lateral spacing of elements.

The usefulness of the three depths in landscape garden design is that "the elements of the composition are not restricted in size by any fixed laws. Important features can be magnified to indicate their significance, while distant features that might otherwise be inconspicuous can also be enlarged."[33] In other words, a particular scene can be given the impression it is far off in the distance, yet it can be portrayed in the kind of detail (or size) that would only be possible if one had a zoom lens or actually approached it to take a closer look.

The multiperspective system inherent in the Chinese method may at first strike some of us as unrealistic. But Jack A. Hobbs's critique of Cézanne's painting *Mont Sainte-Victoire Seen from the Bibémus Quarry* suggests that it actually gives integrity to our experience of the work of art.[34]

> Rather than use a traditional one- or two-point perspective system, Cézanne combined the rock surfaces, trees, and bits of sky into a multiperspective system of several focal points. Such a system may in fact represent the conditions of normal vision more truthfully than traditional perspective.

Two fourteenth-century examples of how the principle of three depths has been used in the Japanese garden are at the temples Tenryūji and Kinkakuji in Kyoto. In each the broad expanse of a pond is broken in the middle distance by a spit of land that runs parallel to the picture plane: the peninsula jutting into the pond from the right at Tenryūji and the long central island directly across from the observation area at Kinkakuji's three-story pavilion. The foreground in the Tenryūji composition is marked by the front shore of the pond—one of the most commonly used devices for this purpose—and the far distance begins with the hill that rises as a backdrop behind the pond.

SIZE-PERSPECTIVE TECHNIQUES

The three depths provide a natural and clear-cut compositional framework for using size-perspective techniques. For example, a garden's distant scenery may be framed by the trunk and branches of a single specimen or of a grove of full-sized trees in the foreground. Much smaller trees of the same variety, pruned to make them look mature, are planted in the middle distance—preferably on an island or other prominent land area located across a level expanse consisting of water or plains—and set against a backdrop of foliage where the shapes of individual trees can no longer be discerned.

Another technique of size perspective in classical Japanese gardens is to place a massive rock, recumbent and stretching out horizontally before the viewer, in the foreground, near the front shore of the pond. The stable mass of the rock helps orient the viewer kinesthetically and serves as a pushing-off point for the eyes. Its size therefore becomes a ruler for measuring the size of the other rocks and associated landforms in the garden. While most of the other rocks are likely to be significantly smaller than the foreground rock, due to their position in the middle or far distance, the viewer assumes that they must be at least as large as the foreground rock and that they look so much smaller only because they are so much farther away. Thus the impression of distance is enhanced.

There is a rounded whitish boulder called the Reclining Moon Rock (Gagetsu-seki) set in a recumbent position on the northeast shore of the pond at Tenryūji. Its qualities are moonlike enough by day, but on nights when the real moon rises in the southern sky, the rock's luminous surface vies for attention with the moon reflected in the pond and helps bring the experience of the distant moon most poignantly to our senses. The Reclining Moon Rock is an excellent example of a large rock in the foreground serving as a *repoussoir* or "pushing off point"—in this case for a vista that incorporates in the far distance the well-known mountain Arashiyama (which by day has the bluish cast of aerial perspective; pl. 25).

A comparable role is played by the large flat boulder in the left foreground of the pond scene viewed from the veranda of the teahouse at Isuien in Nara (pl. 26). These wide-spreading foreground rocks are reminiscent of the type called Worship Rock (*reihaiseki*) used in gardens to underline visually and thereby call attention to an important scene meant to be admired from its vantage point. The appearance and position of the very broad, flat rock pictured at the bottom of figure F of the *Illustrations*, labeled *chinseki* ("precious rock"?), suggest the type of large foreground rock we have been discussing; further research is needed to determine precisely what is intended by it, however.

Another size-perspective device that similarly consists of a large rock set in the foreground of the garden is the *chōzubachi*, an upright water basin meant to be dipped in from the veranda. The water basin named Furisode for its resemblance to the "hanging sleeves" of a kimono is by far the most engaging foreground element in the seventeenth-century garden of Jōjuin at the temple Kiyomizu in Kyoto (pl. 27). This natural stone basin's large size, unusual rounded contours, proximity to the veranda, and human purpose (clearly stated by the water spout and dipper) make it the first element in the garden with which the viewer feels an intimate connection. Add to this the fact that such standing basins generally have a flat top accentuated by the smooth, level surface of the water contained inside, and it is not hard to understand the success of this device as a *repoussoir* for the viewer's visual journey into the garden space beyond.

Because the garden is created in a three-dimensional space, foreground elements close to the principal viewing position—like the broad or flat-topped rocks we have just been discussing—can provide yet another kind of depth cue. Whenever a person moves his head, the closest stationary objects appear to move far more rapidly in relationship to what is behind them than distant objects. We all have experienced this while driving, particularly along a country road where objects like trees and fence posts are often very close by. Called motion perspective, this is one type of depth cue that cannot be duplicated on a two-dimensional surface. Since it can be used by landscape garden designers, however, we shall add it to our list of perspective cues, again with Gibson's explanation:[35]

7. *Motion perspective*:   "If a thing seems to move, or be displaced across other things when the observer moves his head from side to side, it must really be nearer than the other things in proportion to its relative motion."

SINGLE-DEPTH PERSPECTIVE

Motion perspective and the variants of size perspective just discussed all produce the impression of depth by virtue of changes that occur along axes running roughly parallel to the ground plane, from a position near the viewer toward a more distant point on the horizon. There is another, very important way that size perspective is used in classical Japanese gardens; this time the change in size takes place along axes that lie in the elevational plane, perpendicular to the observer's line of sight. The composition that produces the desired effect—one of immensity far beyond the actual size of the elements used—forms along a vertical plane running through the face of the largest and rearmost element, which then serves as a kind of backdrop. The comparison is therefore not between the size of objects at different distances from the viewer along the ground plane, but rather between the different heights and widths of objects closely juxtaposed and nearly the same distance away. Space is stretched as the eyes scan vertically and horizontally, but within a very narrow range in depth. This "single depth" technique for producing a sense of immensity goes even further than the previously discussed two-dimensional cues in rejecting the Cartesian geometric conception of space.

A specific example will help clarify this. The Crouching Tiger Rock (Fukuko-seki) is viewed at a distance of about eighteen feet from the north veranda running along the right side of the main garden of Tenryūji, and at much closer range for a person walking by it on the gravel. By itself it is already a substantial mass—nearly three feet high and five feet wide—whose rough-textured vertical face suggests a rock formation of great proportions (pl. 28). With the addition of the mirrorlike rock barely protruding from the moss below it at the right, the size of the Crouching Tiger Rock seems to increase many times over until it appears as a sheer wall of rock rising to a height of a thousand feet or more. The striped bamboo grass growing up from its base turns into a forest of giant tropical trees, and the moss becomes a lush valley floor.

The sense of immensity is so overpowering here that as viewers we project ourselves into the composition, to roam it as if we stood only an inch or so high by comparison. While this effect is achieved with more than just size perspective—texture gradients are also very important—the impression of an immense landscape is in large part the result of the tremendous deviation between the size of the two rocks. This is but another example of how the eyes operate far more on the basis of comparisons between objects in the visual field than they do on absolute standards of measurement.

There is another technique for using rocks to enhance the sense of space where the depth of the site is severely constricted. Vertical rocks that narrow toward the top—especially when set off by much smaller rocks—have the capacity to trick the eye into believing they are much taller than they actually are. In a narrow space at the northeast corner of the Daisen'in dry landscape, the converging sides of vertical rocks—accentuated by the ripply indentations and grain of the rocks—make them appear to tower precipitously over the stone bridge and gravel stream bed below (pl. 8). This technique of employing linear perspective in the vertical dimension is the same one used in the tapering columns of the Parthenon, the soaring arches of

Gothic cathedrals, and the familiar stepped profile of the Empire State Building.

A number of the dry landscape gardens made in Kyoto in the seventeenth century use the single-depth technique. In each, the designer has constricted the composition into a narrow band running parallel to the veranda of the building from which the garden is viewed. The composition is placed at an appropriate distance from the viewing position, just as the viewer in an art gallery positions himself a comfortable distance from a painting depending upon its size and detail, and the intermediate zone is covered with an unobtrusive ground cover, usually white gravel. The single-depth technique thus produces a relatively flat, two-dimensional effect reminiscent of Gauguin and the primitivists that he admired. The choice of this technique over three-dimensionality may be compared to the preference for monochrome over full color in painting or photography.

Why should the designer limit himself to single depth, particularly when the garden site has ample space to use more complex perspective techniques? Simply put, restricting the composition to a single depth reduces the effort required to view the garden, because the observer is not asked to shift his focus back and forth from near to far. This shift of focus puts to work not only the muscles governing the convergence angle of the two eyes in normal binocular vision, but also the ciliary muscles controlling the shape of the lens to accommodate near and far vision. The reduction in stress gained through single-depth composition frees up the viewer's senses and imagination to savor the more suggestive subtleties of form, texture, and tonality that can be conveyed on a flat, two-dimensional surface. As a result, he is likely to experience an attenuated sense of oneness between his own interior psychic space and the sensory qualities of the garden composition being viewed. This intense personal realization of oneness is a principal goal of many Japanese gardens and works of art in general.

The dry landscape garden of the subtemple Konchi'in, within the Nanzenji monastic complex in southeastern Kyoto, is an excellent example of a single-depth composition. The concentration of design elements in this garden—a rich tapestry featuring two asymmetrically balanced rock compositions at the left and right set against an almost vertical wall of clipped shrubs and elongated broadleaf evergreen trees—occupies a narrow band along the rear of the wide-spreading site, separated from the temple veranda by an expanse of white gravel (fig. 38). Between the two compositions (done in the crane and turtle motif) a large flat rock with its upper surface barely protruding above ground level provides a safe, stable horizontal platform parallel to the viewer's position on the veranda. As such, it not only serves as a visual bridge between the two island compositions, but also functions as a kind of magic carpet Worship Rock (*reihaiseki*) to transport viewers into the mysterious land on the opposite shore of the gravel "sea." The power of such a visual paradise to come to the viewer lies in the fact that the composition conforms to the basic shape of the human senses: the narrow band of the design parallels the visual field and the body's mid-frontal (or "coronal") plane rather than oppose it in perpendicular as a long, deep vista is apt to do. And, as mentioned earlier, the eyes are freed from the fatiguing task of shifting focus back and forth from near to far.

OVERLAPPING AND MIEGAKURE

We have not yet discussed the role of overlapping in Japanese garden design. This is a technique for increasing space perception that Chinese painters have long used with success, as Rudolf Arnheim explains:[36]

> For some painters space is realized best through a continuous series of overlapping objects, which lead the eye like stepping-stones from the front to the back. . . . The space-building role of superposition in Chinese landscape painting is well known. The relative location of mountain peaks or clouds is established visually in this way, and the volume of a mountain is often conceived as a skeleton of echelons or slices in staggered formation. The complex curvature of the solid is thus obtained through a kind of "integral" based on the summation of frontal planes.

In classical Japanese gardens there are not many examples of "the volume of a mountain . . . conceived as a skeleton of echelons or slices in staggered formation." It would have been impractical to use so many rocks, and the Japanese in any case preferred other, more suggestive, techniques for creating the impression of moun-

Fig. 38. "Single-depth" perspective is evident in this woodblock print of the Konchi'in garden. From *Miyako rinsen meisho zue,* an Edo-period guide to Kyoto gardens.

tains continuing back into space. An effective use of overlapping, however, may be found in the composition of lofty peaks that serves as the central focal point at the rear of the Tiger Gorge Garden of Nishi Honganji (fig. 39).

Beginning with the pointed rock that forms the highest peak, three more huge, upright rocks—one at the left and two at the right—provide overlapping echelons moving in steplike fashion, down toward the sides and out toward the front. The overlapping does not appear contrived, because the repetition of the triangle motif lends the composition integrity and stability, and because the balance among the four rocks is natural and asymmetrical.

Related to the above is a technique used far more commonly in Japanese gardens. Called *miegakure,* or "hide-and-reveal," it[37]

> relies heavily on the principle of overlapping perspective and involves making only a part of an object visible, rather than exposing the whole. The purpose is to make the viewer imagine the invisible part and thus create not only an illusion of depth but also the impression that there are hidden beauties beyond. *Miegakure* is, in short, a means of imparting a sense of vastness in a small space.

Fig. 39.   Detail of overlapping peaks in the Tiger Gorge Garden at Nishi Honganji.

One effective way of achieving this, as was mentioned earlier, is to design a meandering watercourse or path so that it now and then fades out of sight behind an object such as a hill or a tree or a rock to reappear at a greater distance from the viewer. In the case of a path, at each turn a new vista is revealed and a new one suggested by the point where the path fades out of sight beyond yet another bend. This is undoubtedly the same technique introduced in the *Illustrations* as the phenomenon of "gnarled trees blocking the path" and described in conjunction with figure K: "As shown in the illustration, it means that you plant contorted trees so close together that it appears a person would not be able to pass through." A device like this almost demands that the designer have a genuine sense of play, and revel in the way the garden can at turns entice and then surprise the observer.

AERIAL PERSPECTIVE

Overlapping and *miegakure* bring us to the threshold of a type of depth indicator different from those we have been dealing with so far—one that relies for its effect as much on what is unseen as what is seen. This is of course true of the above, but here the dividing line between what is hidden and what is revealed is seldom so sharp. For the type of depth indicator we shall now be discussing is based not on the physical characteristics of the solids and liquids that constitute the earth's crust, but rather on the atmospheric effects that result from the illumination of gases and suspended particles in the earth's atmosphere. In our original list of depth cues, Gibson calls this type of indicator "aerial perspective" and differentiates it from the other types when he says, "Unlike the other forms of perspective it is variable with the conditions of illumination and it does not rest on the geometry of optics."[38]

Frederick Law Olmsted, one of America's pioneers in the field of landscape architecture, noticed the important role atmospheric effects play in landscapes of great beauty: "Beauty, grandeur, impressiveness in any way, from scenery, is not often to be found in a few prominent, distinguishable features, but in the manner and the unobserved materials with which these are connected and combined. Clouds, lights, states of the atmosphere, and circumstances that we cannot always detect, affect all landscapes. . . ."[39] The Chinese used atmospheric effects to imbue the small space of a landscape painting with the ineffable vastness experienced when one wanders through certain lake and mountain regions of China. Painters often lived in areas of great natural beauty, such as that of the Hsiao and Hsiang rivers, where they were inspired by the sense of limitless space produced when mountains were viewed across misty lakes as if through a veil. "To further heighten this sense of unknown vastness," says George Rowley, "the Chinese used cloud, mist, light, and weather conditions to make the voids between the three depths more vague, thus suggesting . . . boundless infinity. . . ."[40] Atmospheric effects, of which Gibson's aerial perspective is one variety, often have about them an ineffable or mysterious quality because we are viewing the landscape through a kind of veil or scrim.

How are such hazy or misty effects produced in classical Japanese gardens? If the garden has a pond, the designer may create conditions for real mist to form and trail up an adjacent ridge until it hovers around an upright rock calculated to look just like the kind of peak one would expect to see through the mist. Such a rock does occur in this very context in item 68 of the *Illustrations*, and is appropriately named the Hovering Mist Rock. But it is not always possible, or aesthetically desirable, to reproduce in a garden the requisite conditions for mist to form. Could the effect of mist, or of haze, which makes distant hills appear "bluish and blurred, with less color saturation," be duplicated without mist or haze being present?

This is the type of challenge that must have fascinated a classical Japanese garden designer, particularly with the advent of the dry (that is, waterless) landscape garden in the late fifteenth century. At about this same time the renowned Japanese painter Sōami was using ink washes in the style of the Chinese painter Mu-ch'i to capture the effect of "open water and low mountain ranges extending into distance, with low-lying mists hovering between them."[41] In all probability, Sōami executed his famous landscape panorama *Eight Views of Hsiao and Hsiang* on the sliding-door panels in the abbot's quarters of the Daisen'in in 1513, the same year the former head priest of Daitokuji, Kogaku Sōkō, created a dry landscape garden northeast of the same building. This may be no coincidence. We have already discussed the debt this garden's magnificent rocks and convincing scenic effects owe to Chinese landscape painting styles.[42]

At Daisen'in, a jade-green rock marbled with vertical white striations has been set in the shadowy depth of twin pinnacle rocks to produce the effect of a compound waterfall. Might it not be possible to simulate the effects of mist in such a garden? Mist would surely be present if this scene actually existed in nature. No one would have been more capable of conceiving ways of doing so than Sōami. His paintings show him to be a keen observer of natural phenomena who used graded ink washes on paper to realize a great variety of atmospheric effects. Since Kogaku Sōkō very likely talked with him about the design of the Daisen'in dry landscape, we can imagine Sōami suggesting new ways of using traditional materials to simulate in the garden the effects of water and mist.

Several such techniques are in evidence at Daisen'in. The most obvious is the use of a white plaster wall, which serves as a backdrop for all but the northeast corner of the garden. When the miniature pine on the islet (pl. 9) or the craggy mountain rocks south of the crane island (pl. 10) are viewed against it, the white plaster wall takes on the appearance of a misty, overcast sky just like the blank white paper of an ink painting, and there is the impression of an immense landscape that does not stop at the wall but continues on through the mist.

Less obvious is a technique for creating an impression that a light veil of haze or mist hangs in the air—apropos of Gibson's aerial perspective—between near and far objects, an effect Sōami achieved in painting by using light ink washes. The juxtaposition of two rocks in the Daisen'in dry landscape—one at the southern tip of the crane island and the other set against the white plaster wall behind it and to the right—argues convincingly that a technique for producing the effect of aerial perspective has been used here deliberately (pl. 10). Protruding columnar plates stand out in bold relief from the face of the larger rock in the foreground to give it a strongly three-dimensional quality, and the sharp edges of the plates make it look "in focus," heightening the impression that it is close to the viewer. The rock set against the wall has characteristics that link it to the sharp-edged rock in front: it appears to be of the same geological makeup, and it too has the jagged outline of a mountain peak. But it is diminished in size as if it were more distant, and its sharp edges are rounded off and its face worn smooth to give it a flat, blurred quality as if it were veiled by intervening layers of mist or haze.

A third technique used in dry landscape gardens probably combines the observation that hills on the horizon take on a bluish cast—an aspect of aerial perspective mentioned earlier—and the realization that colors can deepen the sense of space ("forces acting in the direction of depth are present in the color itself," says Johannes Itten in *The Art of Color*).[43] Generally the technique involves the use of plant materials, but the same principle could also be applied to rocks. An example is the way camellia has been used as a backdrop for the waterfall composition in the northeast corner of the Daisen'in dry landscape.[44] It is clipped into a rounded mountain form, and its shade deepens the effect of the waterfall.

Camellia's glossy, very deep evergreen foliage also makes it the perfect choice for producing the effect of mountains receding into the distance, particularly when lighter tones of green are used in front. Because, as Itten says, "light tones on a black ground will advance according to their degree of brilliance,"[45] plant materials like pine trees, azaleas, ferns, and moss—all of which are a much lighter green—advance from the dark ground provided by camellia, thus enhancing the sense of depth. The significant amount of yellow contained in the green of such plants should also bring out any blue in the deep green of camellia, and so contribute to the aerial perspective effect. The effect in this instance is to heighten the sense of distance between nearby and faraway garden elements through the bluing of aerial perspective, and to suggest that the most distant objects are so far away that their details cannot be clearly discerned.

The same technique may also be used in reverse. The water basin next to the veranda before the dry landscape garden at the temple Manshuin in Kyoto is set in the deep shade of a *mokkoku* tree (*Ternstroemia japonica*), which has dark green glossy foliage, and this cool oasis is viewed against the bright ground of white gravel and the bright green foliage of a Japanese red pine (*Pinus densiflora*). Here, the dark foliage of the *mokkoku* advances, for, as Itten reminds us, "on a white ground, the effect is reversed; light tones are held to the plane of the background, and shades approaching black are thrust forward in corresponding degree."[46]

The same effect of a dark foreground viewed against a bright background may be found in the garden outside the Bōsen tearoom of Kohōan at Daitokuji. There a row of camellias provides a shady backdrop for the stone lantern and water basin in the foreground (spread with subdued blue-gray pebbles simulating water), while beyond this the bright tones of a sunny garden are seen in the distance (pl. 29).

REVERSE PERSPECTIVE

All the techniques introduced in this section have been described in terms of their ability to increase the apparent depth of the site. Yet sometimes the designer wants to decrease rather than increase the sense of depth in a garden. In the earlier section on framing, two methods were presented for reducing the effective depth of a narrow, deep site: (1) screening the rear portion of the site from view and putting it to another use, and (2) maximizing the width of the site so as to increase the width-to-height ratio of the frame.

There is another method, or set of methods, for reducing the apparent depth of a narrow, deep site, very useful when the rear portion of a garden site or vista must be incorporated into the design. It simply involves using the perspective techniques described in this section in reverse—turning them into "reverse perspective" techniques. Size perspective, for example, may be used this way. Instead of enhancing the sense of depth by setting a massive rock in the foreground against which much smaller rocks in the distance are measured, a designer can make the rear portion of the site appear closer by using massive boulders in the distance and small or mid-sized rocks in the foreground. This technique will compress a narrow, deep site and make it appear wider than it is deep.

As a matter of fact, in just about every garden, designers consciously adjust the space up and down and from side to side across the visual field, in order to give greater significance to certain parts of the garden while letting other areas fade into the background. One can draw an analogy to the way a cinematographer uses the camera lens in filming a western movie. As the wide-angle lens slowly pans across a barren landscape, we feel the vastness of nature and wonder what forms of life—even human activity—we might discover upon closer examination. Then the lens (imitating a pair of binoculars) begins to zoom in on a rock outcropping that serves as the hideout for an outlaw, until in the details of his face we can sense his predicament. When the camera returns to wide angle, the landscape contains a new significance for us.

A film is viewed sequentially, but that sequential experience is also part of how we take in a scroll garden or painting. Our eyes can focus on only a small area at a time, and require intermittent rests. Areas of strong and weak focus in a garden address that capacity (or limitation) of our eyes.

.   .   .

Throughout the preceding discussion—from factors involving the size and shape of the site all the way to depth cues and atmospheric effects—the intimate relationship between sensory and scenic effects has emerged again and again. Clearly, the landscape garden designer cannot successfully create scenic effects without a thorough knowledge of sensory effects and the principles of perception on which they rest. At the same time, he must remember that sensory effects are first experienced and understood through the scenic effects of our environment, whether in nature or in art. The designer therefore must be a keen observer of both natural phenomena and the workings of the human senses.

Nature creates abundantly, but not expressly for the purpose of providing the senses with aesthetic experiences. The author of *Sakuteiki*, in attempting to answer the question "Which is more beautiful, natural scenery or that produced by human design?" concludes—after observing how even renowned natural scenery invariably has some "worthless views existing close by"—that "in the case of a man-made landscape garden, since only the attractive and best parts of the places are studied and modelled after, meaningless stones and features are seldom provided along with man's work."[47] Borrowing the words of Rudolf Arnheim, we can say that Japanese gardens, like other "works of visual art, . . . are made exclusively for being perceived, and therefore the artist endeavors to create the strongest, purest, most precise embodiment of the meaning that . . . he intends to convey."[48]

THE ART WE SEE:

CULTURAL VALUES

Spirit turtles are carrying the
Fan-chang island on their heads.
Its high peaks rise to majestic heights.
Immortals flutter along the edges of
the island.
Jade maidens play on the slopes of
the mountains.

—Ts'ao Chih
(3rd century B.C.)

So far our investigation of the types of aesthetic experience conveyed in classical Japanese gardens has taken us into the two realms of scenic and sensory effects. We have seen that these two categories, or "levels," of experience can be presented to the viewer's senses by one and the same work of art. One of the measures of an excellent work of art is that it conveys, in its totality and in its parts, more than one level of meaning or experience. It is time now to consider a third level of "meaning" (in the experiential rather than the conceptual sense) traditionally incorporated in the design of Japanese gardens, that of human values as developed in a cultural milieu. The range of these values is wide, and the way they are expressed in art varies from culture to culture. Still, certain core values appear to transcend cultural boundaries, and there is a recurring tendency for people of different cultures to associate certain expressive qualities with certain ideals. Vitality, immortality, enlightenment, courage—such values as these have been worshiped and captured in the arts of many a culture.

How is the garden going to be used? What ideals or stylistic preferences will guide the design? These important considerations are the prerogative of the client. So, as we look at how cultural values are incorporated into the garden design, we should keep in mind that we are talking about the aspect of the design process in which the client is most directly involved.

The Statue of Liberty in New York Harbor is an example of a work of sculptural art that communicates the cultural values of its client (the people of the United States) at an affective level as well as a literal one. The feminine quality of "Lady Liberty" and her victorious gesture holding the torch in an upright pose aptly convey the spirit and ideals of American liberty. The orientation of the statue has been well considered too: it stands at the gateway to America, welcoming those arriving by ship.

Other kinds of cultural values are communicated in the designs of Japanese gardens. At the base of the waterfall at Kinkakuji in Kyoto stands an upright "carp rock" (see fig. 1). It seems to be poised for a final leap toward the top of the waterfall that breaks over it. In Buddhism, the carp is a symbol of the perseverance needed to attain enlightenment (according to legend, carp that leap up such towering waterfalls become dragons and take wing). The rock does not simply "stand for" a carp. Rather, it succeeds because it communicates the qualities of the leaping carp on a sensory level. An observer, therefore, need not know what the carp represents in Japanese culture in order to experience the quality of spiritual aspiration.

The Power of the Garden to Bring Fulfillment

The power of art to convey experientially the deepest values a culture aspires to has long been recognized in East Asia. Early in the Heian period the Japanese priest Kūkai (774–835) established the Shingon sect based on teachings of esoteric Buddhism he had brought back from China. There, his "master, Hui-kuo, had told him that only through art could the profound meaning of the esoteric scriptures be conveyed."[1] Kūkai was himself an artist, and the teachings he promulgated, stressing the close connection between religious and aesthetic experience, went on to provide a philosophical basis for the subsequent development of the fine arts in Japan. Art, said Kūkai, even more than philosophical discourse, has the power to communicate the most profound spiritual truths: "the esoteric doctrines are so profound as to defy their enunciation in writing. With the help of painting, however, their obscurities may be understood. . . . Art is what reveals to us the state of perfection."[2]

In the West, the arts have not always been held in such high esteem as carriers of truth. Traditionally, Western thinkers have made a division between sense perception and cognition, in which "raw sense data" are regarded as inferior to the cognitive faculties of the mind. Rudolf Arnheim notes that "from medieval philosophers . . . the rationalists of the seventeenth and eighteenth centuries derived the notion that the messages of the senses are confused and indistinct and that it takes reasoning to clarify them."[3] He traces the tendency all the way back to ancient Greece: "The high esteem of music and the disdain of the fine arts derived, of course, from Plato, who in his *Republic* had recommended music for the education of heroes because it made human beings partake in the mathematical order and harmony of the cosmos, located beyond the reach of the senses; whereas the arts, and particularly painting, were to be treated with caution because they strengthened man's dependence on illusory images."[4]

There were, of course, periods in Western history when a different attitude prevailed. One of these was the time of the romantic movement in the nineteenth century. The American landscape architect Frederick Law Olmsted (1822–1903), grounded as he was in nineteenth-century romanticism, found in the beauty of natural landscape a healing power capable of tranquillizing and reinvigorating the mind through the senses. Olmsted's discovery of a more holistic interaction between the mind and the body points us toward a practical method for mending the artificial rift between sense perception and cognition that has long existed in the West:[5]

> If we analyze the operation of scenes of beauty upon the mind, and consider the intimate relation of the mind upon the nervous system and the whole physical economy, the action and reaction which constantly occur between bodily and mental conditions, the reinvigoration which results from such scenes is readily comprehended. . . . The enjoyment of scenery employs the mind without fatigue and yet exercises it; tranquillizes it and yet enlivens it; and thus, through the influence of the mind over the body, gives the effect of refreshing rest and reinvigoration to the whole system.

There would have been no need for Olmsted to persuade members of the culture which produced *Sakuteiki* and the *Illustrations* that beautiful natural scenery has the power to reinvigorate the human spirit. He would have found that this culture had achieved a successful marriage between the scenic and the sensory in its landscape art, and had gone so far as to invest the garden with the power to fulfill—based on the power of art to evoke—the hopes and prayers of the people for whom it was created. Item 25 of the *Illustrations* alludes to that power as it explains how the viewer can best appreciate the garden. Buddhism was still the major spiritual philosophy in Japan when the *Illustrations* was set down, and certain key compositions of rocks were given Buddhist names:

> A person who approaches the garden wanting to view it first does so from beside the Reverence Rock [fig. 40]. The reason for this is that, due to the awe-inspiring nature of certain rocks that are set in the garden—the Buddhist Triad Rocks, the Twofold World Rocks, the Mystic Kings Rocks, and the Celestial Beings' Abode Rock—the viewer, with heart full of hope for the fulfillment of his most devout prayers, reverently worships all the Buddhas of the Three Worlds from beside this rock.

Fig. 40.   The entire garden is first viewed from the Reverence Rock.

Fig. 41. Three factors that the designer must bring into a mutually beneficial relationship.

Later in the *Illustrations*, the mention of two more rocks with Buddhist-sounding names reveals the power of Japan's garden art more directly: The Absolute Control Rock (item 27) "protects the people who dwell there. . . . If it is set well, good fortune will come and riches will abound." Similarly, the Fulfillment Rock (item 29) is so named because "this rock, when it is set well, has the power to bring about fulfillment of the master's prayers."

We can imagine what shape those prayers might take. The master might well hope that a finely executed landscape garden would bring him praise as a man of cultivated taste and lofty sentiment; that the garden would refresh and transport him to a paradise far from the pressures of the city that surrounds his estate; that the beauty of the garden might rub off on him and bring good fortune. If he were a man of letters, he might seek to re-create in the garden the poetic moods of his favorite landscapes from classic works of literature.

As we go on to consider some of the different ways in which specific values are presented in classical Japanese gardens, it would be well to bear in mind what was stated at the beginning of chapter 3: that the designer does not create the garden in isolation purely as an expression of personal fancy, but rather takes into account the nature and needs of two masters—the client and the site. Only then can the garden have the power to reinvigorate the human spirit and so "bring about the fulfillment of the master's prayers." How that was to be done is set forth in item 2 of the *Illustrations*. The exhaustive elaboration to be found there is based upon Chinese geomancy and the cosmological theories of Yin and Yang and the Five Elements. In essence, the garden designer is charged with bringing into a mutually productive relationship three basic factors: (1) the client's nature, (2) the nature of the site, including topography and the various cosmic forces that come into play there (sun and moon, weather conditions, prevailing winds), and (3) the aesthetic qualities of the materials used in the composition (fig. 41).

The Quest for an Earthly Paradise

The search for happiness, for health, wealth, and longevity, is no stranger to the East or the West. Ideal happiness, however, is rarely close at hand. Far-off places like tropical or temperate islands, with their exotic quality and sense of mystery plus their remove from the "dusty world" of civilization, have long been associated with paradise in the imagination of people seeking a greater measure of contentment in this life. In the fifteenth and sixteenth centuries, belief in the existence of a worldly paradise, containing such treasures as gold and the Fountain of Youth, sent many a European expedition out across uncharted oceans. For several centuries preceding the West's Christian era, the same thing was happening in China.

For the Chinese—most notably the kings with the wealth and power to send out expeditions—the worldly paradise was the Isles of the Immortals, believed to lie off the east coast of China and thought to be the dwelling place of beings who possessed the secrets of eternal youth. This "Eastern Paradise" was closely associated with the Taoists, many of whom were involved in the search, through alchemy and other methods, for an elixir of immortality.

Perhaps the most ambitious expedition to be sent in search of the mythical isles was that of Ch'in Shih Huang Ti (259–210 B.C.), China's first emperor. Its dismal failure is recorded in the historical annals *Shih-chi*, and no doubt led Ssu-ma Ch'ien, the author of that work, to stress the difficulty of actually reaching the "three spirit mountains," known as P'eng-lai, Fang-chang, and Ying-chou:[6]

> From the age [the fourth century B.C.] of Kings Wei and Hsüan of Ch'i and King Chao of Yen, men were sent from time to time to set out to sea and search for the islands of P'eng-lai, Fang-chang, and Ying-chou. These were three spirit mountains which were supposed to exist in the Gulf of Pohai. They were not very far from the land of men, it was said, but the difficulty was that, whenever a boat was about to touch their shores, a wind would always spring up and drive it away. In the past, people said, there had been men who succeeded in reaching them, and found them peopled by fairy spirits who possessed the elixir of immortality.

It was Emperor Wu of Han (156–87 B.C.) who first "conceived the possibility of enticing the Immortals to his own estates" by imaginatively re-creating the three spirit mountains there.[7] To this end he erected, on three rocky islands in a large lake west of the capital, buildings he appropriately named P'eng-lai Palace, Fang-chang Palace, and Ying-chou Palace. In the seventh century, according to Masao Hayakawa, "the basically Taoist belief in the Isles of the Blest entered Japan to take its place beside Indian-inspired Buddhist thought in the designing of gardens."[8] By the beginning of the eleventh century, not long before the author of *Sakuteiki* was born, the depiction of P'eng-lai (the main island, often used to stand for all three) had come to be considered "a conventional subject" in Heian culture,[9] making it difficult to believe this isle was not also portrayed in the gardens of that time. Yet, for whatever reason, P'eng-lai is not mentioned in *Sakuteiki*, although two related symbols of longevity, the turtle and the crane, do occur there in connection with the shape of the pond.[10]

It is to the *Illustrations* that we must turn our attention if we are to appreciate fully how the idea of immortality was conveyed in classical Japanese gardens through the motif of the mythical Isles of the Immortals. As fortune would have it, we do not have to search far in the *Illustrations* to find what we are looking for: the first named rock to occur there, in item 2, is the Rock of the Spirit Kings (which we shall soon return to), and the second is the Never Aging Rock, which, we are told, is Hōrai (Hōrai is Sino-Japanese for P'eng-lai). To be set below the Never Aging Rock is a low-lying, turtle-shaped rock called the Rock of Ten Thousand Eons. It is the "ancient turtle of Hōrai." The significance of the turtle is twofold. The Isles of the Immortals, according to the legend, were borne on the backs (or heads) of giant turtles. And the turtle was regarded as a symbol of longevity, reputed to live for ten thousand years.

Items 2, 85, and 86 of the *Illustrations* detail the key points with regard to the size, shape, and visual effect of these two rocks. The Never Aging Rock is like a newly formed mountain in that it is "not flattened off on top." It commands our attention from any direction, and has an enchanting scenic atmosphere. The Rock of Ten Thousand Eons "is the ancient-looking rock set below the Never Aging Rock." Like an aged mountain, its upper surface has been worn down so that it resembles a round cushion or the shape of a turtle. The aesthetic technique employed here is a highly effective one involving contrasts—between the steep, jagged profile of a new mountain and the recumbent, rounded form of an ancient mountain eroded for countless eons (fig. 42).

So far, the idea of immortality is being communicated in a purely sensory, immediate way. However, when we are told that the Rock of Ten Thousand Eons is "the ancient turtle of Hōrai" and therefore should be set "so that it bears a striking resemblance to the shape of a turtle," we sense the shift toward symbolism, where there is a one-to-one correspondence between the signifier and what is signified. The viewer can only learn the correspondence between the turtle and immortality in a cultural context.

There is a danger here if one fixes too much on the symbols; over time the original aesthetic significance of the design may be lost. We have already seen one of the more successful renderings of the turtle image in the dry landscape of Nishi Honganji. The turtle island of this garden uses rocks mostly in the recumbent position, like the Rock of Ten Thousand Eons. The effect is that of very old mountains worn down by erosion. Its companion, the crane island, on the other hand, resembles the Never Aging Rock (or the Rock of the Spirit Kings) in its use of sharp-edged rocks in the vertical position—these may be likened to the wings of the crane—to convey the impression of steep, jagged new mountains such as are found in the Himalayas. It is this contrast, between towering newly formed peaks and well-eroded old mountains, that so effectively triggers the aesthetic experience of ageless vitality.

Fig. 42. The turtle and crane originally alluded to "old" and "new" mountains.

In their effort to faithfully represent the anatomy (heads, legs, wings, tail) of the turtle and the crane, designers of some Japanese gardens apparently lost sight of this mountain imagery that was the key to translating the human ideal of paradise into a palpable sensory form. The turtle and crane motif, which has long enjoyed popularity in Japan, may at this point simply lack the precision it needs to convey the original aesthetic function. In the hands of a second-rate designer, it is apt to fall into cliché. This may be sufficient reason to revive from its obscurity in the *Illustrations* the vocabulary of the Never Aging Rock and the Rock of Ten Thousand Eons—the youthful mountain and the old mountain.

THE ROCK OF THE SPIRIT KINGS

Even more worthy of commanding our attention than the Never Aging Rock is the Rock of the Spirit Kings, a tour de force of rock compositions. Interesting here is the degree to which the description and function of these two rocks overlap. As pictured in figures B and C of the *Illustrations* (reproduced here as figs. 43 and 44), the Rock of the Spirit Kings and the Never Aging Rock bear a striking resemblance to one another, particularly in their vertical fissures and steplike jagged edges. Both are described as combining horizontal, diagonal, and vertical forces in their shapes.[11] More telling is the purpose of the Rock of the Spirit Kings as stated in figure O. It is not unlike a description of the Isles of the Immortals: "This rock is the seat of the myriad felicitous spirits and of Benzai Ten, and its purpose is to pray for happiness and prosperity."

No great leap of the imagination is needed to see these felicitous spirits that dwell on the protruding ledge at the front of the rock as the same immortals who make their home on the spirit mountains. The cloudlike form (composed of a few strokes almost like a cipher) floating off to the right of this rock in figure B clarifies its role still further. The passage from the *Shih-chi* quoted above, relating the difficulty of reaching the Isles of the Immortals by boat, continues as follows:[12]

> Seen from afar, the three spirit mountains looked like clouds but, as one drew closer, they seemed instead to be down under the water. In any event, as soon as anyone got near to them, the wind would suddenly come and drag the boat away, so that in the end no one could ever reach them.

Clouds evoke a sense of the unapproachable, supernatural quality that surrounds this island paradise where "high peaks rise to majestic heights/Immortals flutter along

Fig. 43. The Rock of the Spirit Kings shown in figure B of the *Illustrations*.

Fig. 44. The Never Aging Rock shown in figure C.

Fig. 45.   Detail of figure D: the rock labeled "Spirit Kings."

Fig. 46.   Detail of figure E: the rock with pine and cloud.

the edges of the island," in the words of the Chinese poet Ts'ao Chih. The cloud in figure B thus serves as a kind of signature; it is a reminder to the designer of the far-off, mysterious quality that shrouds the Rock of the Spirit Kings—for the richest paradise is that which lies within the viewer's own imagination.

The steep mountain rock in the center of figure E in the *Illustrations* may not be labeled "Spirit Kings" as is the rock in figure D, but the cloud "signature" floating just above and to the right of it conveys that information just as unmistakably (figs. 45, 46). Moreover, the caption below figure E describes the scene as "an immense ocean stretching out before a single mountain." The depicted rock's deep shading, vertical fissures, and steplike jagged edges are all qualities shared by the Rock of the Spirit Kings portrayed in figure B.

The pine tree growing from the base of the rock (below the cloud at the right) in figure E is the final stroke to the spirit-mountain theme. Pines, endowed with evergreen foliage, long life, and expressive gnarled forms of great beauty aptly convey the atmosphere of lofty cliffs far from the haunts of man. The scenic effect pictured in figure L and referred to in item 6 of the *Illustrations* as "craggy mountains with gnarled trees" is precisely what one would expect to find in such a "spirit mountain" paradise.

An example of what might be a Rock of the Spirit Kings can be seen today on an island in the "immense ocean" of Nijō Castle's Ninomaru garden in Kyoto (pl. 30). It has deep furrows, steep sides, and a jagged top.[13] Two cavelike indentations near its bottom suggest the ledge on which immortals dwell. From the right of this rock near its base grows a pine, its trunk reaching diagonally outward and upward to a soft, rounded "cloud" of needles at the top. It requires little imagination to see in this pruned pine both the tree and the cloud pictured to the right of the rock in the middle of figure E. Apparently the designer, and later the gardener who replanted and now prunes this pine, recognized how to capture with a single tree two distinct atmospheric effects—that of lofty cliffs (the tree's gnarled trunk) and that of the clouds which cast their veil of mystery over the Isles of the Immortals (the tree's billowy crown). In the absence of the veiling pine, much of the rock's power to evoke a sense of mystery would vanish.[14]

The cavelike hollows at the bottom of the Rock of the Spirit Kings in the Ninomaru garden may also allude to a later development in the Taoist conception of paradise—the world of light beyond the cave —that supplanted the island as a place of bliss. As Wolfgang Bauer explains,[15]

> For a long time, the idea of the "island" as a place of happiness seemed the ideal compromise. While situated on earth, it was yet adequately detached from it. But as the world began to shrink still further, an even more ideal place was discovered. It was the "cave," or better, the world, the "heaven" *beyond* the cave. For the "cave" was even closer to earth than the island. Like the latter, it could also be connected with the idea of the "mountain," that old place of refuge for the Taoists. Yet it was also otherworldly and, being much more difficult to discover, its magic could not as easily be lost as that of the island.

For the master of this garden, then, paradise is indeed approachable, the more so because stone bridges link the isle on which the rock sits to the distant shore by way of the large, central island. The first to enjoy the mystical power of the Nijō Castle Rock of the Spirit Kings would have been the shogun, Tokugawa Ieyasu, for whom the garden was created. Its construction was in all likelihood completed close to the time of his retirement ceremony, held at the castle in April of 1605. The two rooms of the Kuroshoin (the shogun's private living quarters) that face the garden—the Ni no Ma (Second Room) and the San no Ma (Third Room)—provide the perfect vantage point for viewing this rock. The view from these rooms was a privileged one, for from here the shogun could cast his eyes upon the eternal paradise, be it an island out at sea or a world just beyond the cave.

Literary Landscapes in the Garden

Poets and novelists are often moved to put into words the subtle qualities of landscape, sometimes purely for the beauty of it, and sometimes as a way of alluding to certain human feelings. Landscape design can translate such literary landscapes into three-dimensional form in the garden. Like the poet, the garden designer may allude to human feelings in his portrayals of nature.

Few gardens in Japan owe as much to literature for their inspiration as that of Katsura villa in Kyoto, created in the seventeenth century by Prince Toshihito and his son, Prince Toshitada. As members of the nobility, both men were steeped in the poetry and novels of the Heian period, that Golden Age of aristocratic culture to which they longed to return. The seventeenth-century political reality was iron-fisted rule by the Tokugawa shogunate, and the only escape for the imperial family was through art. Sano Shōeki, a merchant and respected man of culture, records in *Nigiwaigusa*, a collection of essays he published in 1682, that Prince Toshitada "was fascinated with a passage in *The Tale of Genji* that told about a garden where the color of the flowers, the songs of the birds, and the approach to the middle island were all strange and beautiful. . . ."[16] The passage, at the beginning of part 3, chapter 6, "The Butterflies," tells of courtiers venturing out into the lake on pleasure boats built in the Chinese style and later describes the following scene:[17]

> . . . round the Palace even the wistaria that ran along the covered alleys and porticos was all in bloom, but not a flower past its best; while here, where the boats were tied, mountain-kerria poured its yellow blossom over the rocky cliffs in a torrent of colour that was mirrored in the waters of the lake below.

So skillful was Toshitada's re-creation of this scene in the garden at Katsura, Sano tells us, that those who saw it felt almost as if they had been transported to the glorious age of *Genji*.

.   .   .   .

The mingling of the effect of an island-dotted bay on a misty morning and a feeling of longing for a loved one embarking on a journey is the subject both of a famous anonymous poem in the early tenth-century imperial anthology of Japanese poetry, *Kokinshū*, and of a scenic effect mentioned in the *Illustrations*. The poem has been translated as follows:[18]

Honobono to	Dimly, dimly
Akashi no ura no	In the morning mist that lies
Asagiri ni	Over Akashi Bay,
Shimagakureyuku	My longings follow with the ship
Fune o shi zo omou.	That vanishes behind the distant isle.

The composition referred to in item 64 of the *Illustrations* as the Boat-concealing Rocks aims at visually evoking the same combination of scenic atmosphere and human feelings: "The composition should convey the feeling of a boat vanishing behind isles in the bay of Akashi."

The *Illustrations* reveals no more than the essentials of how to compose this scenic effect; the rest is left to the designer. Spatially, the Boat-concealing Rocks are to be set by twos or threes, in a string or as a horizontal triad—fitting methods for capturing the visual impression of offshore islands dotting a bay (pl. 31). The essential quality of the rocks themselves is described as follows: "They must be rocks that look as if they had once towered quite high, but have since crumbled and eroded away." Erosion creates more rounded forms and softer textures. Rocks like this would aptly convey the indistinct quality of islands viewed through morning mist. As they appear to fade away, they might also allude to the drawn-out feeling of loss as the viewer on the shore watches the loved one's boat vanish. Of the repertoire of scenic effects presented in the *Illustrations*, this one comes closest to the aesthetic quality known as *yūgen*—a mysterious, sublime beauty best evoked by techniques of suggestion and paradoxical contrast, and a quality that was raised to an ideal in the arts of Japan's medieval period.

The challenge for the designer here is to use materials that re-create the quality of the mood rather than resort to using objects that merely represent it symbolically (as a boat-shaped rock might). Classical garden designers developed a sensitivity to the atmospheric qualities of natural scenery not only through direct experience, but also indirectly through poetry. Item 32 of the *Illustrations* exhorts the designer to convey those subtle moods of nature that, through a lifetime of sensitive observation, he has made his own: "Recollecting the subtle seasonal moods of *waka* poetry from ancient times up to the present, you must re-create with a quiet, graceful charm those moods that speak to you in your innermost heart."

The Names of Rocks: Toward a Vocabulary of Scenic and Sensory Effects

Names are an important key to what a society values. Anthropologists recognize naming as "one of the chief methods for imposing order on perception."[19] What is not named in a culture very likely goes unnoticed by the majority of its people. The converse is also true: people pay greater attention to things that have been given names. Names tend to cluster in those areas of human life that are highly valued, because with valuation comes the need and desire for greater discrimination. Consider the number of words that we in the United States have for money—the "Almighty Dollar." In other cultures we are struck by the number of names people have to distinguish varieties of snow, or bamboo.

The Japanese language has names for certain aesthetic qualities that are difficult to translate into English. The entire March 1960 issue of *House Beautiful* was devoted to explaining several of these Japanese terms, because at least one of them, *shibui* (meaning "astringent" and therefore of subdued taste), was beginning to creep into the language of American designers and interior decorators, who were applying it with more ingenuity than accuracy. In this section, we will consider the way different names are given to compositions of rocks in the *Illustrations*. Like anthropologists, we have to regard these names as an index to what is significant in the art of classical Japanese landscape gardening.

Item 26 of the *Illustrations* traces the lineage of the art of setting rocks in the landscape garden from its alleged origin in India, through China to Japan. Buddhism followed the same route on its eastward journey from India to Japan, and we can safely say that the author is here motivated less by the need to provide historical accuracy than by the desire to lend an aura of legitimacy to his art. Furthermore, the India referred to here is not so much the geographical country as it is the mythical center of the Buddhist cosmos. When we read in the *Illustrations* that "in India at the lake called Mānasarovara . . . rocks numbering 8,631 were set, with each of the Eight Great Dragon Kings in charge of more than 1,000 rocks," we sense the desire to represent exhaustively, in a one-to-one correspondence, all the multitudinous entities that make up the macrocosm.

The number of named rocks is reduced to 361 in China, and finally to 48 in Japan. There are at least two plausible reasons for this. First, 48 was no doubt a manageable number for a working vocabulary of named rocks, as the Japanese syllabary contained, at least by one count, 48 phonetic characters. Second, and more important, the reduction represents a move away from the encyclopedic listing of entities in the macrocosm toward a more aesthetic presentation of a world in microcosm, where fewer forms are potently used to re-create selected experiential qualities or tones of feeling.

The rocks in the *Illustrations* reveal a whole spectrum of ways in which names can be used to communicate aesthetic values. Some rocks, such as the Hovering Mist Rock and the Water-channeling Rocks, are named for the scenic effect they produce. Others, such as the Horizontal Triad Rocks or the Erect & Recumbent Rocks, are named for their formal sensory qualities (size, spacing, shape, texture, color). Still other rocks, such as the Master Rock and Attendant Rock or the Buddhist Triad Rocks, are given metaphorical names that allude to their aesthetic roles.

The meaning of these metaphorical names may at first elude us, but that is only because we lack sufficient knowledge of the culture from which they have been drawn. Appendix 2 at the end of this book classifies all the rocks mentioned in the *Illustrations* according to the type of name ("scenic," "sensory," or "cultural") and geological zone they represent. Most of the metaphorical names fit into the naming category of "cultural values." There they are further subdivided into Taoist, Confucian, Buddhist, and Shinto—the four major creeds of traditional Japan that were syncretically associated at the time the *Illustrations* was written—and Poetic Allusion, for which the Boat-concealing Rocks serves as the single example.

What aesthetic values are the metaphorical names of rocks in the *Illustrations* intended to communicate? In most cases, the names refer either to scenic effects or sensory effects, the two aspects of aesthetic experience we have looked at in the preceding two chapters. For example, Taoist names, such as the Rock of the Spirit Kings and the Never Aging Rock, allude to a mythical paradise of almost supernatural scenic beauty, and thus by extension direct the designer's imagination to the prospect of creating scenic effects equally magical in the landscape garden. Confucian terms such as "Master" and "Attendant" originally communicated the hierarchical nature of social relationships, but used as names of rocks in the garden figuratively express the formal visual relationships of rocks in a composition. As item 4 of the *Illustrations* puts it, continuing the metaphor of the names, "the Master Rock looks after its Attendants, and the Attendant Rocks look up to the Master." What is being referred to here is a sensory effect resulting from the relative size, shape, thrust, and spacing of the two rocks—qualities that define what *Sakuteiki* calls a rock's "requesting" mood.

Even Buddhist names which reflect a concern with cosmological truths realized in contemplation have been borrowed by classical designers to allude to certain formal, sensory patterns produced by the relationship of two or more rocks. An example is the pair, the Absolute Control Rock and the Mirror Rock, where the smaller rock, the Mirror Rock, "sharpens the image of the Absolute Control Rock." Its important-sounding name reminds the designer that the Absolute Control Rock plays a key role in the composition, so much so that it is considered "king among all the rocks."

Several other Buddhist names are used as metaphors for formal compositions consisting of a specific number of rocks, usually with one rock rising higher than the others. The Twofold World is originally a concept of esoteric Buddhism that also came to be prominently associated with the medieval religious tradition known as Ryōbu Shintō.[20] The *Illustrations* in item 33 capitalizes on the popularity of this concept by giving the name Twofold World Rocks to a prominent group of two rocks, one of which "is set in the pond close to the waterfall, and the other . . . in line with it on the shore." The Buddhist Triad Rocks is a name used to refer to a

Fig. 47. Cloudlike rocks, by Hsiao Chao. From the *Mustard Seed Garden Manual of Painting*.

group of three rocks. And the Mystic Kings Rocks is an example of a name drawn from Buddhism to refer to a group of five rocks.

The names of rocks found in the *Illustrations* did not all survive the test of time. One such name is *tenninkyoseki*, the Celestial Beings' Abode Rock. Other names, such as *sanzonseki*, the Buddhist Triad Rocks, remain in common parlance to this day in Japan. These two names occur in close proximity in the text. In figure H, they are pictured side by side and clearly labeled "Celestial Beings" on the right and "Buddhist Triad" on the left. They appear again in a list of four "awe-inspiring" rocks, all with Buddhist names, in item 25. Since the two compositions appear to be of equal importance, why did the first name die out while the second lives on?

All of item 69 is devoted to describing the placement and formal visual character-istics of the Buddhist Triad Rocks. The Celestial Beings' Abode Rock is never so described in the *Illustrations*. Perhaps this is because "Celestial Beings" is a concept that has no clear spatial configuration associated with it. This is not to say that designers at the time of the *Illustrations* did not enthusiastically embrace the challenge of translating an abstract Buddhist idea into a sensory form for viewers to enjoy in the garden. In doing so, they would have been responding sensitively to the cultural values of their age and, more specifically, to the stylistic preferences of the client. For example, to evoke the qualities of the Celestial Beings' abode, the designer might select a weathered rock of convoluted limestone like the billowy, cloudlike rock formation pictured here (fig. 47). What seems clear in the light of our present discussion, however, is that this is a rock whose name is to be taken at face value and

Fig. 48. Examples of Buddhist Triad Rocks (*sanzonseki*) from classical gardens. Based on drawings by Mirei Shigemori.

not figuratively, and so it cannot serve as a general tool to designers in structuring landscape gardens.

The Buddhist Triad, by contrast, is based on a triangular configuration rising vertically from the ground. It is a name that easily communicates formal visual qualities (fig. 48). The disappearance of the Celestial Beings' Abode Rock suggests that a term borrowed from the predominant culture for the purposes of art will not survive unless it can function as a metaphor for a universal aesthetic value that is rooted in the human senses.

FEELING-TONES

Several of the rocks in the *Illustrations* are named for the effect they have on the viewer. The metaphorical names Fulfillment Rock and the Never Aging Rock, for example, reveal the paradise function of the garden discussed earlier in this chapter. Sometimes names explicitly describe the viewer's physical response to a garden composition. For example, "Looking Back Falls" (Mikaeri no Taki) is the name of the waterfall in the Japanese garden adjoining Jefferson Hall at the University of Hawaii's East-West Center. It was so christened by Kenneth Yasuda when, in descending the stepping-stone path from above the falls, he discovered that not until a precise point about halfway down does the waterfall become audible, at which point the sound compels the viewer to look back and view the falls. Since this "looking back" defines the special nature of the experience one has in viewing the falls, the name is highly appropriate.

A name like Looking Back Falls has an additional advantage: it does not treat the viewer and what he views as two distinct entities, but places these two where they belong—inseparably fused at the heart of the aesthetic experience. Still, it is sometimes helpful to divide aesthetic experience into its so-called subjective and objective components. The experiential quality the composition transmits to the viewer—what it evokes in him—can be called its "feeling-tone" (the term *fuzei* introduced in chapter 2 means almost the same thing). The objective characteristics of the composition can then be regarded separately as its "sensory qualities." Listed side by side in figure 49 are several feeling-tones and the sensory qualities that produce them. The chart is by no means all-inclusive, but is merely a sampling of what are the infinite possibilities open to the designer. The sensory qualities given for each feeling-tone are not absolute. Depending upon the context (site, client, culture, and available materials), other qualities may be more appropriate. Also, while the line drawings here represent rocks, other materials may be similarly employed.

Feeling tones, because they lie at the heart of aesthetic experience, are more at home in an artist's vocabulary than they are in the everyday world. Without a well-developed vocabulary through which to interpret their experience, it is difficult for most people to express the qualitative nature of aesthetic feeling. In the *Illustrations*, the word *fuzei*, meaning "atmosphere" or "mood," comes very close to the concept of feeling-tone. Yet almost every time *fuzei* occurs there, its particular quality is described by referring to some aspect of nature—the ambience of an ordinary pond, the scenic effect of a cherry tree in a village setting, the scenery of steep cliffs—each of which conveys the particular mood desired. When *fuzei* is qualified verbally, it is by nonspecific adjectives like "fascinating" or "enchanting" (Japanese *omoshiroshi*). The Japanese had developed a vocabulary of feeling-tones in conjunction with the art of literature—terms like *aware* (pathos), *okashi* (a diverting or pleasing quality), *yūgen* (a profound, haunting beauty), or *sabi* (resigned solitude), but this vocabulary is unfortunately not reflected in the *Illustrations*. When we consider this omission, we are led to wonder about the author's intentions in referring to poetry at all in the text. Do these references spring from a deep understanding of Japanese poetry? If so, it is unfortunate that the implications for garden design were not further developed. Or, were they added simply to raise the aesthetic validity of the text, and left to the designer to interpret?

The predominant sensory qualities and corresponding feeling-tone of a garden, whether sprightly, heroic, or languid, spring from the designer's understanding of the nature and needs of the two masters —the site and the client. Sometimes it is the client's nature that seems to call for a particular feeling-tone. That was the conclusion Kenneth Yasuda reached after the Tenri Church asked him to design the Japanese garden for a new worship hall in Kasaoka, Japan. According to Yasuda, a scholar of Japanese aesthetics, what characterizes the Tenri faith is living in a spirit of joy, or *yōki-gurashi*. In response, Yasuda decided that the garden should be imbued with a bright and radiant quality.

Feeling-Tones		*Sensory Qualities*

Heroic

 SIZE:	massive
SHAPE:	tall verticals with steep sides, angular lines
SPACING:	close
TEXTURE:	grain running vertically, characterized by deep fissures and boldly outlined plates
COLOR:	subdued colors with quiet strength, such as deep grays and blue-grays, blue-greens, rust and maroon in the reds

Sprightly

 SIZE:	depends upon scale
SHAPE:	diagonal sides with convex and concave curves
SPACING:	further apart than for "heroic"
TEXTURE:	grain running diagonally, with twisting, braided effect
COLOR:	luminous colors, with medium to light saturation

Languid

SIZE:	depends upon scale, but generally fewer rocks of a larger size are used
SHAPE:	recumbent, wide-spreading horizontals with rounded forms
SPACING:	distant; expanses of level land or water predominate, with rocks only here and there
 TEXTURE:	smooth, well worn, rounded
COLOR:	no bright hues; rather, off-shades with low color intensity, such as light to medium grays, blue-grays, and beiges

Fig. 49. Correlation of feeling-tones and sensory qualities.

Yasuda observed that most classical Kyoto gardens, while technically superb, lose a sense of aliveness because they are too neat. When distinctive rocks like the favored blue-green *aoishi* (chlorite schist) are used, there is a tendency to pose them in such a manner that they seem to sit up and say, "Look at me." In gaining people's praise, these rocks deny the composition some of the immediacy so essential to aesthetic experience. So, Yasuda says, he realized that he needed something different to produce the desired bright, sunny quality. He would stay away from the austere *aoishi* (which someone was willing to donate for the garden) and use rocks that were found right there on the site, even though the designers from Kyoto who came to look regarded them as *kuso-ishi*, "worthless rocks" (or, literally, "dung rocks").

These rocks are granite with nothing outstanding about them but a warm, rusty brown color. Even among such homely rocks, however, some were well shaped and more aesthetically appealing than others. All were placed in the composition using the classical proportions, but the posed look was avoided by toning down the outstanding rocks rather than emphasizing them. This produces a quality of naturalness that is conducive to a joyful (*yōki*) spirit.

This spontaneous quality was carried through in the planting. After completing the rock composition, Yasuda staked out areas for varieties of trees that would be at their best in each of the four seasons. Parishioners could plant seedlings of the appropriate types anywhere within the areas staked out. In ten years or so when the trees have gotten larger, some will be thinned out. This process is similar to what takes place in nature. When you enter the garden, Yasuda explains, the quality is so natural—"almost like the air you breathe"—that you are not aware of it. There is nothing philosophical here. It is all apprehended immediately.

By using the so-called "worthless rocks" readily available on the site to create a garden that lacks neither classical beauty nor a rich feeling-tone, Yasuda has made an important statement about both Japanese garden aesthetics and art in general. The value of the work of art does not lie in the perceived value of the materials, but rather in the quality of the experience produced by materials woven into effective sensory relationships. Common sense may lead us into the false belief that splendid rocks will as a matter of course produce a garden of high quality. Unfortunately, many gardens in Japan, particularly from the Edo period on when landscape design became a profession rather than an avocation, were built with at least partial acquiescence to this belief. It is to help us avoid this pitfall that Yasuda cautions "Great rocks do not necessarily make a great garden." When this is understood, the client who wants a fine garden and the designer who is capable of creating it will look first to available local materials, be they ever so humble.

"Worthless rocks" have more than one application in Japanese garden design. In the *Illustrations*, a distinction is made between "named" and "nameless" rocks. The latter, we are told in item 26, "are set without limit, as the garden demands." Nameless rocks, like supporting actors, should be lacking in the special attributes that qualify named rocks for their starring roles in the composition. What aesthetic function might these "worthless" rocks play in the landscape garden?

The term *suteishi*, "discarded rock," which was apparently not used until the end of the Edo period when the Japanese were beginning to reflect upon their own garden tradition, has special significance here.[21] The term was applied to a rock placed so casually that it appeared almost as an afterthought. The aesthetic role of such rocks was clearly to infuse the composition with a free-flowing, spontaneous quality (fig. 50). As the finishing touch to the rock composition at the Kasaoka garden, Kenneth Yasuda used a technique that he considers a variant of the *suteishi* concept. This involved dumping several loads of leftover rocks here and there on the garden site, as needed, to lend the formal composition a sense of naturalness. Rocks used in this way fit easily into the category of nameless rocks (*mumyōseki*) mentioned in the *Illustrations*. The fifteenth-century concept of "nameless rocks" may therefore have been a precursor to the late-Edo idea of "discarded rocks."

The technique at Kasaoka is suitable for a large-scale garden, but other variants of the *mumyōseki/suteishi* concept work better in small gardens where only a limited

Fig. 50.   Example of a *suteishi*, or "discarded rock," in the garden of Tōkaian at Myōshinji in Kyoto. The tiny rock set in front of the triad right of center plays an important role in naturalizing the composition and pulling the elements together in a dynamic balance.

number of "named" rocks are used. For example, an upright rock might be tilted slightly, or an extra rock might be "tossed in" to avoid an arty, posed look. The aim here is no different from that of the Japanese potters who created tea bowls "which relied for their attraction on the charms of their irregular shapes"[22]—that is, to create an irresistible quality of spontaneity and naturalness.

.   .   .

It is time now to return to the courtyard garden of the abbot's quarters at Daitokuji, where we left off at the end of chapter 2. In order to get a sense of where our journey through scenic effects, sensory effects, and cultural values has brought us, we might now ask ourselves, What is the meaning of this garden?

The way the question is asked, of course, begs the question. It sounds almost as though the work of art is like a traffic sign logo, for which there is a specific meaning beyond the symbol that is of greater importance than the sign itself. However, as we have seen, the finest gardens do not resort to signposts to convey their intended meaning to the viewer. Their meaning is instead translated into a totally sensory, experiential form, just as the religious ideal of living with joy was expressed as a bright, sunny quality in the Kasaoka garden.

The meaning of a garden so conceived *is* its sensory effect, its beauty. The meaning is what arises, like the fragrance of a flower, in the intersection of the garden and the viewer. Apart from that, no meaning exists. "Beauty," Santayana has said, "is pleasure regarded as the quality of a thing." It is, in terms of its effect, "something that gives satisfaction to a natural function, to some fundamental need or capacity of our minds."[23]

The Daitokuji garden captivates us through the tension created between two compositions of rocks—the massive, upright "waterfall" at the left rear and the diminutive, recumbent "island" at the right front—diagonally counterpoised across a vast gravel expanse. The sustained force of the one, guided by supporting rocks along the back "shore," is catapulted rightward across the taut stillness of the gravel "sea," finally to be echoed in and reflected back to the left by the other. The tempo and resultant tension bear a striking resemblance to a Noh play cadence in which a sustained cry is punctuated by a sharp drum beat—almost as if that auditory experience had been translated into a spatial medium.

Santayana has speculated that such basic pleasures as breathing have much to do with "our highest and most transcendental ideals. It is not merely a metaphor that makes us couple airiness with exquisiteness and breathlessness with awe; it is the actual recurrence of a sensation in the throat and lungs that gives those impressions an immediate power, prior to all reflection upon their significance."[24]

If Santayana is right, then the power of art to reach down through our senses and touch us deeply becomes less of a mystery. We can understand too what Frederick Law Olmsted said about the power of beautiful scenery to give refreshing rest and reinvigoration "through the influence of the mind over the body." The responsive chord that the tempo and tension of the Daitokuji garden strike within us may well result from a correspondence to the vital sensations we feel in the slow rhythm of our own breathing punctuated by the beating of our heart. In such fundamental rhythms as these lies the kinship between nature and art.

TWO

TRANSLATION:

*ILLUSTRATIONS FOR
DESIGNING MOUNTAIN,
WATER, AND HILLSIDE
FIELD LANDSCAPES*

BY ZŌEN

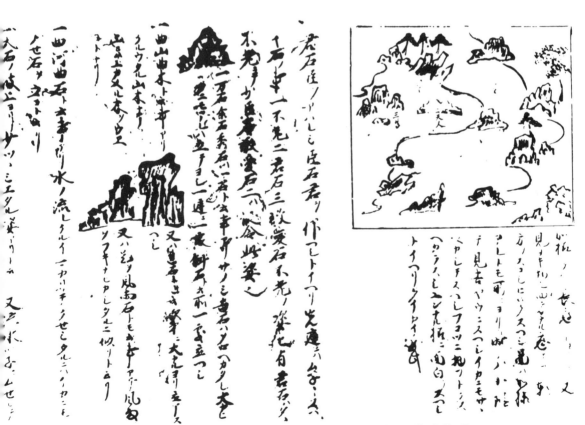

Section of the Illustrations *containing figures H (far right) through N (far left). From a collotype copy of the original Maeda manuscript (1466).*

If you have not received the oral transmissions,
you must not make gardens.

[1]   Here I shall abstract some instructive points from the records and drawings of Tung-fang Shuo's residence.[1] First, when laying out the plains, the mountains and peaks, and the waterfalls and rivers of a garden, you must regard rocks and trees as the structural elements. Hence you must consider fully the relationships of Mutual Destruction and Mutual Production in respect to the Five Colors of rocks.[2] Since the ten thousand stream valleys[3] are nearly always bordered by mountains, you must make two mountains, one on the left and one on the right. The *yang* mountain must be very high, the *yin* mountain somewhat lower. Locate the *yang* mountain opposite the residence at the place where you feel it would stand out the most. If you plan to have a waterfall, it must be articulated with the stream valley design; depending upon the site, however, there are also times when you must adapt the design of the waterfall to the existing topography. Mountains, water, and rocks are like the three legs of a tripod—if even one is missing, there can be no garden.

[2]   Bearing in mind the Five Colors of rocks, you must set them with full consideration of the relationships of Mutual Destruction and Mutual Production. In the cycle of Mutual Destruction, Wood destroys Earth, Earth destroys Water, Water destroys Fire, Fire destroys Metal, and Metal destroys Wood. Let this be your guide. A

person of the Wood nature has blue-green for his color, so you should not set a yellow rock in the direction he faces, since Wood destroys Earth. A person of the Earth nature has yellow for his color, so you should not set a black rock in the direction he ordinarily looks, since Earth destroys Water; but, even though the cycle of Mutual Destruction works like this, you need not so eschew a blue-green rock.[4] A person of the Water nature has black for his color, so you should not set a red rock in the direction he ordinarily looks, since Water destroys Fire. A person of the Fire nature has red for his color, so you should not set a white rock in the direction he ordinarily looks, since Fire destroys Metal. A person of the Metal nature has white for his color, so you should not set a blue-green rock in the direction he ordinarily faces, since Metal destroys Wood. If you do set a blue-green rock, do not place it up close.

In the cycle of Mutual Production, Wood gives birth to Fire, Fire gives birth to Earth, Earth gives birth to Metal, Metal gives birth to Water, and Water gives birth to Wood. Even though according to the cycle of Mutual Production you should set a red rock for a person of the Wood nature, among the Five Colors red rocks are shunned. You should set a yellow rock in the direction a person of the Fire nature ordinarily looks. You should set a white rock for a person of the Earth nature. When you set a black rock for a person of the Metal nature, viewing it will bode well for him. You should set a blue-green rock in the direction a person of the Water nature ordinarily looks. This is the way Mutual Production works.

There is also Mutual Conjunction. It would be exceedingly harmful for a person of the Fire nature to look at a red rock set in the south with a nandina planted facing it, for it is said that when four Fires come together a fire disaster will result.[5] A blue-green rock set in the east and viewed by a person of the Wood nature is a Mutual Conjunction. A yellow rock set in the center of the garden must not be viewed by a person of the Earth nature. It would be harmful for a person of the Metal nature to view a white rock set in the west. And it would be harmful for a person of the Water nature to view a black rock set in the north.

When the water is made to flow from the northeast, water-related misfortunes will be carried away. You should bear this in mind when you make the stream valley of the garden. For the stream valley, you must first of all construct the two mountains, *yin* and *yang*. Make the *yang* mountain very high, and the *yin* mountain somewhat lower. Then there is the matter of the waterfall and river. Since the Green Dragon is on the left and the White Tiger is on the right—the result of siting the house so that it faces south as is standard[6]—you should make the waterfall flow down from the northeast toward the southwest. The water may also be made to flow down from the northwest, in which case it is known as the Water of the Spirit Kings. This is the Water of Wisdom of the myriad felicitous spirits—or Spirit Kings—especially Benzai Ten.[7] A flat-topped rock called the Rock of the Spirit Kings is set in the northwest. But because it is forbidden for this rock to be below the level of the feet, it must not be set there if the land drops off from the edge of the veranda of the house, and so forth and so on.[8] Under no circumstances must the waterfall and river be directed from the southeast. This is called "reverse current" and is what people are referring to when they speak of "water that flows the wrong way." You must not willfully reverse the specified course of a large river to suit the site. The term "reverse current" is applied to this.

When you go to the fields and mountains to get rocks, keep in mind the three forces—horizontal, diagonal, and vertical. A horizontal rock is one that has its grain running lengthwise along the top when lying in a level position. As illustrated, this type of rock may also be used in the vertical position. Only by searching through one hundred and thirty-three rocks for each of these three will you be able to select them well.

A.

A diagonal rock formation may also be created.

Otherwise, the most important rock to get is the Never Aging Rock. It is not flattened off on top, and appears massive from all four directions. If small, it would not command our attention. This rock is Hōrai.[9] The ancient turtle of Hōrai is called the Rock of Ten Thousand Eons and is set beside the Never Aging Rock. Since it is the turtle, this rock should be recognizable as such. First you set the Never Aging Rock and the Rock of Ten Thousand Eons, and only then should you set the other rocks.

B.

Begin with this rock.

This rock is also called the Venerable Seat Rock.

As the Rock of the Spirit Kings, it is the seat of the myriad felicitous spirits. It must be set so it faces from northwest to southeast.

C.

Never Aging Rock

Rock of Ten Thousand Eons

[3]   You should set rocks bearing in mind the three forces—horizontal, diagonal, and vertical—introduced above. These three are equivalent to the triad, Heaven, Earth, and Man. First of all, set these three together at one spot that is to be the focal point. Once you have set the triad—Heaven, Earth, and Man—and then planted an upright tree to complement it, the result is a flawless gem fit for a king.[10] Just as in the ancient expression, "In a country full of wealth, the Five Treasures proceed to the Center,"[11] it is said that when you compose the garden next to the residence in this way, the occurrence of misfortune is avoided by virtue of the garden.

D.

Bufo (river god)[12]

Just as this single piece of paper is titled "Ten Thousand Leagues," you must make the stream valley appear to extend on and on, while at the same time you must reduce it to a small size.

Spirit Kings

Attendant Rock

Master Rock

E.

Boat-concealing Rocks

This is titled "Single Mountain in a Boundless Sea." In a garden like this, the scenery of an immense ocean stretching out before a single mountain is reduced to a small size.

F.

Torii Rocks

protruding rock

flat rock facing this way

facing this way

Barrier Rock on a peak

precious rock[13]

precious rock

Having done as illustrated, you should then plant various wildflowers with an autumn view in mind. In order to capture this impression of hillside fields in autumn, be sure to arrange these wildflowers so that they catch the eye in the foreground.

G.

It is invariably diffi-
cult to design a gar-
den for a site that is
narrow and runs
deep such as the
one illustrated. You
should leave it open
at the back.

H.

Buddhist Triad

Celestial Beings

A garden site that is wide across the front such as the one illustrated is easy to work with
and pleasing to look at. If the garden site is square, make it a little wider at the eaves in
front of the residence. The sketch simply illustrates these points. If you are to make an attractive garden, the design must be a highly sensitive response to both the site and the situation, with nothing clumsy or coarse about it. The result must be fascinating in a quiet,
graceful way. These are the main points.

[4]   The Master Rock looks after its Attendants, and the Attendant Rocks look up to the Master.[14] The rocks you should first of all give your attention to in the garden are (1) the Never Aging Rock, (2) the Master Rock, and (3) the Respect & Affection Stones. The figure of the Never Aging Rock occupies the highest position. The Master Rock resembles the Never Aging Rock but is somewhat smaller. The Attendant Rock and the two Respect & Affection Stones, in the proportional relationship of larger to smaller, follow the model of the first two.

[5]   Treasure Rock, Castaway Rock, and Rock of Perfect Beauty are all names for one type of rock.[15] Fine rocks of this type are difficult to find. Generally, it is good to set one even if it is small. Set it at a place in the garden that lends itself to such a diagonally shaped rock.

I.

J.

Sometimes referred to as the Colonnade Rocks, this formation is created by setting rocks in gradually descending fashion from the largest on down. It is also called the Wind & Rain Rocks for its resemblance to rain blown slantwise by the wind.

[6]   There is the phenomenon of "craggy mountains with gnarled trees," mountains and trees with twisted forms. For this you plant contorted trees on the mountains.

[7]   There is the phenomenon of "rocks at the bend of a twisting river." This means that you set rocks at eccentric angles where the water flows turbulently as it makes a turn.

[8]   We are told of the phenomenon of large rocks scarcely visible above the water, and of flowing water, constantly obstructed as it seeks the sea. This being so, you should narrow the watercourse here and there, and then widen it so it appears like the sea. Simply keep such things in the back of your mind.

K.

There is the phenomenon of "gnarled trees blocking the path." As shown in the illustration, it means that you plant contorted trees so close together that it appears a person would not be able to pass through.[16]

This shows how you must plant the trees—like parents watching over their child.[17]

L.

Craggy mountains should have the general feeling shown in the illustration.[18]

[9]   When you search for trees, select them with the three forces—horizontal, diagonal, and vertical—well in mind.

M.
It is good to plant trees that have few lower branches and graceful forms such as those shown here:

This example shows a tree whose branches center on a vertical trunk.

This is a tree whose trunk extends out horizontally. It plays a supporting role.

This is a tree that combines both diagonal and vertical lines. It is good when the lower part of the trunk curves out and then straightens back up at the top.

There are places where even trees such as this[19] can be planted to good advantage.

N.

Never Aging Rock

another example of the same

[10]   In the planting of trees and herbs, you make their natural habitats your model. You will not go astray so long as you bear in mind the principle of planting trees from deep mountains in the deep mountains of the garden, trees from hills and fields in the hills and fields, herbs and trees from freshwater shores on the freshwater shores, and herbs from the seashore on the seashore. For the landscape garden mirrors nature. And thus it is said that in each and all we must return to the two words, natural habitat.

[11]   The Japanese apricot has no difficulty growing on mountain peaks, mountainsides, or in villages. Even so, since it is at home on snow-covered mountains, bear the north in mind when planting it. You may have some ideas of your own.

[12]   There is an instruction that says you are not to change the position of a rock from what it was in the mountains. Placing a rock so that the part which was underneath in the mountains is on top is called "reversing the rock," and is to be avoided. To do this would anger the spirit of the rock and would bring bad luck.

[13]   In setting rocks and planting trees, you should never use any that are exotic or showy, nor should you plant trees with dead or drooping branches in the area right in front of the bamboo blinds where the master, the eldest son, and the other family members reside. Respect the area the occupants live in and use such materials only in the other areas as befits the more striking topographical features found there.[20]

[14]   The Respect & Affection Stones are two stones set slightly apart with their brows inclined toward one another.[21]

[15]   Disharmonious rocks must not be used. All the rocks should go well together.

[16]   There is a rock resembling a toad, called the Bufo Rock. It does not stand out above the other rocks. With the Rock of the Spirit Kings facing southeast from the northwest, the Bufo Rock [faces northwest from the southeast and] embodies the fierce, meddlesome god, Kōjin.[22]

[17]   There is an expression, "ten thousand trees in a single glance." If asked what this means, I would reply that you must plant the trees in a garden so that all are visible without exception in just one glimpse. No matter how fine a tree you plant up close to the eaves, it must not conceal the smaller trees in the distance.

O.

[center] Set one rock out in front of the lower veranda where you feel it will not stand out.

north

[Spirit Kings]

male, female

west

east

[Bufo]

south　　　　southeast

[left] In this interval between the Rock of the Spirit Kings and the Bufo Rock, the rocks and trees must never lean or topple over even after the passing of many ages. As the Rock of the Spirit Kings you set a rock of the general form shown here, facing southeast so that it appears to be instructing the river god. This rock is the seat of the myriad felicitous spirits and of Benzai Ten, and its purpose is to pray for happiness and prosperity.

[bottom] As illustrated, set the rock resembling a toad so it is hidden from sight, facing the northwest. You must set it so as not to interfere visually with the harmony of the *yin* and *yang* couple. The river god embodied in the Bufo Rock is the fierce god Kōjin who renders a place propitious but who also causes trouble in all human affairs. Hence a certain interval is maintained, as shown, between the embodiment of Kōjin and that of Benzai Ten, the deity of earth.

The above landscape garden illustrations have presented the various aspects of designing mountains and stream valleys.

[18]　Excavating the pond. In the design of the pond, you may take as your model the shorelines of an ocean, or you may model it after the configuration of a river flowing out into a bay. You need not make the pond very deep; the depth will depend on the size of the pond. Excavate the pond so that the contour from the edge to the bottom of the pond is shaped like a druggist's mortar.[23] Then, even when the water level is low, the surface of the water will retain the shape of the original pond. If fish are to be put into the pond, there is no problem in its being a little deeper than

ordinary. For a pond where such fish as cyprinin carp are to be raised, you generally make a small pond alongside the main pond, with a corresponding shape. Construct it by laying up rocks in an interlocking fashion so that they will not collapse into the pond. Set the rocks so that those at the top retain the earth and look like mountains along a shore, while those toward the bottom obscure the pond from view. If in this way you prepare a place for the fish to spawn, they will naturally give birth to their young, and they will thrive. You can conceal from above the channel through which the fish enter and exit, by arranging rocks in an interesting and natural way. If around one pond you create two or three such places for the fish to seek shelter, they will flourish. For a pond that is to be stocked with crucian carp, you need not make the special ponds to provide cover such as you do for a pond in which cyprinin carp are to be released.[24] You need only prepare two or three places with an interesting and natural quality so that the crucian carp can find cover within the main pond, and they will thrive. Furthermore, if a pond to be stocked with water birds is constructed in this way, the fish will be able to take cover. They will neither be caught by the birds nor leap out of the pond when frightened, and thus they will thrive. When the pond is stocked with water birds, they may be harmed by a fox that lies in prey along the shore. So, while you are closely interweaving scenic rocks to create a pleasing effect along the shore, set some commonplace rocks just offshore to create the impression of frolicking birds.[25]

There is also the marsh-pond, which has the feeling of just an ordinary pond. The scenic effect of a marsh-pond is achieved by composing plantings of sweet flag, rabbit-ear iris, eurya, kerria, azalea, wisteria, and gromwell along the shore of the pond so as to create an interesting ambience. Rocks must be visible only here and there. Or you must set them to produce an effect where they are not even noticed.

Another type of shoreline scenery is the ebb-tide beach, which has no striking features but simply creates the impression of the tide constantly ebbing and flowing. Here, if just by spreading fine and coarse grades of sand and without setting any rocks you can visually re-create a single scenic ambience—that of a beach rising to a knoll where a pine or some such tree alternately appears at high tide to be out in the middle of the sea, and at ebb tide to tower as if suddenly borne high above the beach that is now exposed so far into the distance that one cannot tell where it ends and the sea begins—you have nothing more to learn. The visual impression of an ebb-tide beach is produced simply by the way the tree is planted and the way the fine and coarse grades of sand are spread.

[19] On the seashore, one should not find such plants as sweet flag, rabbit-ear iris, and kerria. It is common practice nowadays to use such plants when creating the scenic effects of the seashore, but this matter should be taken more seriously. People who are discerning with regard to this type of scenery are rare. It is all the more important, therefore, that you view the garden with a discerning eye, always bearing in mind that a mountain is a mountain, an ocean is an ocean, and a stream is a stream.

[20] The term "stream valley" merely refers to the scenic effect of foothills running along a stream valley. For this effect, you must not set rocks too conspicuously, but rather, principally by planting trees and herbs, you must aim at creating the scenic atmosphere of hills and fields. You should simply make the stream valley ever so gently rolling and utterly ordinary.

[21] If there is a pond in the garden, such birds as the white egret may naturally alight on the roof and eaves with the intention of feeding on the fish, without cause for concern. However, in the event that they are perched on the roof where no pond exists, an exorcism must immediately be performed.

P.

Here it is good to plant large trees of the upright varieties that grow in the mountains.

The scenic effects of the stream valley must be ever-changing. Herbs must be planted to lend a gentle, refreshing touch. Above all, be sure to plant flowering herbs at the foot of the mountains ——————

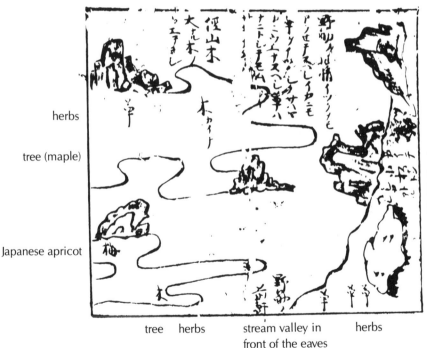

herbs

tree (maple)

Japanese apricot

There must by all means be azaleas, kerria, maples, small pines, etc.

tree   herbs   stream valley in front of the eaves   herbs

With a stream valley like that shown above, you must set the rocks to produce a fascinating scenic effect—not setting them in profusion, but here and there, with regard for their visual balance. They say it would be very bad to do this in a clumsy way.

[22] In the landscape garden, you must regard rocks and trees as the structural elements. When obtaining either trees or rocks, you must keep uppermost in mind the three forces—horizontal, diagonal, and vertical. Do not position a rock in such a way that it has a sharp point sticking out in the direction of the position from which the master customarily faces the garden, no matter how fascinating the scenic effect. You must prune out, with consideration for the overall effect, any superfluous branches of trees and herbs growing too close together, one above the other, and sticking out in the direction of the master's position, even though they may have a scenic effect. If the branches are too sparse at the tips, it is unsightly. At the same time, there must be as few branches as possible. It is said there is a reason for this.

[23] In setting the rocks, first of all, when you are about to set the Happiness & Prosperity Rock for the master, select with consideration for its place in the overall balance a nameless rock, so that people will not know which is which. Then, after the hole is dug, with the hands in the Touching the Earth mudra under the sleeves of one's robe, the proper mantra is invoked.[26] This is a secret matter. (—oral transmission) Have ready about 1 *shō* of rice (depending upon the size of the garden) and when you set the named rock, with the rice still in the measuring box put it into the hole.[27] Here again, so that people will not know it is the named rock, after you have had the hole dug for the nameless rock, put the rice while still in the measuring box into it too, then remove the measure and put a little rice into each hole. This is done so that people will not be able to distinguish between the named rock and the nameless rock. This is a secret matter! (—oral transmission)

Even if it is the master's desire, you should not make a scene in which a sandspit and the watercourse of the stream flowing around it project out toward the front of the house, as this would be inauspicious for the master. The size of the garden must be determined on the basis of the master's financial situation. If the master lacks the financial means, he may be defeated by the garden. Such matters are of great importance. Keep them firmly in mind. Also, when you begin setting the rocks in the garden, be sure to select an auspicious day and begin from an auspicious direction.

[24] Unless there is a place to draw up an ox-cart at the middle gate, bushclover must not be planted there. Bushclover is planted where it will come into view just as one passes through the middle gate. Asters, white chrysanthemums, and the like must not be planted within the landscape garden proper, even if the master expresses such a desire, since they customarily evoke feelings of melancholy. When in the course of constructing the garden master's house a gate is erected, the Torch-cleaning Stone is set 10 *shaku*[28] to the left of the gate. It must not be set if there is no gate. This stone is in general appearance flat on top and naturally rough on all four sides. It is set at a height of 0.7 *shaku* above the foundation stones of the gate. The reason it is called the Torch-cleaning Stone is that when guests make an excursion up into the hills at night, the person who greets them comes out, lights a pine torch, and then knocks the embers off by striking it on this stone. You must knock off the embers

of the pine torch on the top of this stone. Such matters are secret. You must never divulge them to those who have not received the transmissions.

[25] A person who approaches the garden wanting to view it first does so from beside the Reverence Rock. The reason for this is that, due to the awe-inspiring nature of certain rocks that are set in the garden—the Buddhist Triad Rocks, the Twofold World Rocks, the Mystic Kings Rocks, and the Celestial Beings' Abode Rock—the viewer, with heart full of hope for the fulfillment of his most devout prayers, reverently worships all the Buddhas of the Three Worlds from beside this rock.

Now after offering words of greeting to the master, a person thoroughly views the garden by first surveying the scenery in the direction of the waterfall; he then makes the rounds following the direction of the water's downward flow, stopping to view along the way; and once again approaches the Reverence Rock. A person ignorant both of the direction of the water's downward flow and of how things are laid out in a correctly ordered garden, is so lacking that he simply will not be able to see anything. He who cannot distinguish between the named rocks and the nameless rocks must by all means not step on top of any of the rocks, so as to avoid stepping on a named rock. When viewing a garden of a person whose rank is higher than his own, a person must not praise it in a loud voice, no matter how captivating it may be. But whenever this involves a person of his own rank, he should offer praise freely. It is with attentiveness to such things that a person must view the landscape garden.

[26] The art of setting rocks in the landscape garden originated in India at the lake called Mānasarovara where rocks numbering 8,631 were set, with each of the Eight Great Dragon Kings in charge of more than 1,000 rocks.[29] From that origin, it took root in China, where, in accord with the relatively smaller size of that country, the number of rocks was reduced to 361, set on the banks of the Hsün-yang.[30] After that, the art was introduced into Japan during the reign of Emperor Kagamiyama, and the number 66 was decided upon.[31] In a still later age, this number was considered inappropriate, and it was reduced to the 48 that have been selected as the named rocks. The Great Teacher Kōbō has said that though the names of rocks are many, the scale drawing of a garden must accurately reflect their number.[32] Nameless rocks, on the other hand, should be set without limit, as the garden demands.

[27] The Absolute Control Rock is set in the middle of the pond. In shape, it is flat-topped. The right side, as one faces it, slants outward toward the base. It is 3 *shaku* in height, that being to scale for an estate of 8 *chō*.[33] This rock protects the people who dwell there. It is king among all the rocks. If it is set well, good fortune will come and riches will abound. Because this rock possesses such magical powers, another name for it is the Miraculous Rock. However, it is correctly called the Absolute Control Rock. (—oral transmission)

[28] Mirror Rock. This rock accompanies the Absolute Control Rock. Because in its shape it mirrors its companion, the Mirror Rock sharpens the image of the Absolute Control Rock, thereby bringing out its powers. This is the reason that it is set to accompany the Absolute Control Rock. In shape, it is flat-topped and resembles a person saying something. Depending on the composition, it should be set at a height of anywhere from 1 *shaku* down to 0.32 *shaku*. You will know the proper height by virtue of the model that the other rocks provide. There are oral transmissions.

[29] The Fulfillment Rock is set in front of the main hall, pagoda, or abbot's quarters of a temple. Because this rock, when it is set well, has the power to bring about fulfillment of the master's prayers, it is called the Fulfillment Rock. In shape, it is a vertical rock. With no defects on any of its four sides, it is a rock endowed with compassion.

[30] The Reverence Rock is set to the left of the Fulfillment Rock. In shape, it is a vertical rock. Its height is 0.33 *shaku*. You will know which way to adjust this standard height by virtue of the model of the rocks mentioned above.

[31]   Names of Rocks[34]
Supplication Rock* [V], Human Form Stones [V], Current-impeding Stone [R], Constant Waters Rock [R], Status Rock [V], Companion Rock [R],
Frolicking Birds Rocks [R], Drip Line Paving Stones* [R], Rock of the Right* [V], Rock of the Spirit Kings [V], Never Aging Rock [V], Rock of Ten Thousand Eons [V],
Master Rock [V], Attendant Rock(s) [V], Barrier Rocks [V], Flowing Water Rocks [R], Water-collecting Rock* [V], Respect & Affection Stones [V],
Bufo Rock [R], Waterfall-deepening Rocks* [V], Paving Stones* [R], Stream-rippling Rock [R], Falling Water Rocks [R], Buddhist Triad Rocks [V],
Bridge-anchoring Rocks [R], Water-dividing Rock [R], Wind & Rain Rocks [R], Erect & Recumbent Rocks*, Water-channeling Rocks [V or R], Flying Birds Rocks* [R],
Ducks' Abode Rocks* [R], Torii Stones [R], Twofold World Rocks [V], Mystic Kings Rocks [V], Subordinates Rocks [R], Folding Screen Rocks [V, R],
Waiting Rock(s),* Water Striking Rocks, Horizontal Triad Rocks, Frolicking Fish Rocks,* Cormorants' Abode Rocks* [R], Hovering Mist Rock [V],
Guardian of the Mansion Rock* [V], Taboo Rock [V], Boat-concealing Rocks [V]
[V = vertical, R = recumbent]

[32] Complying with the illustrations for these rocks, you must set them with great care. Keep in mind that the dimensions of the rocks depend on the size of the landscape garden. The landscape illustrations presented above are for estates of between 4 and 8 *chō*. Now even if it means the dimensions of the rocks will differ somewhat from what is prescribed, set them in accordance with their assets and faults. If you do not grasp this, you will not be able to set them in a composition. The

illustrations presented here must be followed today just as they were in the past. Recollecting the subtle seasonal moods of *waka* poetry from ancient times up to the present, you must re-create with a quiet, graceful charm those moods that speak to you in your innermost heart. As a rule, first set the largest rock, and then set each succeeding rock in proportion to it. This can only be done intuitively. Without continual cultivation, your work will be inferior. There must be oral transmissions concerning this.

[33] Twofold World Rocks. One is set in the pond close to the waterfall, and the other is set in line with it on the shore. The reason for this is that the one set on the shore embodies the Tathāgata of the Diamond World. It is the rock that gives rise to the herbs and trees and the ten thousand things. The one set in the pond embodies the Tathāgata of the Womb Treasury World. It gives visual form to the fluidity of corporeal reality and the nonduality of conceptual categories. Together they manifest the Vairocana of the Twofold World, and contain the Five Agents and the Five Colors. Even so, in general shape these rocks are flat-topped, and beautiful from all four directions. They are set at heights of 3 *shaku* and 2 *shaku*.

[34] Mystic Kings Rocks. This composition of rocks is set in the courtyard garden that the master faces. The rocks form a configuration akin to the Five Great Mystic Kings, each in its respective position. The rock in the center is the seat of the Mystic King Fudō, and is 2 *shaku* in height. The remaining rocks are all set at a height of 1.6 *shaku*, and combine vertical, horizontal, and diagonal forces. You must inquire thoroughly into the oral transmissions on such matters.[35]

THE WAYS OF PLANTING TREES

[35] The pine tree is not averse to making its home on mountainsides, mountain peaks, hillside fields, or plains. Still, you must plant it to harmonize visually with the landscape scene. It is especially important that the pine be planted correctly in the auspicious direction. As a rule, it is difficult to imagine a landscape garden, even one in an enclosed courtyard, without a pine tree. Only the pine tree can be planted in so many different ways to interesting effect. There ought to be some oral transmissions on this matter.

[36] While there are no fixed places for using camellia in the landscape garden, you will do well to plant it in association with pines so as to create a scenic effect. Whatever that may be, these two must be planted in perfect harmony. Surely there are oral transmissions on this.

[37] The Japanese apricot has no difficulty growing on mountain peaks, in valleys, or in villages. Still, when determining its direction, you must bear in mind the north. Of two or three Japanese apricots to be put in a garden, you must plant the finest specimen in a location that preserves this directional orientation. The others should then be planted to harmonize visually with the scenic atmosphere. Since the Japanese apricot has an inviting fragrance, plant it in the direction from which the prevailing breezes blow with respect to the living quarters, keeping in mind the scenic effect. The reason for this, it is said, is that Japanese apricot blossoms have an exceptional fragrance. Surely there are also oral transmissions on this.

[38] While the Japanese cherry may be found most anywhere, on mountain peaks, mountainsides, or in the deep mountains, you must chiefly bear in mind villages when you plant it. The cherry is also fascinating when planted in the juncture between the deep mountains and the verdant hills. For its "home site," bear in mind the south. You may also plant one or two cherries in the shade of trees that are associated with high or remote mountains, so that one feels there is a village nestled deep in those mountains. Really, the cherry, possessing the special qualities that it does as a tree, may be planted in any location whatsoever without difficulty, so long as you plant one specimen in the cherry's home environment. A person who has not received the transmissions, even when given two or three trees to work with, will plant them so indiscriminately that not one will be in the cherry's home site, and thus will incur the blame of those who have received the transmissions.36 In all such matters, you must act with a similar discernment.

[39] The willow is ordinarily not much favored for planting in the landscape garden. When it is used, however, it is planted on the northwest side of the island. If there is no island, the willow is not planted. There are also cases of its being planted as a river willow at the point where a bridge crosses the river in a marsh-pond landscape—a scenic effect sometimes found in large-scale landscape gardens. It is a scenic effect that is ordinarily not used, and should not be favored.

[40] It is unthinkable to plant wisteria without pines. Nevertheless, because of the fascinating effect, it is fine to plant it in the umbrage of other trees such as hinoki cypress. It is also fascinating when in bloom, if planted so that it extends out over the water in a marsh-pond landscape.

[41] Kerria is best planted chiefly in the marsh-pond landscape. When used in an ordinary landscape garden, it should be planted beside a fence or some such spot.

[42] Winged euonymus is especially striking when the leaves turn red in autumn. It makes hills and fields its principal home. As a rule, it is also striking when planted in among podocarpus and hinoki cypress. When planting it, you must bear in mind the northeast as its principal direction.

[43] Azaleas are woody plants that make hills and fields their principal home. Nevertheless, there is general agreement that it is good to plant azaleas as the undergrowth in the deep mountains. They are fascinating when hidden away among rocky crags or when planted on the banks above a pond. They make both *yin* and *yang* mountains their principal home.

[44] The peach tree is not considered very desirable. Nevertheless, being an auspicious tree, it is acceptable to plant it in a large-scale landscape garden, in the concealment of other trees. Its direction is east.

[45] Pomegranate. This is a tree of the village. In the landscape garden, it should be planted at a place where you intend to create the impression of hills bordering a village. However, since pomegranate has an exotic scenic quality when it bears fruit, you should set it off by planting it in an unobtrusive spot, in harmony with its surroundings. As a rule, you must be sure that this tree bears fruit before you plant it.

[46] The pear tree. This tree, too, is not of the deep mountains, but rather makes hills and fields and villages its principal home. Varieties like the Chinese pear are particularly appealing.

[47] Maple. Keep this tree uppermost in mind when planting. It is primarily a tree of the deep mountains, and not found in villages. Even so, do plant it there so that it is attractive and harmonizes with the surrounding scenery. Bear in mind the northeast as its principal direction. With this tree too, after locating one in a spot that corresponds to the maple's home site, you should plant the others in accordance with the scenic effect. The maple is an especially attractive tree.

[48] Bear in mind that, as a rule, trees from hills and fields are to be planted in the hills and fields of the garden, trees from deep mountains are to be planted on the large mountains, and trees from villages are to be planted in village settings.

[49] As a rule, in landscape gardens that feature an island, you should plant willows to the northwest, maples to the northeast, pines to the southeast, and cryptomerias to the southwest. By saying this, I do not mean to imply you must strictly follow it. These rules are intended for a large-scale landscape garden with a broad island. In these matters, you must listen to the dictates of your heart and then design in whatever way you feel best suits the scenic effect being created.

[50] Bamboo must be planted to the north, in accordance with the visual impression it makes there.

[51]   Pines are striking when clustered along the flanks of the waterfall in whatever numbers the scenic effect calls for. Even if there is no waterfall, it is a good idea to plant clusters of pines along the descending ridges of hillside fields and mountain capes—scenery typical of the foothills of deep mountains—in whatever numbers are needed to produce a striking scenic effect. Consider the west as the pine's principal home, and plant it in accordance with the situation.

[52]   In the deep mountains you should plant mainly such trees as podocarpus, cryptomeria, hinoki cypress, cinnamon and camphor, castonopsis, paulownia, oak, daphniphyllum, pine, and wild cherry. As the undergrowth beneath these trees, a mix of plants like azaleas, ilex, eurya, wild sumac, and bamboo grass will look splendid when they are growing luxuriantly together with no patch of ground exposed. But if either the trees above or the undergrowth below is unkempt, the scenic effect will be without merit. You must achieve the scenic effect of deep mountains, in which the trees and underbrush are growing luxuriantly together (but not *too* thickly) with a fresh, quietly graceful, natural feeling. Without a keen sensibility, this is impossible.

[53]   Plant citrus trees so as to capture in a single scenic ambience the impression of a village bordering on hills and fields. Keep in mind that the pattern of a formal wooden fence extending out from the eaves can serve to recall this image. Such fruit-bearing trees as loquat, tangerine, mandarin orange, citron, and chestnut are charming when planted to create this domestic effect.

[54]   As for the smaller herbs, it is good to plant chiefly such varieties as calanthe, wasabi, *hyakunansō*, *kinkisō*, and *nekusa*, all herbs that do not grow tall.[37] When planting such herbs, you will do well to select those rich not only in scenic qualities, but also in poetic associations.

[55]   White chrysanthemums and asters have a magical affinity like that of the intimate converse between a man and a woman. When the effect would be appealing, prepare a special place that suits them and plant them there to good advantage. Or, plant them on opposite sides of a formal wooden fence, so that they appear to be peeking at one another through the fence.[38]

[56]   As a rule, when thinning out the branches of trees, first thoroughly observe the shape of the tree, giving priority to the front. As you do so, remember that branches sticking out in the same direction, one above the other, on the side of the tree the master faces are undesirable, and begin by pruning out the branch of lesser quality in any such pair.[39]
When pruning vertical trees, as a rule you must not cut off the central leader that extends heavenward, for it is fundamental to the tree's natural growth; leave it erect.

When it comes to horizontal trees, observe the natural growth pattern of the tree, and then prune it to bring out its inherent scenic qualities. Do the same for diagonal trees and vertical trees. Do not prune back the longer of those branches inherent to a tree's natural growth pattern.

For trees whose main interest lies in their foliage, all the branches with leaves on them, from the upper part of the tree down to the base, are considered desirable; do not remove them. Prune out only those branches that wander erratically or are long and unkempt, so as to achieve a visually harmonious effect.

It is bad to cut off the branches of a tree indiscriminately. You should not prune out gnarled branches, even if they are somewhat unsightly.

[57] When pruning back the roots of trees during transplanting, you must treat the larger ones as follows: First apply a hot iron to the cut ends of the roots. Then grind some pine resin into a powder and mix it with sulphur, and after coating the cut ends of the roots with birdlime, spread the mixture over this. As a rule, you should treat the cut ends of branches in the same way. When you are about to plant the tree, thoroughly coat the roots with red clay that has been kneaded vigorously into a sticky paste. Then put this same soil into the hole as you plant the tree. If the roots are plentiful, you do not necessarily have to do it this way.

[58] Alternately, in transplanting a tree, fill the hole with soil from where the tree was originally growing. After planting the tree, water it and then pack the soil down well with your feet. Such care assures the successful transplanting of a highly valued tree.

In moving and planting trees, it sometimes happens that the bark of a tree is peeled back, or a tree is abraded or cut part way through. In such instances, apply the preparation mentioned above. Always give the proper care to a newly planted tree, constantly watering it, shading it from the sun, spraying it with water in the morning, and removing spider webs. You must be ever attentive. These are secret matters relating to the planting of trees.

[59] As a rule, when you make a garden on a site where the soil is excessively fertile, there will be no end to pruning the branches of trees and herbs growing ever taller and closer together. If you coat the cut ends of the branches with a mixture of rat droppings and sulphur, and then lightly apply a hot iron to this, the new growth will diminish and appear normal. If you want to keep herbs and the like delicate, make a powder of rat droppings and dust it over them from time to time. Particularly when you want to keep a plant like sweet flag delicate, do as follows: First clip off the tops. Next, spread a cloth over the plants. Then, after preparing a powder of rat droppings, get some on the tip of a toothpick and work it around on the cloth. Some will sprinkle down onto the plants. If you coat a toothpick and play it over the surface of the new shoots whenever they appear, the new growth will remain delicate.

[60] As a rule, when varieties of trees first removed from the wilds are pruned back, do as before: Coat the cut ends with birdlime, pine resin, and sulphur, and apply a hot iron. Next, make a powder of betel-nut, add some powdered licorice, mix in birdlime, and coat the cut ends with this preparation. Then sprinkle pine resin over this, and again apply a hot iron.

[61] When planting a tree that has been in transport, or that has been dug up and left out of the ground for as many as five or even ten days, first coat the cut ends of both the branches and roots with the preparation above and lightly apply a hot iron. Then, after digging the hole and planting the tree, cover the area around the tree with a thick mulch of finely shredded arum root.

[MORE WAYS OF SETTING ROCKS][40]

[62] You must never, never neglect the place in which the felicitous named rock is to be set for the master—make a mental note of this.

[63] Even if it happens that a snake slithers down a tree and disappears in the direction that the Rock of the Spirit Kings is facing, toward where the Bufo Rock is to be set,[41] you must not trample on the roots of the tree. When you make a landscape garden, maintain an attitude of reverence and respect, giving each aspect your full attention. You should solicit the skills and learning of others, and not simply do what you alone find interesting. Never treat lightly what you feel are secret matters. The placement of herbs and trees may appear simple, but there is not one person in a thousand who knows how to do it. Although numerous landscape garden scrolls have been handed down, keep only the one scroll that you consider most suited to your sensibility. The illustrations concerning rocks, the locations for setting rocks, and the locations for planting herbs and trees must be kept absolutely secret. In fear of the Eight Great Dragon Kings, it is forbidden to make gardens without observing the principles. These are priceless treasures, which you must never, never divulge! There are oral transmissions concerning this.

[64] Boat-concealing Rocks. These rocks are set in the middle of the pond. By way of illustration, you may set the rocks by twos or threes, in a string with slight intervals between them, or you may set them in the horizontal triad configuration. The height of these rocks is not fixed—you should set them higher or lower depending on their shapes. They must be rocks that look as if they had once towered quite high, but have since crumbled and eroded away. Turning the possibilities over thoroughly in your mind, set them in a fascinating composition. The composition should convey the feeling of a boat vanishing behind isles in the bay of Akashi. This scenic effect is a secret matter. So be it! So be it!

[65] Taboo Rock. This rock is flat-topped and vertical. Set it so that it is inconspicuous from afar, and only comes into view when one draws near. The reason for this is that in the front part of the pond many tall rocks are set on a projecting spit of land to create the impression of a boundless sea; this rock is set at a sufficient interval to be separate from them. It is placed on the south side of the pond, and visually depicts Mount Fudaraku. Therefore, it is also called the Kannon Rock.[42] Set it at the height of a man's elbows.

[66] The Folding Screen Rocks look as if a folding screen had been unfurled. With no fixed size, they are set back behind the rocky coast where the water from the falls flows out into the pond, at a point where one might find the scenery of steep cliffs. Continually unfolding like an escarpment, they represent scenery of great variety. The same composition may be used in the northwest part of the garden.

[67] Subordinates Rocks. This name refers to smallish rocks in a bed of white sand. They are set so that they barely protrude, almost as if one took no account of them. Still, it is fine if they stick up a little. Use them in any number, in the horizontal-triad or the crescent configuration. Set them helter skelter, to create an intriguing quality like that of gently rustling leaves. They may also be set at the base of a tree.

[68] Hovering Mist Rock. This rock is set beside and slightly above a Barrier Rock. It is a vertical rock. In height, it should be set 0.3 *shaku* above the Barrier Rock. Yet it must be used at a point close to the pond where one might find the trailing ridge of a lower peak. This is because the mist always rises from a point close to the pond. If you do not keep this fully in mind, you will not be able to set it properly.

[69] Buddhist Triad Rocks. These three rocks are set to one side or the other of the waterfall, depending on the composition. How they are set depends on whether the composition is to represent the Shaka triad, the Amida triad, or the Fudō triad. The central figure is set at a height of 3 *shaku*, the others at 2.5 *shaku*. The composition must not be lacking in substance, nor must it be used in the garden of a secular residence. Here too, depending upon the garden, you may need to set the central rock at a height of only 1 *shaku*, and then set the other two rocks in proportion to it. These rocks must never be set carelessly.

[70] Water-channeling Rocks. These are used to imitate the effect of water being channeled between rocks at the point where a stream or river flows out from the mountains. This is not a scenic effect for which the shapes of the rocks are specified; you should just set rocks with highly distinctive features so as to bring out these particular qualities.

[71] Torii Stones. These stones are set in the pond, toward the east shore close to the Water-dividing Rock. They are flat-topped, and there are three of them, set in the horizontal triad configuration. They stand 1.3 or 1.2 *shaku* above the water.[43]

[72] Dragon's Abode Rocks. These rocks number thirty-three, and are set off to the east of the central island in a crescent-shaped configuration. The rock at one end of the crescent should be set so as to resemble the dragon's head, and the rock at the other end should resemble the dragon's tail. The first is set at a height of 1 *shaku*, the last at 0.6 *shaku*. This configuration of rocks is not very desirable; with the dragon as master of the pond, if they are set poorly, it would not bode well for the master of the house.

[73] The Water Striking Rocks must be set just slightly away from the shore of the pond at a point that is in the path of the current, so that as the water flows by, it strikes against them. These rocks combine both diagonal and vertical shapes. Two or three are placed out along the edge of a sandspit in front of the master's house. As the water flows along, it will naturally strike up against them. The height at which these rocks are set depends upon the breadth of the pond. These are fascinating rocks. You must bear these things in mind when you position them.

[74] Wind & Rain Rocks. This composition is used at a choice location in the central area of the garden. Flat-topped rocks are used to create a diagonal formation. You establish this diagonal quality with the principal rock, and then set four or five more rocks in descending fashion. Begin by setting the largest, which is 1.5 *shaku* in height. After that, set the others in gradually descending sizes of 1 *shaku*, 0.8 *shaku*, 0.6 *shaku*, 0.4 *shaku*, and 0.2 *shaku*. Because they are set like this, in imitation of the pattern of wind-driven rain, they are called the Wind & Rain Rocks. This is a dynamic composition. Bear these things well in mind when you make it.

[75] Water-dividing Rock. This rock has diagonally sloping sides. You must set it so that it looks splendid when the water is flowing at full volume. Because it is the rock that stands in the middle of the current where the water flows out into the pond, do not set the Falling Water Rocks until you have set the Water-dividing Rock.

[76] Barrier Rocks are set on the peaks. You may set them facing in any direction, at any place on the mountain tops. Their shapes include all three forces—horizontal, diagonal, and vertical. These rocks greatly resemble mountain peaks and create a striking scenic effect. You should set each at the height best suited to it. Because they simulate peaks, it is difficult to specify how many you will need. Construct steep mountains and set these rocks to create the impression that a path along which a person might journey winds among the peaks. Keep these things fully in mind as you set these rocks.

[77] The Flowing Water Rocks are set in the middle of the pond, out in front of the main viewing position. The special feeling of these rocks cannot exist without water. They are "water bottom rocks," set at the bottom of the water in the horizontal triad configuration, so that the tips of two or three are just barely visible above the waves.

Here, too, there are no specified dimensions. They should simply be set harmoniously, with an eye to their own special scenic qualities and the way they will look in respect to the surrounding water surface.

[78] The Respect & Affection Stones must be set to the northeast, in the seclusion of other rocks so they cannot be seen from farther away. There are two stones, whose shapes create the impression of a man and a woman engaged in intimate conversation. They are set at heights of 1 *shaku* and 0.85 *shaku*, respectively, but this may vary depending on the height of the other rocks. This composition is used primarily in the garden of a secular residence.

[79] The Bufo Rock is set in the southeast facing the northwest, also in the seclusion of other rocks so that it is not seen together with the Rock of the Spirit Kings, and is inconspicuous. It resembles a toad, yet its size may vary. Thoroughly consider its relationship to the other elements when you set it.

[80] Stream-rippling Rock. There is no specified shape for this rock. But it must have a scenic quality and be set so that ripples are formed as the water flows around it. This rock is also called the Stream-dividing Rock. It is one of the fascinating scenic effects that employ rocks. Keep these things fully in mind when setting it.

[81] Falling Water Rocks. These rocks are set so that the water falling from the upper level of the pond flows around and over them. They are diagonally shaped rocks, with one set 0.62 *shaku* above the water, and the other immersed in the water. A third may be set just 0.02 or 0.03 *shaku* above the water.

[82] Bridge-anchoring Rocks. These are set next to the onion-flower-shaped bosses at both ends of the bridge that crosses to the central island. There are two different shapes. One type is flat-topped and the other has diagonally sloping sides. They are placed 1 *shaku* away from the bosses, or, depending upon the size of the bridge, only 0.7 or 0.5 *shaku* away, whichever the proportional balance calls for.

[83] Master Rock. The most suitable place to set this rock is at the point where a projecting cape of the island meets the island proper, or off to the northwest, to the right of the residential buildings. In shape, this rock is neither flat-topped nor a vertical. Rather, from nearby, it has an understated elegance that commands people's respect. It should be set at a height of 3 *shaku* or, depending upon the garden and the desired effect, at a height of 2 or even 1 *shaku*.

[84] The Attendant Rocks are set to either side of the Master Rock. If there is only one, it is set to the right of the Master Rock. In shape, these are flat-topped rocks, resembling persons with their heads lowered, respectfully saying something to the Master Rock. Their height is 1 *shaku* for a 3-*shaku* Master Rock. Adjust their height based on that proportion. Set them in postures of deep respect for the Master Rock.

[85]   The Never Aging Rock may be set either in the pond or in the garden proper. In shape, it combines all three forces—horizontal, diagonal, and vertical. You should by all means use this rock. Its height is 2.5 *shaku*. Below it the Rock of Ten Thousand Eons is set. The Never Aging Rock must have an enchanting scenic atmosphere. Keep these things fully in mind when you set it.

[86]   The Rock of Ten Thousand Eons is the ancient-looking rock set below the Never Aging Rock. It has the shape of a turtle. Set it so that its upper surface is like a round cushion laid on the ground. There is no specified size; here too, it depends on the size of the Never Aging Rock. Set it so that it bears a striking resemblance to the shape of a turtle.

[87]   The Rock of the Spirit Kings is set in the northwest. It is a flat-topped rock with a ledge in front and a balanced form from the front and both sides. You can find detailed descriptions of it in written compilations of the oral transmissions. On top it has the shape of a vertical rock, and in front, that of a diagonal rock. It should be set at a height of 3 *shaku* or, depending upon the garden, as little as 1 *shaku*, 0.8 *shaku*, 0.6 *shaku*, 0.7 *shaku*, or even 0.3 *shaku*. These are very important rocks. You must set them with an eye to their harmonious balance.

[88]   The Frolicking Birds Rocks are set between the central island and the shore of the pond out in front of the house. These rocks have both horizontal and diagonal lines, and rather resemble the shapes of birds. They should be set 0.5 *shaku* above the water, so that the diagonal sides are partly submerged. Three, four, or five in number, they should compose a scene reminiscent of birds at play. These rocks make an especially intriguing scenic effect in the landscape garden.

[89]   Companion Rock. This rock is set to the left of the Status Rock. Flat-topped, it is set at a height of 0.62 *shaku*. But you must vary its height in proportion to the height of the Status Rock. Bear this fully in mind and set it with an eye to its balance with the Status Rock.

[90]   The Status Rock is set slightly away from and to the left of the Fulfillment Rock. It has diagonally sloping sides and is flat-topped. Its standard height is 1 *shaku*, but there are times when it is set at 0.6 *shaku* or even 0.3 *shaku*. This is decided on the basis of the master's rank and the overall situation. If done well, it will contribute to the scenic quality.

[91]   Constant Waters Rock. This rock is set as a rocky point on the central island of the pond, on a sandspit extending out from the island's south side. It is diagonally shaped, with no specified size. Set it in an interesting way that goes well with the shape of the island, and so that the water in passing washes up against it. To create this effect, it is always best to use a rock in the upright position.

[92] Current-impeding Stone. This stone is set as if it were a bridge pillar. There are no specifications as to its shape. It is set 0.3 *shaku* above the water. Another opinion says it is set at the same height as the bridge, but 0.3 *shaku* is the accepted standard.

[93] Human Form Stones. These stones are set 0.75 *shaku* away from the edge of the veranda of the master's house. They may be set in a large-scale landscape garden, but their use should not be especially favored. These are stones with equal power to bring both good and bad luck. When mountain rocks are used, the indwelling spirits must be exorcised. You must not place them in the garden of an ordinary lay person's residence. In shape, these stones are flat-topped and have the look of two people standing face to face engaged in conversation. One stone is 3.5 *shaku* in height, the other is 3.2 *shaku*. This composition should never be used in the garden of an ordinary person's residence, no matter how much it is desired.

[94] The stump of a willow tree may be left there to view, but the stump of a pine tree must be speedily dug up and disposed of.[44]

You must never show this writing to outsiders.
You must keep it secret.

CHART OF THE TRANSMISSION

Zōen Sōjō

Enchū Sōjō

Chūkai Sōjō

En'un Risshi

Rengaku Kō

Renchū Hōin

Ren'i Sōjō

Chōi Sōjō

Zōshō Risshi

Kakuben Sōzu

Kakuren Sōjō

Chōi Hōin

Jitsuen Sōjō

Kūken Hōin

Kenshin Sōjō

En'en Ajari (grandson of the Ichijō Regent of State, son of Middle Counselor Yoshichika)

Toshitsuna (son of the Lord of Uji)

The Lord Lay Monk of the Chishakuin

The Great Lord of the Hosshōji

Tokudaiji [corr: Ninnaji] no Hōin Jōi (son of Lord Kyōgoku)

Rinken (styled Ise no Bō)

Seikū (styled Ajari)

Shinkai Sōzu

Moroaki

Morouji

Ujiyasu

Yasunobu

Shigekata

Kōson Risshi

Gyōsen Hōin

Ieuji

Iechika

Moriie

Ieyasu

Yasuyuki

Hisataka

Keisen

Lord Yoshinobu

Ryōi

Shōi

Raimyō Sōzu

Ryūmon Oshō (Musō)

Jinkan Hōin

Sōshō (Fumyō Kokushi)

Chūnin Oshō

Jōki (Mima no Shōgen)

Because I wished to make an elaboration on the instructions for garden making, I have transmitted the above without leaving anything hidden from the five scrolls of secret teachings and transmissions that have been passed down from the Priest Chūnin.

Bun'an 5 [1448], first month, on a propitious day

signed, Jōki (Lay Monk of Mima)

The aforementioned scroll has been passed down from the venerable Zōgo (of the Pure Land Sect temple Jōgein). In this elaboration not only have the five scrolls been transmitted in their entirety, but in most cases oral instructions have been transmitted as well. The Venerable Priest [Zōgo] had the above transmitted by the Lay Monk Jōki of Mima, and the genealogy of the provenance is as previously listed.

Bunshō 1 [1466], seventh month, twenty-eighth day

Hōin Shingen [monogram]

THREE

REFERENCE MATERIALS

DESCRIPTIONS OF GARDENS MENTIONED IN THE TEXT

Daisen'in. Subtemple of Daitokuji. Daitokuji-chō, Murasakino, Kita-ku, Kyoto. Ca. 1513. The work of the priest Kogaku Sōkō, probably in collaboration with the artist Sōami. Dry landscape composed on an L-shaped site northeast of the abbot's quarters of a Zen monastery.

Daitokuji Honbō. Headquarters of Daitokuji. Daitokuji-chō, Murasakino, Kita-ku, Kyoto. Ca. 1636. By the abbot Ten'yū? Dry landscape south of the abbot's quarters of a Zen monastery. The focal point—a rock triad representing a waterfall and located in the southeast corner—is counterpoised by a rock islet located in the right foreground.

Entsūji. Hataeda-chō, Iwakura, Sakyō-ku, Kyoto. Mid-seventeenth century. Thought to be the work of Gyokuen. Dry landscape east of the abbot's quarters of a Zen monastery connected with the imperial family. The composition is of mostly recumbent rocks loosely arranged on a level expanse of moss. A clipped hedge across the back frames the distant view of Mount Hiei. Tree trunks just beyond the hedge draw the mountain with its distant bluish cast into the design.

Isuien. Suimon-chō, Nara. 1900. Completed by Jirō Sekifuji. Large-scale stroll garden with tea garden elements, built around two ponds in a naturalistic style characteristic of the Meiji period (1868–1911).

Jōjuin. Headquarters of Kiyomizudera. 1-chōme, Kiyomizu, Higashiyama-ku, Kyoto. Ca. 1629 or Genroku era (1688–1703)? Compact pond garden north of the *shoin* (study) of a Hossō-sect Buddhist monastery. The repetition of stone lanterns is used as a device to "borrow" the wooded hillside beyond the garden.

Jōnangū Rakusuien. Jōnangū, Miyanomae-chō, Fushimi-ku, Kyoto. 1954–61. Designed by Kinsaku Nakane. Arranged sequentially along the stroll path are gardens composed in the Heian, Muromachi, and Momoyama styles.

Kasaoka Tenri Church (Daikyōkai). Mochinoe, Kasaoka City, Okayama Prefecture. 1972. Designed by Kenneth Yasuda. Pond garden on a one-acre site adjoining the reception hall. The focal point is a two-tiered waterfall eighteen feet high.

Katsura Rikyū. Misono, Katsura, Nishikyō-ku, Kyoto. 1620–45. The creation of Prince Hachijō Toshihito and his son, Toshitada. Stroll garden with several teahouses and ever-changing vistas laid out along a path circumscribing the pond.

Kinkakuji (Temple of the Golden Pavilion). Kinkakuji-chō, Kita-ku, Kyoto. 1397. Built by Ashikaga Yoshimitsu as part of his Kitayama Villa. A pond garden lies south of the Golden Pavilion. The villa became a Zen monastery called Rokuonji upon Yoshimitsu's death.

Kohōan. Subtemple of Daitokuji. Daitokuji-chō, Murasakino, Kita-ku, Kyoto. Ca. 1644. By Kobori Enshū. Here the quintessential elements of a tea garden—a humble stone lantern and a water basin—have been incorporated poetically in a landscape view enjoyed from the Bōsen tearoom. A camellia hedge screens this intimate space from the western sun, but a portion is left open to the brightness beyond so that the shade of this secluded oasis is all the more cherished.

Konchi'in. Subtemple of Nanzenji. Fukuchi-chō, Nanzenji, Sakyō-ku, Kyoto. 1632. By Kobori Enshū. A dry landscape garden with turtle and crane islands set against a backdrop of clipped shrubs and trees, and separated from the veranda of this Zen monastery by a gravel "sea."

Kōrin'in. Subtemple of Daitokuji. Daitokuji-chō, Murasakino, Kita-ku, Kyoto. 1960s. Designed by Kinsaku Nakane. Dry landscape located to the south and west of the abbot's quarters of a Zen monastery.

Manshuin. Takenouchi-chō, Ichijōji, Sakyō-ku, Kyoto. 1655. Dry landscape that merges into a wooded backdrop, located south of the *shoin* (study) of a Tendai monastery.

Nijōjō Ninomaru. Nijō Horikawa, Nijōjō-chō, Nakagyō-ku, Kyoto. Ca. 1605, for Tokugawa Ieyasu; 1624 renovations were directed by Kobori Enshū. The Daishoin (Great Study) and Kuroshoin (Black Study) of Nijō Castle make an L-shape around the east and north of a pond-centered garden, where grassy banks and massive boulders form a striking contrast.

Nishi Honganji. Monzen-chō, Honganji, Shimogyō-ku, Kyoto. Ca. 1632. Attributed to Asagiri Shimanosuke, the Kokei no Niwa (Tiger Gorge Garden) is a dry landscape east of the Daishoin of a Jōdo Shin sect temple. Notable are the massive boulders, many with diagonal lines, and the use of Sago palms rather than pines.

Okayama Kōrakuen. Kōrakuen, Okayama City, Okayama Prefecture. 1686–1700. Planned by the daimyo Ikeda Tsunamasa and executed by Tsuda Nagatada. Large-scale "daimyo" garden distinguished by its parklike lawn and stroll paths.

Ritsurin Kōen. Ritsurin-chō, Takamatsu City, Kagawa Prefecture, Shikoku. Begun in 1587 by Ikoma Chikamasa, enlarged in 1673 by Matsudaira Yorishige, and completed in 1741 by Matsudaira Yoriyasu. A large-scale "daimyo" garden with stroll paths and numerous artificial hills built around six ponds.

Ryōanji. Goryōnoshita-chō, Ryōanji, Ukyō-ku, Kyoto. 1499 or late sixteenth century? Anonymous. Dry landscape consisting of five groups of rocks in a rectangular court south of the abbot's quarters of a Zen monastery.

Sanpōin. Daigoji, Higashiōji-chō, Daigo, Fushimi-ku, Kyoto. 1598. Built by Toyotomi Hideyoshi. Garden with a complex rock composition laid out along a pond south of the buildings of a Shingon monastery.

Taizōin. Subtemple of Myōshinji. Myōshinji-chō, Hanazono, Ukyō-ku, Kyoto. 1965. By Kinsaku Nakane. Located in a dale south of the abbot's quarters of a Zen monastery, the composition centers around a stream that cascades down into a gourd-shaped pond at the viewer's feet.

Tenryūji. Susuki no Banba-chō, Saga Tenryūji, Ukyō-ku, Kyoto. 1256, by Rankei Dōryū; 1344 renovation by Musō Soseki. Pond garden with a masterful waterfall rock composition set against artificial hills and incorporating into the scene the two mountains, Arashiyama and Kameyama. The garden is located west of the abbot's quarters of a Zen monastery.

Tsuki no Katsura. Katsura Residence, Tsukahara, Shimomigita, Hōfu-shi, Yamaguchi Prefecture. 1712. Created by Katsura Unpei Tadaharu. Dry landscape employing rocks with predominantly horizontal and vertical lines in an L-shaped court southeast of a private residence. The design is said to have been inspired by the rock garden at Ryōanji.

Yabunouchi Sōke Roji. Nishinotōin, Shimogyō-ku, Kyoto. Mid-seventeenth century. Built by Yabunouchi Jōchi II. Tea garden built for the Ennan teahouse in the Oribe style. Among its design innovations are a walk with a single monolithic stone running its entire length, and a "musket barrel" bamboo fence.

R O C K S   M E N T I O N E D
I N   T H E   *I L L U S T R A T I O N S*

Listed by Naming Category and Geological Zone

English Name	Japanese Name	Geological Zone	Orientation/ Remarks	Item, Figure
SCENIC EFFECTS				
Barrier Rocks	*seki-ishi*	A	on peaks/suggesting mountain path	F, 31, 68,76
Hovering Mist Rock	*kasumi-kakeishi, kakenseki*	AaD by N	above Barrier Rock where mist rises	31, 68
Folding Screen Rocks	*byōbuishi*	C by FaH	also in northwest	31, 66
Waterfall-deepening Rocks*	*ryūinseki*	E		31
Water-channeling Rocks	*mizukayoi-ishi*	FaM		31, 70
Stream-rippling Rock	*nagarenami-ishi, ryūha-seki*	(F), NM	so that ripples form as the stream flows around it	31, 80
(Stream-dividing Rock)	*(nagare-wakeishi)*			80
Water-dividing Rock	*mizuwake-ishi*	FaNM	near east shore	31, 75
Falling Water Rocks	*mizuochi no ishi*	ELN	below mid-pond falls/set after Water-dividing Rock	31, 75, 81
Flowing Water Rocks (Water Bottom Rocks)	*nagareishi (mizu no soko ishi)*	NM	in front of main viewing position	31, 77

PEAKS

CLIFFS

FALLING & FLOWING WATER

	English Name	Japanese Name	Geological Zone	Orientation/ Remarks	Item, Figure
SHORE WATER	Current-impeding Stone	*nakasawari-ishi, chūshō-seki*	NM	near bridge/like old bridge pillar	31, 92
	Water Striking Rocks	*mizuuchi-ishi*	HHbM	first point water strikes, in front of master's house	31, 73
ISLAND SHORE	Constant Waters Rock	*suijōseki*	BaJHbM	island south point	31, 91
	Bridge-anchoring Rocks	*hashibiki-ishi*	HJ	near bridge posts	31, 82
	Boat-concealing Rocks	*funekakure-ishi, funeka-kushi-ishi*	JK	/poetic allusion	E, 31, 64
OFFSHORE SHORE	Dragon's Abode Rocks	*tatsui-ishi, ryūkyoseki*	(Ja), NQ	east of main island /crescent pattern	72
	Cormorants' Abode Rocks*	*ui-ishi*	(N)		31
	Ducks' Abode Rocks*	*kamoi-ishi*	(N)		31
	Frolicking Birds Rocks	*toriasobi-ishi, chōyūseki*	HJNQ	in front of main viewing position	31, 88
	Frolicking Fish Rocks*	*gyoyūseki*	(N)		31
	Flying Birds Rocks*	*toritobi-ishi, chōhiseki*	? Q		31
	Water-collecting Rock*	*mizutamari-ishi*	?		31
	Wind & Rain Rocks (Colonnade Rocks)	*fūuseki (renseki)*	Q	conspicuous spot	5, J, 31, 74

SENSORY EFFECTS

	English Name	Japanese Name	Geological Zone	Orientation/ Remarks	Item, Figure
	Crescent Configuration [Rocks]	*kamoji [-ishi]*	e.g., Dragon's Abode Rocks	horizontal plane	67, 72
	Horizontal Triad Rocks [Composition]	*shinamoji [-tate], hin-bonseki*	e.g., Torii Rocks	horizontal plane	31, 64, 67, 71, 77
	Erect & Recumbent Rocks*	*tatefuseishi*		vertical plane	31
	Castaway Rock	*yoseki*		single rock, set	5
	Treasure Rock	*banseki*		alone/diagonal form	
	Rock of Perfect Beauty	*shūseki*			

CULTURAL VALUES: TAOIST (nature-oriented, quest for immortality)

	English Name	Japanese Name	Geological Zone	Orientation/ Remarks	Item, Figure
	Rock of the Spirit Kings	*shinnōseki*	(ABJO)	facing SE from the NW	2, B, D, (E), 16, O, 31, 63, 79, 87

English Name	Japanese Name	Geological Zone	Orientation/ Remarks	Item, Figure
Never Aging Rock	*furōseki*	(ABJO)	pond or garden proper/Hōrai	2, C, 4, N, 31, 85, 86
Rock of Ten Thousand Eons	*mangōseki*	(BaJO)	below Never Aging Rock/Hōrai's turtle	2, C, 31, 85, 86
Bufo Rock	*gamaishi*		facing NW from SE /resembles toad	D, 16, O, 31, 63, 79

CULTURAL VALUES: SHINTO (nature-oriented, animistic)				
Torii Stones	*torii-ishi*	NM	near east shore and Water-dividing Rock	F, 31, 71

CULTURAL VALUES: CONFUCIAN (anthropocentric, hierarchy of social relationships)				
Master Rock	*kunseki*	JG	to right of living quarters, NW	D, 4, (N), 31, 83, 84
Attendant Rock(s)	*shinseki*		looking up to the Master Rock	D, 4, 31, 84
Respect & Affection Stones (Male & Female Stones) (Yin & Yang Stones)	*keiaiseki* *(danjoseki)* *(inyōseki)*		NE/inconspicuous	4, 14, O, 31, 78
Status Rock	*kanseki*		left of Fulfillment Rock	31, 89, 90
Companion Rock	*renseki*		left of Status Rock	31, 89
Happiness & Prosperity Rock	*fukkiseki*		/for the master	23
Guardian of the Mansion Rock*	*goteiseki*			31
Human Form Stones	*ningyōseki*		next to veranda /large-scale garden, nonsecular residence	31, 93
Subordinates Rocks	*kenzokuishi*	(Ha) or:	at the foot of a tree	31, 67

CULTURAL VALUES: BUDDHIST (cosmological truths realized in contemplation)				
Buddhist Triad Rocks	*sanzonseki*	near E		H, 25, 31, 69
Absolute Control Rock (Miraculous Rock)	*sōjiseki* *(fushigi-ishi)*	N	/king among rocks	27, 28
Mirror Rock	*kagami-ishi*		next to Absolute Control Rock	28
Taboo Rock (Kannon Rock)	*imi-ishi* *(kannonseki)*	(B), N	south side of pond /inconspicuous from afar; Mt. Fudaraku	31, 65

English Name	Japanese Name	Geological Zone	Orientation/ Remarks	Item, Figure
Twofold World Rocks	*ryōkaiseki*	N near E, H	/beautiful from all four sides	25, 31, 33
Celestial Beings' Abode Rock	*tenninkyo-seki*		to right of Buddhist Triad Rocks	H, 25
Fulfillment Rock	*jōjuseki*		in front of temple building	29, 30, 90
Reverence Rock	*reiseki*	(front HN)	to left of Fulfillment Rock	25, 30
Mystic Kings Rocks	*myōōseki*		in courtyard master faces/group of five rocks	25, 31, 34

CULTURAL VALUES: ALLUSION *(geographical, poetic)*

Boat-concealing Rocks	*funekakure-ishi, funeka-kushi-ichi*	JK	rear portion of pond/islands in Akashi Bay	E, 31, 64

UTILITY

Torch-cleaning Stone	*rakkaseki*		to left of gate	24
Paving Stones*	*tataki-ishi*		pond bottom?	31
Drip Line Paving Stones*	*migiri-ishi*		below the eaves	31

The asterisk denotes names of rocks listed in item 31, but nowhere explained in the text. Three other such rocks, the Supplication Rock *(negai-ishi)*, Rock of the Right *(useki)*, and Waiting Rock *(taiseki)*, have not been included above, as the names do not provide enough information to categorize them. When both Japanese and Sino-Japanese names are given, the Japanese reading occurs first.

Key to Abbreviations of Geological Zones

A   mountain peak, *mine;* (a) lower peak, *nomine*

B   mountain, *yama;* (a) mountain rock, *yamaishi*

C   escarpment, *sakiyama*

D   trailing ridge (of mountain), *osuji*

E   waterfall, *taki*

F   mountain stream or river, *yamakawa;* (a) outlet or river

G   cape, headland, *saki*

H   shore, coast, *iso;* (a) sandy beach, *suhama;* (b) sandbar, pebble-strewn spit of land, *susaki*

I   hills and fields, *noyama*

J   island, *shima*

K   inlet, bay, *ura*

L   falling water, *mizu no nagareochi*

M   flowing water, *mizu no nagare*

N   pond (body of water), *ike*

O   sea, *umi*

P   marsh, *numaike*

Q   figurative/imagistic

PLANTS MENTIONED
IN THE *ILLUSTRATIONS*

Listed by Size and Habitat

Botanical Name	Japanese Name in the *Illustrations*/today	English Name	Habitat	Orientation/ Remarks	Item, Figure
CANOPY: TREES					
Camellia japonica	*tsubaki*	camellia		with pines	36
Castonopsis cuspidata	*shii-no-ki*	chinquapin	C		52
Chamaecyparis obtusa	*hinoki*	hinoki cypress	C		52
Cinnamomum camphora	*nioi-no-ki /kusunoki*	camphor tree	C	/aromatic	52
Cinnamomum sieboldii	*nioi-no-ki /nikkei*	cinnamon tree	C	/aromatic	52
Cryptomeria japonica	*ayasugi/sugi*	cryptomeria	C	SW	49, 52
Daphniphyllum macropodum	*yuzuriha*	daphniphyllum	C		52
Paulownia tomentosa	*kiri*	royal paulownia	C		52
Pinus spp.	*matsu*	pine	ABCD EFIJQa	SE, *W*	18, P, 35, 36, 40, 49, 51, 52, 94
Podocarpus macrophyllus	*maki*	podocarpus	C		42, 52
Prunus jamasakura	*yamazakura*	wild cherry	C		52
Quercus dentata	*kashiwagi*	oak	C		52
Acer palmatum	*kaede, keikan-boku*	maple	C, (K)	NE	P, 47, 49

DEEP MOUNTAINS

Botanical Name	Japanese Name in the *Illustrations*/today	English Name	Habitat	Orientation/ Remarks	Item, Figure
Prunus spp. of cherry	*sakura*	Japanese cherry	ABa, CxG, K	south	38
Prunus mume	*ume*	Japanese apricot	ABKL	north	11, P, 37
Euonymus sieboldianus	*mayumi*	euonymus	H	podocarpus, cypress; NE /fall color	42
Pyrus culta, spp.	*nashi*	pear	HK		46
Castanea crenata	*kuri*	chestnut	K by H	wooden fence	53
Citrus medica	*yuzu*	citron	K by H	wooden fence	53
Citrus tachibana	*tachibana*	mandarin orange	K by H	wooden fence	53
Citrus unshiu	*kōshi/unshū mikan?*	tangerine	K by H	wooden fence	53
Eriobotrya japonica	*biwa*	loquat	K by H	wooden fence	53
Prunus persica	*momo*	peach	(K), Ra	east/large-scale garden	44
Punica granatum	*zakuro*	pomegranate	K (by H)	/red flower and fruit	45
Salix spp., esp. *babylonica*	*yanagi*	willow	MNO (P)	NW/large-scale garden	39, 49, 94
Bambusaceae, mostly of genus *Phyllostachys*	*take*	bamboo		north	50

MIDDLE STORY: WOODY SHRUBS & VINES

Botanical Name	Japanese Name	English Name	Habitat	Orientation/ Remarks	Item, Figure
Ilex crenata	*yadome /inutsuge*	(bush) holly	C		52
Rhus trichocarpa	*yamaurushi*	wild sumac	C	/fall color	52
Sasa kozassa	*ozasa/kozasa*	bamboo grass	C		52
Rhododendron spp., esp. *kaempferi*	*tsutsuji*	azalea	BaBb CM(P)		18, P, 43, 52
Eurya japonica	*hisakaki*	eurya	CM(P)		18, 52
Kerria japonica	*yamabuki*	kerria	M(P)		18, 19, P, 41
Wisteria floribunda	*fuji*	wisteria	(C), M (P)	pine or cypress	18, 40
Lespedeza spp.	*hagi*	bushclover		inside gate	24

Botanical Name	Japanese Name in the *Illustra-tions*/today	English Name	Habitat	Orientation/ Remarks	Item, Figure
GROUND LEVEL: NON-WOODY PLANTS (herbs)					

MARSH

Botanical Name	Japanese Name	English Name	Habitat	Orientation/Remarks	Item, Figure
Acorus gramineus	*sekishō*	sweet flag	M(P)		18, 19, 59
Iris laevigata	*kakitsubata*	rabbit-ear iris	M(P)		18, 19
Lithospermum erythrorhizon	*murasaki*	gromwell	M(P)		18

VILLAGE

Calanthe discolor	*ebine*	calanthe	K by H?		54
Wasabia japonica	*wasabi*	wasabi	K by H?		54
?	*hyakunansō*		K by H?		54
?	*kinkisō*		K by H?		54
?	*nekusa*		K by H?		54

SENTIMENT

Aster tartaricus	*shion*	aster, Michaelmas daisy	(K), Rbc	wooden fence; not in garden proper	24, 55
Chrysanthemum morifolium (white)	*shiragiku*	white chrysanthemum	(K), Rbc	wooden fence; not in garden proper	24, 55

Key to Abbreviations of Habitats

A   mountain peak, *mine*

B   mountainside, *yama;* (a) high, *yō;* (b) lower, *in*

C   deep mountains, *shinzan*

D   waterfall, *taki*

E   foothills, *tanzan*

F   cape, projecting point of land, *saki*

G   verdant hills, *aoyama*

H   hills and fields, *noyama;* along stream valleys, *nosuji*

I   hillside fields, *no*

J   plains, *hara*

K   village, *sato*

L   valley, *tani*

M   marsh, *numaike*

N   river, *kawa*

O   island, *shima*

P   freshwater shore, *suihen*

Q   seashore, *umibe;* (a) ebb-tide beach, *hikata*

R   cultural values; (a) auspicious; (b) romantic; (c) melancholy

APPENDIX 4

"MAKE IT YOUR OWN": LISTENING TO NATURE AND ART

A book can lead us to water, but we have to do the drinking ourselves. Each of us will find our own way to do that. This book has introduced a set of design principles and techniques used in making Japanese gardens. But without human purpose and deep feelings born of experience to guide their use, these design tools are worthless, and may even be a curse. A technically accomplished musician may be able to play a Beethoven sonata perfectly; yet it will be devoid of feeling if the musician has not himself been transported by the spirit of the piece and made it his own.

Every lesson we have learned so far suggests that the Japanese garden is a kind of ballet, where the patterns of human response are subtly interwoven into the very fabric of forms and rhythms provided by the rocks and plants in a composition. The designer cannot achieve this in an actual garden unless he has internalized the principles and techniques of the art in an authentic personal way. In chapter 1 we looked at how this was done in Japan. I believe that traditional model can be useful to landscape design students today. And while there is no substitute for serving an apprenticeship, there is yet much a sensitive student can learn by letting nature and existing gardens be his teacher, two ways the art has traditionally been learned in Japan.

Learning from nature in this case does not mean attempting to identify in natural phenomena the principles and patterns presented here or in other books. As long as you are focused this way, on a narrow band of experience, the natural listening mode of your senses will be impaired. As a result, you probably will not even find what you are looking for. In reality, you must let it find you. All you need do is come to nature in a receptive mood, and let your senses be your guide. You might decide to hike up along a stream bed, where natural phenomena like waterfalls, rock formations, and a variety of water and plant life are found in abundance. Or you might choose to set out against the grain of the landscape, crossing streams, hills, fields and woodlands to see what lessons nature will reveal that way. When you let nature speak to you through your senses, you will begin to feel the weight and thrust of a rocky cliff or a mammoth boulder, the feather-light touch of a fern, the playful rippling movement of water round rocks in a stream, the dignity of a gnarled trunk of an ancient cedar. If you allow yourself, your senses will guide you on a journey unknown to your conceptual learning.

Bashō says, go to the pine if you want to know the pine. The best way to learn from nature—or a garden—is to go and experience it for yourself. We all have our predilections, habits of observation, things we respond to, and I do not pretend that the suggestions I offer here will work for everyone in the same way. But I do hope that they will at least encourage readers to rely upon their senses more and let nature and art be their teachers.

All you need to take with you is a sketchbook and a pen or pencil. I usually carry an 8½ × 11 inch sketchpad, because it is not cumbersome yet it is big enough to allow me to sketch freely. You may prefer something else, and whatever you have on hand will do. There are times when it is good to go for a walk in the woods, or up a mountain path, and simply see what you can see. Other times you may prefer to look for specific types of natural phenomena. You may, for example, choose to concentrate on water-related phenomena, in which case you would first want to find a good stream and then seek out the best places to observe the various aspects of falling and flowing water the stream provides.

Once you have set out, what do you look for? You may start out with one thing in mind and end up being totally absorbed by another. The point is to look for everything and nothing, to simply relax and open your mind. As you stroll along, what kinds of things might you see, hear, or feel? If the path is near a stream, perhaps you will notice the mossy contours of a bank where it meets the level surface of a limpid pool. An overhanging tree may arch across the top of your field of view and create a natural frame. Or perhaps you will respond more to other sensory qualities: the turbulence of water rushing around a half-sunken boulder, the confusion of forest sounds, or the way light glints off the water and then is lost in the deep shade of evergreens above. The fact is, if you set out to see just one thing, or are intent only on identifying a particular design principle, you will likely miss everything else and come home feeling that what you gained was not worth the trouble. You will be far more likely to make something your own if you let it find you.

The same manner of looking with a "listening" heart can be applied at any range. You might be brought to your hands and knees by a delicate wildflower growing out of a clump of moss, to view it from the perspective of a tiny animal. (Once when I was crouching down planting clumps of velvet moss to form a ground cover in one of Kinsaku Nakane's gardens, I had just this experience for an extended period of time. Looking down from only a couple of feet above the freshly planted moss, the tiny seedlings that grew up here and there from the dappled green carpet seemed to tower high above a rolling landscape of hills and fields.) Or you might emerge from a dark wood onto a rocky ledge overlooking a distant panorama, and sense not only

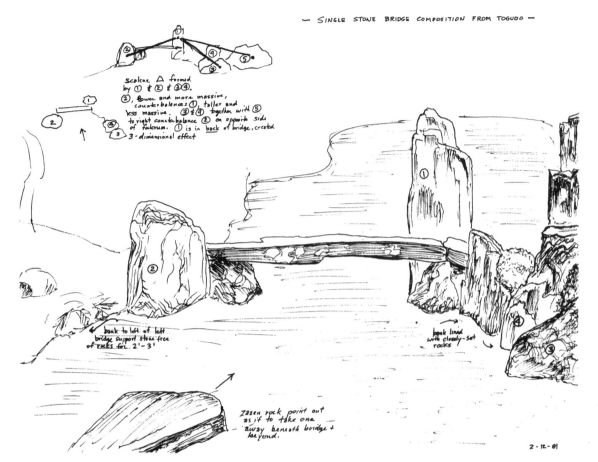

Fig. 51.   Page from author's sketchbook dated February 12, 1981: Single stone bridge and island composition, viewed from Tōgudō at Ginkakuji, Kyoto.

the expressiveness and grandeur of far-off peaks and valleys, but the added ethereal quality as the wind sweeps down through a stand of firs.

Once you have gotten a feel for the features and sensory qualities of the landscape before you, it is a good time to take out your sketchpad and pencil. Your sketch need not be a work of art or a detailed representation. What you are after is the feeling of the scene, and that is best conveyed with a sketchy quality anyway. Here and there detail a few essentials, and complete the rest in a quick-sketch outline of the general forms. Use short jagged strokes or long flowing lines—whatever the feeling-tone of what you are experiencing suggests. After you have captured on your sketchpad what initially attracted you, jot down beside the sketch any thoughts or feelings you have. What, for example, are the qualities (shapes, textures, horizontal or vertical emphasis, light and shadow, sense of movement) that made you stop and take notice? What feelings do these qualities evoke in you? For example, the tops of young pines viewed against the sky may remind you of a village dance troupe frolicking hand-in-

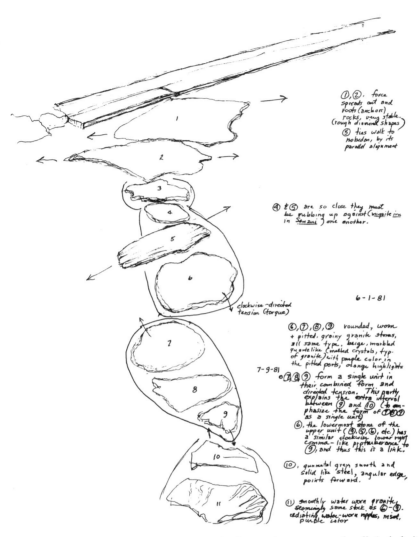

①,②. force
spreads out and
roots (anchors)
rocks, very stable.
(rough diamond shapes)
③ ties walk to
nobedan, by its
parallel alignment

④ & ⑤ are so close they must
be rubbing up against (*migaite iru*
in *Senzui*) one another.

6-1-81

clockwise-directed
tension (torque)

7-9-81

⑥,⑦,⑧,⑨ rounded, worn
+ pitted. grainy granite stones,
all same type. beige, marbled
quartz-like (melted crystals, typ.
of granite) with purple color in
the pitted parts, orange highlights

⑦,⑧,⑨ form a single unit in
their combined form and
directed tension. This partly
explains the extra interval
between ⑨ and ⑩ (to em-
phasize the form of ⑦⑧⑨
as a single unit)

⑥, the lowermost stone of the
upper unit (④,⑤,⑥, etc.) has
a similar clockwise lower right
comma-like protuberance to
⑨, and thus this is a link.

⑩, gunmetal grey smooth and
solid like steel, angular edge,
points forward.

⑪ smoothly water worn granite,
seemingly same stock as ⑥-⑨.
radiating water-worn ripples, msd.
purple color

Fig. 52.   June 1, 1981. Stepping-stone path leading to the stone-paved walk (*nobedan*) in front of the shelter at Sago Palm Hill, Katsura villa, Kyoto.

hand, snaking this way and that along the crest of a hill. What about the aspects of water when it flows around and over rocks in a mountain torrent? Where do eddies form? Sandbars? Quiet pools?

Nature is an endless source of both scenic and sensory effects. Not only are there the lessons taught by various waterfalls and craggy rock formations with their gnarled trees, but there is much to be learned from the visual patterns of birds in flight, animals grazing in a pasture, children at play in a park, or dancers practicing

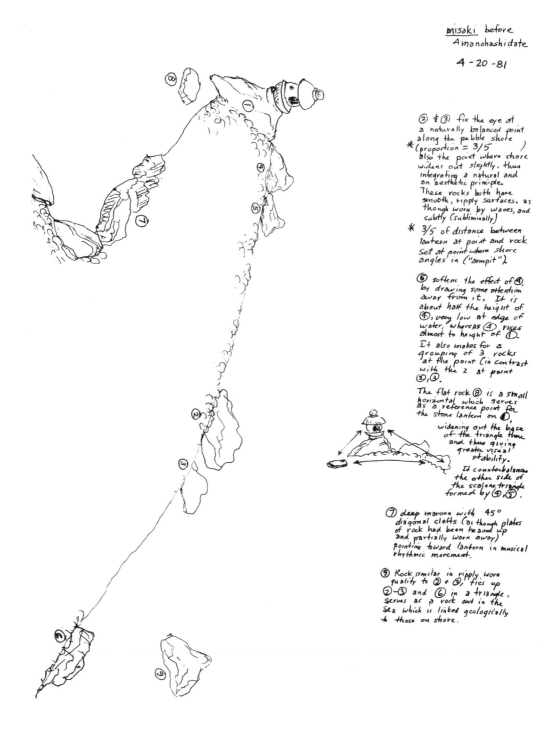

misaki before
Amanohashidate

4 - 20 - 81

② & ③ fix the eye at a naturally balanced point along the pebble shore
* (proportion = 3/5   )
also the point where shore widens out slightly, thus integrating a natural and an aesthetic principle.
These rocks both have smooth, ripply surfaces, as though worn by waves, and subtly (subliminally)

* 3/5 of distance between lantern at point and rock set at point where shore angles in ("armpit")

⑤ softens the effect of ④ by drawing some attention away from it. It is about half the height of ④, very low at edge of water, whereas ④ rises almost to height of ①.
It also makes for a grouping of 3 rocks at the point (in contrast with the 2 at point ②, ③).

The flat rock ⑧ is a small horizontal which serves as a reference point for the stone lantern on ①, widening out the base of the triangle there and thus giving greater visual stability.
It counterbalances the other side of the scalene triangle formed by ④, ⑤.

⑦ deep maroon with 45° diagonal clefts (as though plates of rock had been heaved up and partially worn away) pointing toward lantern in musical rhythmic movement.

⑨ Rock similar in ripply worn quality to ② & ③, ties up ②-③ and ⑥ in a triangle, serves as a rock out in the sea which is linked geologically to those on shore.

Fig. 53.   April 20, 1981: Cape before Amanohashidate, Katsura villa.

their art. When it comes to actually directing the placement of rocks and trees in a composition, making such patterns your own can be just as important as what you have learned from the direct observation of rocks and trees in nature. In fact, *Sakuteiki* instructs that rocks placed at the foot of a hill or on a hillside field should resemble a pack of crouching dogs, running and scattering pigs, or children playing tag.

A work of art can be your teacher in the same way nature can, if you will come to it in a receptive frame of mind and let your senses guide you. Landscape paintings are valuable because they show us that the experience of nature can be conveyed by very restricted means. The idea that a landscape garden is like a painting in three dimensions suggests that we can learn a great deal about perspective techniques and other means of rendering a landscape experience by studying two-dimensional visual arts. The more standard representational forms of art are instructive for the way they employ such techniques as size and linear or aerial perspective to create an integrated perceptual universe. In Oriental painting, ink washes are often used to suggest great distance. Abstract painting and other "nonrepresentational" art forms are useful because their impact is often purely sensory, and so by observing them we learn to see *bon'yari shite*, without the usual impulse to identify or conceptualize what we are looking at.

Works of art that defy categorization as representational or nonrepresentational and instead hover somewhere in between, like the impressionist and postimpressionist paintings of the late nineteenth century, have much to teach us. An example is Gauguin's *Jacob Wrestling with the Angel*. Here the rich red background on which two men are wrestling vibrates with the same intensity as the white-bonneted women looking on in the foreground, and as a result near and far hover together on the flat surface of the picture plane, and we feel a heightened sense of immediacy.

When you are studying a landscape garden, the same process of looking with an open mind, sketching, and jotting down verbal notes to yourself to describe your experience applies. One note of caution: If you intend to photograph the garden you are studying, it has been my experience that this involves a very different relationship to your subject than firsthand study, and is best done at a different time. If you can visit a garden only once, then I would suggest that you take photographs after you have first come to know the garden through viewing, sketching, and jotting down your impressions. The discipline of proceeding through these steps will make for better photographs and fewer wasted shots. Be sure to photograph the scenes you sketched, and then anything else you would like to record.

Figures 51 through 54 reproduce some sketches and notes I made in 1981 while I was studying in Kyoto. My insights and ideas came directly out of the experience of viewing each garden scene. Occasionally, in order to fill out a feeling I had, I drew upon my knowledge of the culture.

On Apprenticeship

An artist never goes from the verbal statement of a principle directly into a design. First he must make that principle his own by learning it through his body. The most

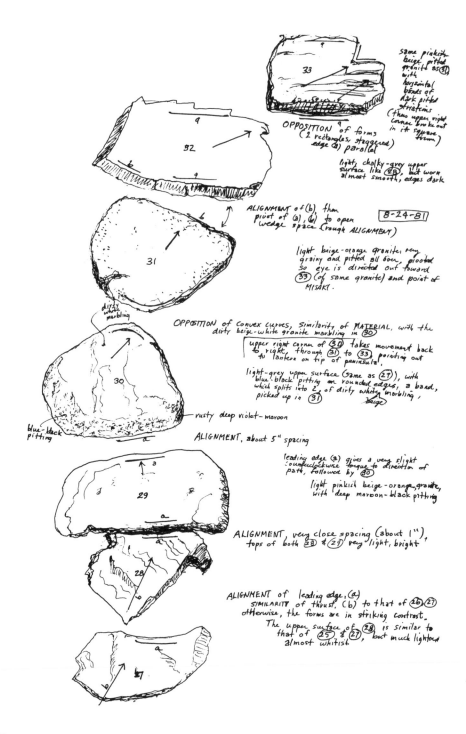

same pinkish beige pitted granite as (31) with horizontal bands of dark pitted striations (these upper right corner broke out in its square form)

OPPOSITION of forms (2 rectangles, staggered) edge (a) parallel

light, chalky-grey upper surface like (28), but worn almost smooth, edges dark

ALIGNMENT of (b) then pivot of (a), (b) to open wedge space (rough ALIGNMENT)

8-24-81

light beige-orange granite, very grainy and pitted all over, pivoted so eye is directed out toward (33) (of same granite) and point of MISAKI.

dirty white marbling

OPPOSITION of convex curves, similarity of MATERIAL, with the dirty beige-white granite marbling in (30)

upper right corner of (30) takes movement back to right, through (31) to (33), pointing out to lantern on tip of peninsula!

light-grey upper surface (same as (27)), with 'blue-black' pitting on rounded edges; a band, which splits into 2 of dirty white beige marbling, picked up in (31)

rusty deep violet-maroon

blue-black pitting

ALIGNMENT, about 5" spacing

leading edge (a) gives a very slight counterclockwise torque to direction of path, followed by (30)

light pinkish beige-orange granite, with deep maroon-black pitting

ALIGNMENT, very close spacing (about 1"), tops of both (28) & (29) very light, bright.

ALIGNMENT of leading edge, (a) SIMILARITY of thrust, (b) to that of (26)(27) otherwise, the forms are in striking contrast. The upper surface of (28) is similar to that of (25) & (27), but much lighter, almost whitish.

Fig. 54. August 24, 1981: Stepping stones on pebble-strewn cape before Amanohashidate, Katsura villa.

effective ways of doing this are learning from nature and art, as explained in the previous section, and serving an apprenticeship. The latter is the type of opportunity that needs to be more fully developed for American students. This is a subject that deserves a great deal more thought. Here I would like to add just a few words based upon my own experience in Japan.

I have asked myself, is a fifteen-year apprenticeship (or five-year, as is common today) the only way to master the art of Japanese gardens? And, more to the point, can a training program be devised that is better adapted to Western students who have the necessary sensitivity and desire to learn the art?

It occurs to me that there are two basic areas in which the traditional Japanese apprenticeship might more fully tap the student's potential. First of all, the principles might be studied more systematically. The principles of an art cannot be, as Rudolf Arnheim says, "absorbed again in intuitive application" unless they have first been identified. Yet the traditional apprenticeship sets aside precious little time for the teacher to impart theoretical knowledge to his apprentices, much less for discussions of theory to take place between teacher and students. Ideally, this area should be given full treatment academically, in the classroom. There the principles of the art should be studied in the context of their application, so that students become aware of how successful design solutions—often regarded in retrospect as this or that "style"—are really creative responses to changing social and environmental conditions. What distinguishes good designers is their ability to apply the basic principles in new ways to solve certain problems and thus bring about aesthetic satisfaction. When students realize this, they will better grasp the importance of studying the principles, and sense their own role in the design process.

The second area in which the traditional apprenticeship falls short is the very area where its strength supposedly lies—the "learn by doing" approach. While a garden is being made, apprentices learn to serve as the master-designer's "arms and legs," deftly following his every signal, to facilitate the creation of the design that is in his imagination. But they receive only token opportunities to personally direct the setting of rocks and planting of trees in the composition. The traditional "learn by doing" approach is thus really much too passive, and students get almost no firsthand experience in implementing a design.

There are two ways of giving students a more active role during the training period. The first would be to create projects in the studio that simulate the process of implementing a design in the field. Students would move artificial materials representing rocks and plants of different shapes and sizes into position in their own compositions, verbally present their aesthetic rationale, and critique one another's work. This step would allow students to internalize the knowledge of the principles gained in the classroom. The premise behind this "hands on" form of learning is the same as that for a chemistry or physics lab—students must experience the principles at work with their own senses in order for the knowledge to be internalized. Only in this way is the ability to perform this most important aspect of landscape design developed. The final period of training would be conducted on an actual garden site, most likely during summer vacations. Students would direct the implementation of a design from start to finish, including the placement of rocks and trees, under the supervision of the instructor.

Listening to Nature and Art: A Reading List

The following books are suggested for readers who wish to explore further the approach to learning the art of Japanese gardens set forth here. All are available in paperback editions.

Adams, Ansel. *Yosemite and the Range of Light*. Boston: New York Graphic Society, 1979.
> Images of Yosemite and the Sierra Nevada by one of America's great landscape photographers. An essay traces the nineteenth-century movement to protect these natural wonders.

Bachelard, Gaston. *The Poetics of Space*. Translated by Maria Jolas. Boston: Beacon Press, 1969.
> Here Bachelard carries his phenomenology of the imagination into the realm of felicitous space, and examines how the human soul responds to places we love—from the refuge of a hermit's hut to the limitless vastness of the sea.

Bush, Susan, and Hsio-yen Shih, comps. and eds. *Early Chinese Texts on Painting*. Cambridge, Mass.: Harvard University Press, 1985.
> See chapter 5, "Sung Literati Theory and Connoisseurship," particularly the sections titled "The Tao and Painting," "Naturalness in Painting," and "Spontaneity in Painting." Translated excerpts from one of the world's greatest landscape traditions exhort the artist to immerse himself in the subject of his study until it becomes a part of him; then what is stored within will be released unconsciously in his art.

Chang, Chung-yuan. *Creativity and Taoism: A Study of Chinese Philosophy, Art, and Poetry*. New York: Harper and Row, 1970.
> Not merely a book *about* Taoism; Chang uses concrete examples to show how artists achieved a direct awareness of the qualities of things that they then expressed in their art.

Koffka, K. *Principles of Gestalt Psychology*. New York: Harcourt, Brace and World, 1935.
> Those willing to tackle this theoretical work on the psychology of human perception will find, especially in its "environmental field" sections, a wealth of behavioral principles applicable in design.

Matsuo Bashō. *The Narrow Road to the Deep North and Other Travel Sketches*. Translated by Nobuyuki Yuasa. Harmondsworth, England: Penguin Books, 1966.
> Japan's best-known haiku poet travels and records his impressions of the landscapes and people he encounters along the way, in both poetry and prose.

Muir, John, ed. *West of the Rocky Mountains*. Philadelphia: Running Press, 1976.
> Inspired descriptive essays and paintings and pen-and-ink drawings portraying some of America's most striking landscapes.

Mustard Seed Garden Manual of Painting, The. Translated by Mai-mai Sze. In *The Tao of Painting: A Study of the Ritual Disposition of Japanese Painting*. Bollingen Series, vol. 49. 2nd ed. Princeton, N.J.: Princeton University Press, 1963.

A seventeenth-century manual with numerous examples illustrating the types of brushwork Chinese landscape painters used to depict rocks, trees, and flowering plants; accompanied by the translator's introductory essay on the *tao* of painting.

Roberts, Jane. *The Nature of the Psyche: Its Human Expression*. New York: Bantam Books, 1984.

See chapter 6, "The Language of Love: Images and the Birth of Words," pp. 108–21. Can modern man rediscover a primal union with the forces of nature? The powerful image this chapter presents of early man's capacity for merging his consciousness with that of a rock, a tree, or an animal challenges us to reclaim this lost portion of the human psyche.

Thoreau, Henry David. *The Valiorum Walden*. Annotated and with an introduction by Walter Harding. New York: Twayne Publishers, 1962.

An American classic on listening to nature.

Tuan, Yi-fu. *Topophilia: A Study of Environmental Perception, Attitudes, and Values*. Englewood Cliffs, N.J.: Prentice-Hall, 1974.

A comprehensive analysis of how human cultures and the physical environment shape one another, documenting the many ways in which cultural values are expressed in city planning, architecture, and the landscape garden.

Watts, May Theilgaard. *Reading the Landscape of America*. New York: Macmillan, 1975.

Watts takes us on a narrative journey (well illustrated with sketches) through one habitat after another and, like a native guide, points out subtle cues along the trail to show us how plant communities adapt to their environment. Landscape designers will have little trouble translating this lore into the scenic effects of a garden.

Yasuda, Kenneth. *The Japanese Haiku: Its Essential Nature, History, and Possibilities in English, with Selected Examples*. Tokyo: Charles E. Tuttle, 1957.

This penetrating study of the aesthetics of haiku reveals through concrete examples how the poet's experience of nature is encapsulated in the brief duration of seventeen syllables ("one breath") so that others may reexperience the quality of that moment.

N O T E S

Preface

1. See the March 1977 issue of *Landscape Architecture* for an interview with Kinsaku Nakane by two of his American students, Julie Moir (Messervy) and Renny Merritt.
2. Josiah Conder, *Landscape Gardening in Japan*, 2nd rev. ed. (Tokyo: Maruzen, 1912), p. vi. Originally published by Messrs. Kelly and Walsh Limited in 1893.
3. Samuel Newsom, "Writer's Note" to *Japanese Garden Construction* (Tokyo: Domoto, Kumagawa and Perkins, 1939).
4. Shigemaru Shimoyama, trans., *Sakuteiki: The Book of Garden* (Tokyo: Town and City Planners, 1976). Grateful acknowledgment is due Mr. Shimoyama for allowing me to quote liberally from his translation in this book. I have occasionally included my own translation of *Sakuteiki* where I thought it necessary for consistency with my translation of the *Illustrations*.

Transmission of the Art

The epigraph is from Matsuo Bashō, *The Narrow Road to the Deep North and Other Travel Sketches*, trans. Nobuyuki Yuasa (Harmondsworth, England: Penguin Books, 1966), p. 33.

1. *Sakuteiki*, in *Kodai-Chūsei geijutsuron*, ed. Tatsusaburō Hayashiya, Nihon Shisō Taikei, vol. 23 (Tokyo: Iwanami, 1975, 2nd printing), p. 224, sec. 1; hereafter cited as NST 23. Shimoyama, p. 1.
2. Akira Kurosawa, *Something Like an Autobiography*, trans. Audie E. Bock (New York: Alfred A. Knopf, 1982), p. 195.
3. *Sakuteiki*, in NST 23:224, sec. 1. Shimoyama, p. 1.

4. *Senzui narabi ni yagyō no zu*, in Yasushi Egami, ed., "'Dōji kudensho tsuki Senzui narabi ni yagyō no zu' kōkan," *Bijutsu kenkyū* 247 (July 1966): 37; hereafter cited as *SYZ*.

5. *Sakuteiki*, in NST 23:227, sec. 7 (technique is first introduced); 235, sec. 19 (actual citation). Shimoyama, p. 20.

6. *Sakuteiki*, in NST 23:243. Shimoyama, p. 33.

7. *Sakuteiki*, in NST 23:247, sec. 37.

8. *SYZ*, in *Bijutsu kenkyū* 250 (January 1967): 22 (sec. 16, *omote*); 23 (sec. 17, *ura*); 27 (top, line 1; top, n. 11; sec. 23, *omote*, n. 6). Items 23, 24, 58, 63, and 64 of the translation.

9. *Ibid.*, 27 (top, n. 11). Item 63 of the translation.

10. *Sakuteiki*, in NST 23:238, sec. 24. Shimoyama, p. 25.

11. *Sakuteiki*, in NST 23:241, sec. 29. Shimoyama, p. 31.

12. Shimoyama, p. viii.

13. *Sakuteiki*, in NST 23:238–39, sec. 24. Shimoyama, p. 26.

14. Edward T. Hall, *Beyond Culture* (Garden City, N.Y.: Anchor Press/Doubleday, 1976), p. 79

15. Rudolf Arnheim, *Visual Thinking* (Berkeley: University of California Press, 1969), p. 192.

The Art We See: Scenic Effects

The epigraph is from Lafayette H. Bunnell, *Discovery of the Yosemite, and the Indian War of 1851* (Chicago: Fleming H. Revell, 1880), p. 54.

1. A concise history of Japanese gardens may be found in Kinsaku Nakane, *Kyoto Gardens*, trans. Money L. Hickman (Osaka: Hoikusha, 1965). For a more lengthy treatment in English, see Loraine Kuck, *The World of the Japanese Garden: From Chinese Origins to Modern Landscape Art* (Tokyo: Walker/Weatherhill, 1968).

2. For more on Shinto and Japanese gardens, see Masao Hayakawa, *The Garden Art of Japan*, trans. Richard L. Gage (Tokyo: Weatherhill/Heibonsha, 1973), pp. 27–29, and Teiji Itoh, *The Gardens of Japan* (Tokyo: Kodansha International, 1984), pp. 31–32, 74–77.

3. *Sakuteiki*, in NST 23:224, sec. 1. Shimoyama, p. 1.

4. Murasaki Shikibu, *The Tale of Genji*, trans. Arthur Waley (New York: Modern Library, 1960), pp. 478–79.

5. Kuck, *World of the Japanese Garden*, p. 130.

6. The Japanese word for tree, *ki*, includes also the woody shrubs.

7. Seven marsh-pond plants are listed in item 18 of the *Illustrations*. The beautiful effect of wisteria blossoms reflected by the surface of the pond is what is intended by the second way of planting it—"so that it extends out over the water in a marsh-pond landscape"— in item 40.

8. The Japanese black pine, *Pinus thunbergiana*, has long been the popular classical choice, and for good reason: "This tree actually grows well within a few feet of the high water mark at the seashore, where it is exposed to occasional drenchings of salt-water spray!" (*Wyman's Gardening Encyclopedia*, ed. Donald Wyman [New York: Macmillan, 1972, 2nd printing], p. 838).

9. See appendix 3. Most of the plants for these two habitats are presented in items 52, 53, and 54 of the translation.

10. The use of an organic growth retardant, the chemical efficacy of which has yet to be established scientifically, is detailed in item 59 of the *Illustrations*.

11. Jens Jensen, *Siftings: The Major Portion of "The Clearing" and Collected Writings* (reprint; Chicago: Ralph Fletcher Seymour, 1956), p. 46.

12. Darrel G. Morrison, "Utilization of Prairie Vegetation on Disturbed Sites" (unpublished article), p. 5.

13. *Ibid.*, p. 6. Another good source on the subject of re-creating the visual essence of a prairie, cited by Morrison, is Robert Dyas, "Landscape Design with Prairie Plants," in *Prairie: A Multiple View*, ed. Mohan K. Wali (Grand Forks: University of North Dakota Press, 1975), pp. 411–16.

14. For "dramatic scenery" in the *Illustrations* see, for example, the Folding Screen Rocks (item 66) and the Barrier Rocks (item 76). For the "gentle scenery" of hills and fields, see item 20. See item 18, paragraph 2, for the use of rocks in a marsh-pond scene.

15. This is further validated by the fact that the word for rock (Japanese *ishi* or Sino-Japanese *seki*) occurs 424 times in the approximately 7,500-word text of the *Illustrations*, a frequency of 5.7 percent. All general and specific terms for plants come to a total of 193 occurrences, a frequency of 2.6 percent.

16. *Sakuteiki*, in NST 23:239, sec. 25. To facilitate the comparison being made here between passages from *Sakuteiki* and the *Illustrations*, I have revised Shimoyama's translation (p. 26) to be consistent with my own. The Japanese word *ishi* (Sino-Japanese *seki*) can be translated into English as either "rock(s)" or "stone(s)." Here is my rationale for choosing one or the other:

    Japanese *ishi* (*seki*) I translate as "rock(s)" when they are used in the garden to suggest rock formations in nature, and "stone(s)" when they are used (for their naturally or artificially flattened upper surfaces) as stepping stones or paving stones, or when they have been sculpted (stone lanterns, water basins, pagodas) or split or sawed (stone slabs used for bridges, paving, curbing). Quarried stone obtained by blasting—known as riprap—I call "rock(s)" when it is used in a landscape to suggest rock formations in nature. On the other hand, natural "rocks" that have been domesticated or tamed (like a "worry stone" worn smooth by its owner's touch) by forces of erosion and that are used in a landscape anthropomorphically, to convey human forms or ideas, I call "stone(s)." The Human Form Stones of item 93 is a case in point. Here natural rocks from the mountains are used to suggest human forms, not a natural rock formation. The fact that "the indwelling spirits" of rocks from the wilds "must be exorcised" before such rocks can be used anthropomorphically suggests that classical Japanese garden designers made a distinction in the way *ishi* are used similar to the one I am making here between "rock(s)" and "stone(s)."

17. *Sakuteiki*, in NST 23:235, sec. 19. Shimoyama, p. 20. A sketch illustrating this composition of rocks may be found in Katsuo Saitō, *Zukai Sakuteiki* (Tokyo: Gihōdō, 1979, 7th printing), p. 72, fig. 44.

18. In *Sakuteiki*, as has been mentioned previously, eight types of waterfalls and seventeen types of waterscapes are named and explained. Only two of the waterscapes found in *Sakuteiki*, the marsh-pond and the ebb-tide beach, and none of the waterfall types, occur in the *Illustrations*. Rather, the emphasis is on the forty-four types of rock compositions and forty-two varieties of plants that are named and explained.

19. We use the word "air" itself that way ("a dignified air"). The word "atmosphere" is composed of the Greek *atmos*, "vapor," plus *sphaira*, "sphere," while the word "aura" is akin to the Greek word *aer*, "air."

20. Carol Donnell-Kotrozo, *Critical Essays on Postimpressionism* (Philadelphia: The Art Alliance Press, 1983), p. 37.

21. Albert Chatelet, *Impressionist Painting* (New York: McGraw-Hill, 1962), p. 16.

22. Yoshiaki Shimizu and Carolyn Wheelwright, eds., *Japanese Ink Paintings from American*

Collections: The Muromachi Period (Princeton, N.J.: The Art Museum, Princeton University, 1976), p. 25.

23. While it is likely that this earliest extant version was copied from earlier manuscripts, these copies may have gradually incorporated the changing approach that manifested itself in such arts as poetry and painting.

24. A discussion of the Daisen'in dry landscape and the historical milieu in which it was created may be found in Kuck, *World of the Japanese Garden*, pp. 154–62.

25. Yoshinobu Yoshinaga, *Composition and Expression in Traditional Japanese Gardens* (Tokyo: Shōkokusha, 1962), p. 14.

26. Kuck, *World of the Japanese Garden*, p. 162.

The Art We See: Sensory Effects

The epigraph is from Rudolf Arnheim, *Art and Visual Perception: A Psychology of the Creative Eye* (Berkeley: University of California Press, 1954), p. 28.

1. *Sakuteiki*, in NST 23:224, sec. 2. Shimoyama, p. 2.

2. *The Focal Encyclopedia of Photography*, ed. A. Kraszna-Krausz *et al.*, vol. 2 (London: Focal Press, 1965), p. 1065.

3. *The Focal Encyclopedia of Film and Television Techniques*, ed. Raymond Spottiswoodie *et al.* (New York: Hastings House, 1969), pp. 978–81.

4. *The Foundations of Ophthalmology*, vol. 7 of *System of Ophthalmology*, ed. Stewart Duke-Elder (St. Louis: C. V. Mosby, 1962), p. 409.

5. *Focal Encyclopedia of Film and Television Techniques*, p. 975.

6. More information on the Tenryūji garden may be found in Marc Treib and Ron Herman, *A Guide to the Gardens of Kyoto* (Tokyo: Shufunotomo, 1980), pp. 105–6.

7. Charles Barr, "CinemaScope: Before and After," *Film Quarterly* 16 (Summer 1963): 10.

8. James J. Gibson, *The Perception of the Visual World* (Boston: Houghton Mifflin, 1950), p. 83.

9. *Ibid.*

10. This style is magnificently exemplified in the works of the mid-fifteenth-century Japanese painter Shōkei Ten'yū. See his *Landscape with Distant Mountains* in the Kimiko and John Powers Collection, published in Shimizu and Wheelwright, *Japanese Ink Paintings*, no. 11, p. 103, and his *Small Scene of Lake and Mountains* in the Fujii Collection, also published in Shimizu and Wheelwright, fig. 36, p. 104.

11. *Sakuteiki*, in NST 23:231–32, sec. 13. Shimoyama, p. 14.

12. *Sakuteiki*, in NST 23:237, sec. 22.

13. *Ibid.* My revision of Shimoyama, p. 23.

14. All during the day there was a strong wind blowing, and it is interesting to note that Nakane said the wind interfered with his directing of the rock composition, due to the sensitive visual balance involved. The aural sensation created by the wind apparently disturbed the sense of equilibrium located in the inner ear. The wind may also have disturbed the kinesthetic sense of balance. This anecdote indicates the designer's absolute dependence on the guidance of his senses, and how closely the sensory modes can impinge upon each other.

15. A reference to Nobunaga's obtaining the Fujito Rock during the building of the Nijō Castle may be found in the near-contemporary chronicle of his deeds, *Shinchō kōki*, ed. Takahiro Okuno and Yoshihiko Iwasawa (Tokyo: Kadokawa, 1970, 2nd printing), pt. 2, sec. 3, p. 95; entry for Eiroku 12 (1569), 2.27.

16. One wonders why the height given for the largest rocks is little more than 3 *shaku*. Even if the "foot" measure used at the time of the *Illustrations* was not the present Japanese *shaku*, which almost exactly equals the English foot, but a larger one, sometimes referred to as the *kujira-jaku* ("whale foot") and equal to 1.25 feet, a 3-*shaku* rock comes to only 3.75 feet. Yet rocks as large as 8 feet in height may be found in the fourteenth-century gardens of Tenryūji and Kinkakuji. Fortunately, this disparity does not alter the significance of the proportional relationships set forth in the *Illustrations*, for such relationships are not dependent on absolute measurements.

17. A full discussion of the subject may be found in Christopher Williams, *Origins of Form* (New York: Architectural Book Publishing Company, 1981), pp. 114–20.

18. In fact, there is an ambiguity in the description of the Rock of the Spirit Kings in item 87 that allows either the single-rock or the multiple-rock interpretation. This dual interpretation may be carried back to the classical triad, that "flawless gem fit for a king" which was the subject of item 3. In the Japanese text of the *Illustrations*, item 3 appears next to the top right corner of figure D, which shows a pine tree and a rock formation labeled "Spirit Kings." This would seem to indicate that the "Heaven, Earth, and Man" triad is none other than the Rock of the Spirit Kings.

19. Arnheim, *Art and Visual Perception*, pp. 340–41.

20. *Ibid.*, p. 342.

21. *Ibid.*

22. *Ibid.*

23. *Ibid.*

24. The walkway appears in a woodblock print showing a bird's-eye view of the grounds of Ryōanji in the 1780 guide to Kyoto, *Miyako meisho zue*, comp. Ritō Akisato (reprint; Tokyo: Jinbutsu Ōrai Sha, 1967), pp. 684–85.

25. Gibson, *Perception of the Visual World*, pp. 138–44. Strictly speaking, five of the thirteen cues are given lesser status and regarded not as stimuli for the perception of space, but as "probable signs." The ratio of the two types remains roughly the same among those that are presented here.

26. *Ibid.*, p. 21.

27. *Ibid.*, p. 107.

28. *Ibid.*, p. 108.

29. *Ibid.*, p. 53.

30. Teiji Itoh, *Space and Illusion in the Japanese Garden*, trans. and adapted by Ralph Friedrich and Masajiro Shimamura (Tokyo: Weatherhill/Tankosha, 1973), p. 49.

31. Published in Shimizu and Wheelwright, *Japanese Ink Paintings*, fig. 17, p. 36.

32. George Rowley, *Principles of Chinese Painting* (Princeton, N.J.: Princeton University Press, 1959), p. 64.

33. Mitchell Bring and Josse Wayembergh, *Japanese Gardens: Design and Meaning* (New York: McGraw-Hill, 1981), p. 185.

34. Jack A. Hobbs, *Art in Context*, 3rd ed. (New York: Harcourt Brace Jovanovich, 1985), p. 246.

35. Gibson, *Perception of the Visual World*, p. 21.

36. Arnheim, *Art and Visual Perception*, p. 201.

37. Tadahiko Higuchi, *The Visual and Spatial Structure of Landscapes*, trans. Charles S. Terry (Cambridge, Mass.: M.I.T. Press, 1983), p. 84.

38. Gibson, *Perception of the Visual World*, p. 141. Gibson does not think that aerial perspective will ever be proved a "stimulus" for the perception of space, but believes it may be an indicator. To be classed as a stimulus, a depth cue must "rest on the geometry of optics."

39. [Frederick Law Olmsted], *Walks and Talks of an American Farmer in England*, vol. 2 (New York: G. P. Putnam, 1852), p. 154. Cited in Laura Wood Roper, *FLO: A Biography of Frederick Law Olmsted* (Baltimore: Johns Hopkins University Press, 1973), p. 70.
40. Rowley, *Principles of Chinese Painting*, p. 64.
41. Shimizu and Wheelwright, *Japanese Ink Paintings*, p. 174.
42. *Ibid.*, p. 170, and Kuck, *World of the Japanese Garden*, p. 161.
43. Johannes Itten, *The Art of Color: The Subjective Experience and Objective Rationale of Color*, trans. Ernst van Haagen (New York: Reinhold Publishing, 1967, 4th printing), p. 122.
44. The same technique has been used in the dry landscape gardens located at the headquarters (*honbō*) of Daitokuji and at Taizōin in the Myōshinji monastic complex, both in Kyoto.
45. Itten, *The Art of Color*, p. 122.
46. *Ibid.*
47. *Sakuteiki*, in NST 23:242, sec. 31. Shimoyama, p. 32.
48. Arnheim, *Visual Thinking*, pp. 270–71.

The Art We See: Cultural Values

The epigraph is from Wolfgang Bauer, *China and the Search for Happiness: Recurring Themes in Four Thousand Years of Chinese Cultural History*, trans. Michael Shaw (New York: Seabury Press, 1976), p. 187.
1. Ryusaku Tsunoda, Wm. Theodore de Bary, and Donald Keene, comps., *Sources of Japanese Tradition* (New York: Columbia University Press, 1961, 5th printing), p. 141.
2. *Ibid.*, p. 142. Cf. Yoshito S. Hakeda, *Kūkai: Major Works, Translated, with an Account of His Life and a Study of His Thought* (New York: Columbia University Press, 1972), pp. 145–46.
3. Arnheim, *Visual Thinking*, p. 2.
4. *Ibid.*
5. Frederick Law Olmsted, "The Yosemite Valley and the Mariposa Big Trees: A Preliminary Report (1865)," ed. Laura Wood Roper, *Landscape Architecture* 43 (October 1952): 20–21 .
6. Burton Watson, trans., *Records of the Grand Historian of China, Translated from the Shih-chi of Ssu-ma Ch'ien*, vol. 2 (New York: Columbia University Press, 1961), p. 26.
7. Kuck, *World of the Japanese Garden*, p. 43.
8. Hayakawa, *Garden Art of Japan*, p. 13.
9. William H. McCullough and Helen Craig McCullough, trans., *A Tale of Flowering Fortunes: Annals of Japanese Aristocratic Life in the Heian Period*, vol. 1 (Stanford: Stanford University Press, 1980), p. 280.
10. *Sakuteiki*, in NST 23:241, sec. 29.
11. Items 85 and 87 of the translation. Also see the discussion of the Rock of the Spirit Kings in connection with the Heaven, Earth, and Man triad in chapter 3.
12. Watson, *Records of the Grand Historian*, p. 26.
13. A color reproduction of this rock may be found in Kinsaku Nakane and Shigeo Okamoto, *Kyūtei no niwa, daimyō no niwa*, vol. 5 of *Nihon no teien* (Tokyo: Kōdansha, 1981), p. 53, lower right of photograph.
14. For a photograph of this rock without the pine, see Shūji Hisatsune, *Kyōto meien ki*, vol. 1 (Tokyo: Seibundō Shinkōsha, 1969), p. 118, bottom photograph, rock just above the one at the lower right.

15. Bauer, *China and the Search for Happiness*, p. 111.
16. Akira Naito, *Katsura: A Princely Retreat* (Tokyo: Kodansha International, 1977), p. 123.
17. Murasaki Shikibu, *The Tale of Genji*, trans. Arthur Waley (New York: Modern Library, 1960), p. 479.
18. Robert H. Brower and Earl Miner, *Japanese Court Poetry* (Stanford: Stanford University Press, 1961), p. 214.
19. Stephen A. Tyler, ed., *Cognitive Anthropology* (New York: Holt, Rinehart and Winston, 1969), p. 6.
20. Assumed into Shinto, sc. Ryōbu Shintō, a Shinto school that developed in the Kamakura period (1185–1333) and that applied the Shingon Buddhist graphical device of the two mandalas (diamond and womb) to a systematization of the Shinto pantheon.
21. See Keiji Uehara, ed., *Zōen daijiten* (Tokyo: Kajima Shoten, 1978), s.v. *suteishi*.
22. Soame Jenyns, *Japanese Pottery* (London: Faber and Faber, 1971), p. 251.
23. George Santayana, *The Sense of Beauty: Being the Outlines of Aesthetic Theory* (New York: Charles Scribner's Sons, 1936), p. 39.
24. *Ibid.*, p. 44.

Illustrations for Designing Mountain, Water, and Hillside Field Landscapes

BIBLIOGRAPHICAL NOTE

The basis of what is considered the standard text of *Senzui narabi ni yagyō no zu* is a scroll that bears the seal of Shinren'in, a subtemple of the Shingon-sect temple Ninnaji in Kyoto. The two colophons of the manuscript are dated Bun'an 5 (1448) and Bunshō 1 (1466). After the title, the name of the priest Zōen is given as the compiler of the text. That name occurs also at the beginning of the Chart of the Transmission that immediately precedes the two colophons. The attribution to Zōen is dubious. Even if the text was handed down from Zōen, (who, it would appear, predates the famous eleventh-century priest-gardener En'en Ajari), it exhibits many linguistic features of the fifteenth century.

The *Kokusho sōmokuroku*, vol. 3 (Tokyo: Iwanami, 1969), p. 808, lists five extant variants: in the Kyoto University Libraries, in the Historiographical Institute of Tokyo University, in the Nihon University Library, in the Sonkeikaku Library (the 1466 Maeda manuscript), and another copy formerly in the possession of the Shōkōkan Library of the Mito daimyo. It omits mention of the copy in the Mudōji Library of Enryakuji in Shiga Prefecture.

The basis of my translation was a collotype reproduction of the Maeda manuscript: *Senzui narabi ni yagyō no zu*, Sonkeikaku Sōkan (Tokyo: Ikutoku Zaidan, 1930). I collated this text with the variorum edition prepared by Yasushi Egami, "'Dōji kudensho tsuki Senzui narabi ni yagyō no zu' kōkan," in the journal *Bijutsu kenkyū* 247 (July 1966), pages 32–41, and 250 (January 1967), pages 22–40.

Four of the extant variants of *Senzui narabi ni yagyō no zu* date to the Edo period (1603–1868). On the basis of his textual collation, Egami has concluded that these four trace their origins not to the Maeda manuscript, but to an earlier variant of that manuscript no longer extant. The four Edo-period manuscripts are:

1. The Ōta manuscript, which derives its name from Professor Shōjirō Ōta of the Historiographical Institute of Tokyo University. The colophon is dated Jōō 3 (1654). Egami's textual study has produced evidence that suggests it was written soon after 1654.

2. The Nichidai manuscript, in the Nihon University Library in Tokyo. There is no colophon providing the date. Noting that the style of calligraphy is almost identical to that of the Ōta manuscript, Egami places it in the early Edo period, prior to the Mudōji and Kyōdai manuscripts. Like the Maeda manuscript, it is titled *Senzui narabi ni yagyō no zu*. Library records indicate the manuscript was obtained from Isseidō Shoten, a used book store in Kanda, Tokyo, on April 23, 1955.

3. The Mudōji manuscript, in the Mudōji Library of Enryakuji in Shiga Prefecture. The colophon is dated Kanpō 2 (1742) and, according to Egami, the copy is datable to that year. It bears the interior title *Gion-kyō narabi ni Sakuteiki, ryōkan gassatsu*, and the exterior title *Gion-kyō Senzui narabi ni yagyō no zu*.

4. The Kyōdai manuscript, in the Library of the Faculty of Agriculture of Kyoto University. There is no colophon providing the date, but the Kyōdai manuscript very closely resembles the Mudōji manuscript. Like the Mudōji manuscript, it bears the exterior title *Gion-kyō Senzui narabi ni yagyō no zu*. Library records indicate the manuscript was obtained from Hakushūdō, a used book store in Kyoto, on June 30, 1943.

All four Edo variants are very similar in content, but they differ from the Maeda manuscript in at least two important ways—they omit certain sections of the Maeda text, and they include an additional text entitled *Dōji kudensho*, at the end of which is found a substantial portion of the eleventh-century garden manual *Sakuteiki*. The illustrations in the Mudōji and Kyōdai manuscripts are simplified line drawings that lack the shading found in the Maeda illustrations. Those of both the Ōta and Nichidai manuscripts have light shading and are less stiff and more curvilinear than illustrations in the Maeda manuscript. The Edo variants enable us to substitute characters in the worm-eaten blanks of the Maeda manuscript, but it is not certain that they conform precisely with the text digested by the worms. All four Edo variants were originally bound with folded sheets in *fukurotoji* ("accordion") fashion. The Nichidai manuscript was later converted into a scroll.

Along with Egami's edition, I consulted the following:

1. Tokifuyu Yokoi, *Nihon teien hattatsu shi* (Tokyo: Sōgensha, 1940).

2. Osamu Mori, *Heian jidai teien no kenkyū* (Kyoto: Kuwana Bunseidō, 1945). Mori rearranges the text, and assigns the names of rocks that occur there to the unlabeled rocks in the illustrations.

3. Keiji Uehara, ed., *Kaisetsu Senzui narabi ni yagyō no zu, Sakuteiki* (Tokyo: Kajima Shoten, 1972). Although this is the most widely available, inexpensive, and portable edition, it is not entirely satisfactory. The annotation is rudimentary, and the author repeatedly begs the question by shrugging off problem areas as uncomplicated or reflections of mere superstition. Uehara apparently was unaware of Yasushi Egami's textual collation published in *Bijutsu kenkyū*, for he has not relied upon it to fill in the blanks in the Maeda manuscript.

4. Katsuo Saitō, *Nihon teien dentō no kiban*, vol. 1 of *Saitō Katsuo sakutei gihō shūsei* (Tokyo: Kawade Shobō Shinsha, 1976), pp. 88–132. The text is not reproduced in its entirety. Saitō's annotation is helpful; regrettably, however, sources are seldom cited for the author's interpretations. Included in this edition are high-quality reproductions of all of the illustrations in the Maeda manuscript.

TEXTUAL NOTES

1. Tung-fang Shuo was born in 160 B.C. in Shantung, China. In 138 B.C. he responded to an imperial proclamation issued by Emperor Wu of Han (Han Wu Ti) for men of genius to assist in the government. Han Wu Ti was the emperor who first conceived the idea of enticing the Immortals to his own estate—rather than sending expeditions in search of them—by re-creating the three Isles of the Immortals in his garden. Tung-fang Shuo's own intimate connection with the search for immortality may be judged from the following anecdote: "On one occasion he drank off some elixir of immortality which belonged to the Emperor, and the latter in a rage ordered him to be put to death. But Tung-fang So smiled and said, 'If the elixir was genuine, your Majesty can do me no harm; if it was not, what harm have I done?'" (*A Chinese Biographical Dictionary*, ed. Herbert A. Giles, s.v. "Tung-fang So").

2. The Five Colors—blue-green, red, yellow, white, and black—are associated with the Five Elements of Chinese cosmology. This fivefold division is extended also to directional orientation (east, west, north, south, and center) and to human nature (a person of the "Wood nature," and so forth, comparable to the Western astrological signs). These relationships are shown in figure 55. To "consider fully the relationships of Mutual Destruction and Mutual Production in respect to the Five Colors of rocks" means nothing less than bringing into a harmonious relationship in the garden three essential factors: (1) the client's nature, (2) the nature of the site, as determined by the various cosmic, geological, and climatological forces that come into play there, and (3) the aesthetic qualities of the materials used in the composition. These relationships are elaborated in item 2.

Fig. 55. The Five Elements of Chinese cosmology, correlated with the Five Colors and the Five Directions.

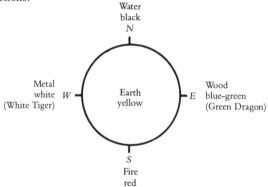

3. Stream valleys: *nosuji*, literally the "veins of the land." Geologists refer to these channels etched in the land as "stream valleys": "Stream valleys can be divided into two general types. Narrow V-shaped valleys and wide valleys with flat floors exist as the ideal forms, with many gradations between. In arid regions narrow valleys often have nearly vertical walls, while in humid regions the effect of mass wasting and slope erosion caused by heavy rainfall produce the typical V-shaped valley" (Frederick K. Lutgens and Edward J. Tarbuck, *Essentials of Geology* [Columbus, Ohio: Charles E. Merrill, 1982], p. 95).

4. Blue-green rock: the author is anxious to point out that there is no need to avoid the reverse relationship in the cycle of Mutual Destruction. That is, for a Wood person (blue-green) to face a yellow rock is destructive, but for an Earth person (yellow) to face a blue-green rock is fine. The reason for the special attention given blue-green rocks both here and at the end of the paragraph no doubt has to do with the fact that blue-green rocks were highly appreciated in China and Japan.

5. Red rock and nandina: the Japanese term *nantenjiku*, which refers not only to the plant but also to southern India, further reinforces the association with the direction south and the element Fire. The nandina (*Nandina domestica*) has terminal clusters of bright red fruits, one-quarter inch in diameter, and it is this characteristic that gives it "Fire." Note that only in the case of the red rock does Mutual Conjunction involve four (rather than three) elements. The number four is regarded as inauspicious in Japan, the rationale being that the Sino-Japanese word for four, *shi*, is homophonous with the word for death. The choice of four elements here rather than three is no doubt a way of especially cautioning the designer against the use of red rocks, which were as much to be avoided as blue-green rocks were appreciated. As stated above in the cycle of Mutual Production, "among the Five Colors red rocks are shunned."

6. The wisdom of siting a residence located in the Northern Hemisphere so that it faces south was, according to Xenophon, also recognized in Europe and by no less than Socrates, who asks rhetorically: "Now, supposing a house to have a southern aspect, sunshine during winter will steal in under the verandah, but in summer, when the sun traverses a path right over our heads, the roof will afford an agreeable shade, will it not?" (Xenophon, *Memorabilia*, bk. 3, ch. viii, in *The Memorabilia and Apology, the Economist, the Symposium, and Hiero*, trans. H. G. Dakyns, vol. 3, pt. 1 of *The Works of Xenophon* [London: Macmillan, 1897], p. 108).

7. Benzai Ten (Sarasvati) "in Hindu theology was the deity of a river bearing her name. Because of the destruction wrought by the river in flood time, she was associated with the violence of the natural elements and sometimes with warfare. On the other hand, because of the melodious murmurings of the river in its more placid moods, she also came to be worshiped as a goddess of music" (Takaaki Sawa, *Art in Japanese Esoteric Buddhism*, trans. Richard L. Gage [Tokyo: Weatherhill/Heibonsha, 1972], p. 30). Benzai Ten was first worshiped in Japan during the Nara period (710–94). It is unknown how popular the deity remained during the Heian period; however, in the late Kamakura period there was a renewed interest in Benzai Ten, and her popularity was fully restored in the Muromachi period (1392–1568). She was regarded as one of the Seven Gods of Fortune and, as the sole female deity among them, stood for feminine beauty and wealth. Her messenger is the white snake. *(Kodansha Encyclopedia of Japan* 5:296.)

8. The expression "and so forth and so on" (*unnun*), occurs in the *Illustrations* in items 8, 24, 31, 40, 41, and 52 (it has been dropped from the translation everywhere except in item 8). Its use is an indication that the author is not recording exhaustively all that he knows or has heard, but is instead selectively writing down what he regards as the key points.

9. Hōrai is the Sino-Japanese for P'eng-lai, one of three spirit mountains or Isles of the Immortals—P'eng-lai, Fang-chang, and Ying-chou—said to exist off the east coast of China and supposedly borne on the heads of giant turtles.

10. King: in his "The Three Obligations of the Ruler," the Han-period thinker Tung Chung-shu (ca. 179–104 B.C.) links the strokes composing the Chinese character *wang* 王, king, with the concepts Heaven (*t'ien* 天), Earth (*tu* 土), and Man (*jen* 人) as follows: "Those who in ancient times invented writing drew three lines and connected them through the middle, calling the character 'king' [王]. The three lines are Heaven, earth, and man, and that which passes through the middle joins the principles of all three. Occupying the center of Heaven, earth, and man, passing through and joining all three—if he is not a king, who can do this?" (*Ch'un-ch'iu fan-lu*, sec. 43, 11:5a–b; sec. 44, 11:6b–9b, in Wm. Theodore de Bary, Wing-tsit Chan, and Burton Watson, comps., *Sources of Chinese Tradition* [New York: Columbia University Press, 1960], p. 179). The character 玉, "gem," is created by adding a vertical stroke at the lower right corner of the character 王, "king."

11. The "ancient expression" 上玉國五賓中至 remains obscure to me, as I have not been able to find the original context in which it occurs.

12.   Bufo: *ka(ga)maku*. One can make sense of this word by assuming that it is a combination of *gama* (Bufo [Rock]) and the *ku* of *kahaku* (the "river god" referred to below figure O in lieu of the Bufo Rock). Osamu Mori does label the rock at the upper left corner of figure D the Bufo Rock (*Heian jidai teien no kenkyū*, fig. 23, p. 352). Mori assigns names of the rocks occurring in the text to all of the unlabeled rocks in the figures of the *Illustrations* (pp. 342–60). Unfortunately, he does not give his rationale for labeling the rocks as he does.

13.   Precious rock: *chinseki*. The size and shape of this horizontal foreground rock suggest it may be the type of rock that served as a key position for appreciating the garden and was referred to as a *reiseki* (Reverence Rock) or *reihaiseki* (Worship Rock). Mori labels it the *kagami-ishi*, or Mirror Rock. (*Heian jidai teien no kenkyū*, fig. 25, p. 355.)

14.   Master Rock. Compare figure N, where two examples of a pair of rocks—with the Never Aging Rock in the higher position—are shown. In each there is a somewhat smaller but similarly shaped rock to the lower right of the Never Aging Rock. From the explanation in item 4, we can assume that the smaller rock is the Master Rock.

15.   These three names occur nowhere else in the text. A rock of very special character such as is indicated here might well be of the type that is used in a tray landscape, or *bonseki*. Such a rock would command a rather large space, even though it is small. It should therefore be set at some distance from the other rocks in the composition.

16.   In figure 56, a path has been added to the grove of trees pictured in figure K. The plan view shows how the trees might be planted at the curve in the path so as to create the desired effect. The technique works psychologically to enhance the sense of depth.

Fig. 56.   How the trees in figure K might be planted at the curve of a path.

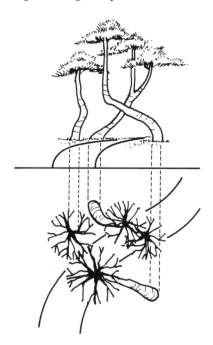

17. An alternate interpretation of the phrase "like parents watching over their child" is possible if one conjectures that the Chinese character 子, "child," is an error for 字, "Chinese character." In this case, the instruction to the initiate would be to plant the trees "as if you were composing the Chinese character 心, 'heart.'" The upright strokes of the character do bear a close resemblance to the pattern of the tree trunks in figure K, as may be judged from figure 57.

Fig. 57. The Chinese character for "heart" resembles the pattern of tree trunks in figure K.

18. Craggy mountains: the scenic effect pictured in figure L is not as far-fetched as it may appear. Along the coast of the Sea of Japan are scenes that bear a striking resemblance to this representation (see pl. 3).
19. Even trees such as this: the tree pictured, with twin leaders resembling a wishbone, is considered undesirable because it lacks a strong central leader.
20. In a garden viewed by the occupants of a residence on a daily basis, exotic or showy materials would become tiresome; yet, viewed only occasionally and in the proper setting, those same materials might produce a fascinating effect. A garden viewed by the members of a family in their daily life should be like their "daily bread," bland rather than spicy.
21. This pair of rocks is alternately referred to as the Yin & Yang (Stones) and the Male & Female (Stones). They are pictured in the upper right corner of figure O.
22. "Bufo" is short for *Bufo bufo*, one of the largest toads in Japan. Kōjin "fall into the category of malevolent deities (*aramitama*) which are juxtaposed in the Shintō tradition against beneficent deities (*nigimitama*). If properly reverenced, they are believed to protect worshipers" (*Kodansha Encyclopedia of Japan* 4:252). In figure O, we find that Kōjin, in the form of the Bufo Rock, is juxtaposed against the beneficent deity Benzai Ten, in the form of the Rock of the Spirit Kings.
23. Druggist's mortar (*yagen*): a utensil for crushing herbs used in traditional East Asian medicine, consisting of a hull-shaped metal trough and a wheellike roller on an axle that serves as the crusher (fig. 58). The contour of the pond bed from the shore to the lower

Fig. 58. Druggist's mortar (*yagen*), side view and cross-section.

level of the pond should resemble the shape of a *yagen* in cross-section—first convex and then concave as it reaches the lower level. This contour is also likened to a turtle's belly (*kamebara*) by Japanese garden makers. The proper pond bed shape is shown on the left (*a*) in figure 59. The contour on the right (*b*) is unacceptable, since it would require rocks twice as tall as those for the turtle belly contour to achieve the same effect, and these taller rocks would have to be braced with smaller rocks to keep them from toppling into the pond in the course of time. In traditional Japanese gardens, the pond bed was formed by tamping layers of clay and small stones to a thickness of one foot or so. This produced a highly durable, water-impermeable seal that was superior to present-day concrete in that it was not subject to cracking.

Fig. 59.   Desirable (*a*) and undesirable (*b*) contours for a pond bed.

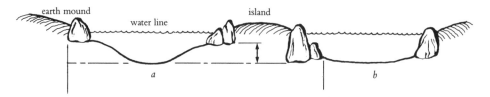

24.   Cyprinin carp (*Cyprinus carpio*) or *koi* have been bred as ornamental fish for nearly a thousand years in China and Japan, and tend to be high-strung. Crucian carp (*Carassius carassius*) or *funa* are less temperamental than *koi*, and therefore do not require the special hiding places. Nowadays, shelter for the carp is generally provided within the pond proper. The pond is dug a little deeper there, and a floating mat of rush or bamboo furnishes cover from above. The deeper water, along with the shade provided by the mat, keeps the area cooler in the summer and warmer in the winter.

25.   The commonplace rocks (*mumyōseki*) set offshore to create the impression of frolicking birds are no doubt the Frolicking Birds Rocks described in item 88 (see also fig. 11). As for the connection between the frolicking birds composition and the fox that lies in prey along the shore (*iso-gitsune*), the implication may be that the impression of birds taking wing should be so compelling that it would fool even a fox. Any birds alighting there would be protected, for the fox seeks to take its prey off guard. *Mumyōseki* are literally "nameless rocks," rocks with nothing special about them. The proper sense of *mumyōseki* may be grasped by juxtaposing it with the term *myōseki*, of which it is the negation. In item 26 the term *myōseki* ("named rocks") is used to refer to those rocks that play the leading roles in the garden composition. Such rocks have distinctive character-istics. For example, they may combine vertical and diagonal forces, or be three feet high and flat-topped. A significant portion of the *Illustrations* is given to discussing these named rocks. *Mumyōseki* may be compared to the nameless actors who serve as extras in a stage drama, such as for a milling crowd around the central action. Their presence contributes to the sense of naturalness and realism. Henceforth *mumyōseki* will be referred to as "nameless rocks" in order to maintain the contrast with *myōseki* that is present in the text.

26.   *Chi-musubi no in* most likely refers to the Touching the Earth mudra (*sokuchi-in*), a gesture of the right hand observed in seated Buddhist statues and described as follows: "It is formed by presenting the hand pendant in front of the right knee with the palm turned inward, the fingers extended downward touching or 'designating' the ground" (E. Dale Saunders, *Mudra: A Study of Symbolic Gestures in Japanese Buddhist Sculpture* [New York: Pantheon Books, 1960], p. 80). This gesture, by one account, symbolizes the Buddha's suppression of the demons, aided by the gods of earth. Such a ritual seems an appropriate one for consecrating the site at which a garden is to be built. Considering

that the named rock, the Happiness & Prosperity Rock (*fukkiseki*), occurs only in this context, and that the word *fukki* occurs elsewhere in the text only in regard to the Rock of the Spirit Kings (to the left of figure O we are told that "its purpose is to pray for happiness and prosperity"), it is tempting to speculate that the Happiness & Prosperity Rock is none other than the Rock of the Spirit Kings.

27.   One *shō* equals 0.477 U.S. gallon.

28.   The traditional Japanese system of linear measure used in the *Illustrations* is as follows:

$$10 \ bun = 1 \ sun$$
$$10 \ sun = 1 \ shaku$$
$$10 \ shaku = 1 \ j\bar{o}$$

The present *shaku* equals 0.99 foot; however, it is likely that the *shaku* used for surveying and therefore for laying out gardens at the time of the *Illustrations* was the *kujira-jaku* ("whale foot"), which equaled 1.25 *shaku*. For that reason, I have chosen to retain the word *shaku* in the translation. In addition, for the sake of simplicity and comparison, I have rendered *sun* and *bun* measures as decimal-point proportions of a *shaku* (e.g., 6 *sun*, 2 *bun* = 0.62 *shaku*).

29.   Mānasarovara, the "lake without heat" (Sanskrit: Anavatapta; Japanese: Munetsunochi) is present-day Manasarovar, located at 31° N., 81° 3' E., and is said to lie south of the Gandha-mādana mountains. (William Edward Soothill and Lewis Hodous, comps., *A Dictionary of Chinese Buddhist Terms* [Taipei: Ch'eng Wen Publishing Company, 1975], s.v. "Mānasarovara.") Lake Manasarovar now lies within the Chinese border in what was formerly Tibet, not very far from the borders of India and Nepal.

30.   The Hsün-yang is part of the Yangtze River near the city of Chiu-chiang in Chiang-hsi province. Mention of the Hsün-yang occurs in the first line of Po Chü-i's "Song of the Lute" (*P'i P'a Hsing*): "Hsün-yang on the Yangtze, seeing off a guest at night" (Burton Watson, trans. and ed., *The Columbia Book of Chinese Poetry: From Early Times to the Thirteenth Century* [New York: Columbia University Press, 1984], p. 249). Po Chü-i (772–846) has been a favorite Chinese poet in Japan ever since the Heian period. The Hsün-yang River is referred to in an allusion to Po Chü-i's "Song of the Lute" in the classic early thirteenth-century work by Kamo no Chōmei, *Hōjōki* (see *Hōjōki, Tsurezuregusa*, ed. Minoru Nishio, Nihon Koten Bungaku Taikei, vol. 30 [Tokyo: Iwanami Shoten, 1957], p. 38).

31.   There is no Emperor Kagamiyama among the emperors of Japan. Just which emperor the author intended is a matter of conjecture. A note in the margin suggests Emperor Kameyama (1259–74).

32.   Kōbō Daishi (also known as Kūkai, 774–835) introduced the Shingon sect of Buddhism to Japan. See chapter 4.

33.   A *chō* was a standard unit of land measuring 360 *shaku* by 360 *shaku*, or about 2.9 acres (or 4.6 acres if the larger *kujira-jaku* is adopted). It was used in laying out the Japanese capital (Heiankyō, now Kyoto) on the Chinese model. Aristocrats in the Heian period were allotted residential plots of so many *chō*, depending on their official rank and social position. A once-famous Heian garden, Shinsen'en, of which only a small portion remains today, "extended to a total of eight of these *cho* units: two on the east-west side and four on the north-south side" (Hayakawa Masao, *The Garden Art of Japan*, p. 35). In item 32, we are informed that the "illustrations presented above are for estates of between 4 and 8 *chō*." A 4-*chō* estate would probably have been in the shape of a square, with two units per side; an 8-*chō* estate would probably have been shaped like Shinsen'en, with its longest side oriented along an east-west axis.

34.   The asterisk denotes a rock mentioned nowhere else in the text. Edo variants of the *Illustrations* label the Attendant Rock(s) as recumbent.

35. There is a mandala-like arrangement of the Five Great Mystic Kings in the lecture hall (*kōdō*) at the temple Tōji in Kyoto, which, incidentally, is the temple of Kūkai. Four statues of this ninth-century wooden sculpture—Daiitoku, Kongō Yasha, Gundari, and Gōzanze—are grouped around the central image, Fudō (Acala). (*Kodansha Encyclopedia of Japan* 1:198, 200.)

36. Jens Jensen, the Danish-born American landscape designer who has been called "the Thoreau of the twentieth century," similarly recognized the value of respecting a plant's "home site" (*zashiki*), or home environment: "To try to force plants to grow in soil or climate unfitted for them and against nature's methods will sooner or later spell ruin. Besides, such a method tends to make the world commonplace and to destroy the ability to unfold an interesting and beautiful landscape out of home environment. Life is made rich and the world beautiful by each section developing its own beauty" (Jensen, *Siftings*, p. 46).

37. *Hyakunansō, kinkisō*, and *nekusa* are plant names that are no longer in the Japanese vocabulary. I have not yet been able to ascertain what plants these names refer to.

38. White chrysanthemums and asters may be seen peeking at one another through a fence in the *fusuma* (interior sliding wall panel) paintings located at the far left corner of the Chrysanthemum Room (Kiku no Ma) at Nishi Honganji in Kyoto.

39. Parallel branches may rub against one another and are aesthetically redundant. The upper of any two such branches should generally be shorter and lighter in feeling than the one below it. To this undesirable type of growth may be added two others that equally demand the pruner's attention: Crossing branches may rub against one another and are unattractive. And excess branches radiating from their "hubs" along the trunk should be pruned so as to leave no more than three or four "spokes." Generally, of course, whenever branches are crowded, the less desirable ones should be pruned to open up the the tree to air and sunlight.

40. This section may be regarded as a continuation from item 34, above.

41. The Rock of the Spirit Kings is, as the explanation on the left of figure O tells us, "the seat of . . . Benzai Ten." Considering that Benzai Ten's messenger is the white snake, the appearance of the snake here is perhaps not so surprising.

42. Kannon (Avalokitesvara) personifies compassion and is one of the most popular bodhisattvas in Japan. While it can take either male or female form, it is almost always represented as feminine in painting and sculpture. Mount Fudaraku (Sanskrit: Potalaka) is the paradise of Kannon known as the Pure Land, and was believed to exist in the sea off the southern coast of India. Kannon is often depicted in paintings seated on top of Mount Potalaka in her island paradise.

43. It may be that this composition of three flat-topped stones is an allusion to a three-posted torii like that of the Kaiko no Yashiro shrine in western Kyoto (torii are gatelike structures marking the entrance to a Shinto shrine or, as in the present case, a sacred space within the shrine compound). The torii at Kaiko no Yashiro is made of stone and enshrines a spring that is supposed to bubble up from the stream bed just beneath the pile of stones placed in the center of the three posts. There is a three-posted (actually, four-posted, as there is an extra column in the center) torii pictured in the Edo-period garden manual *Ishigumi sonoo no yaegaki den*. According to the explanation, it is located in the western part of Kyoto. (Keiji Uehara, ed., *Ishigumi sonoo no yaegaki den, kaisetsu* [Tokyo: Kajima Shoten, 1971], p. 14.) It is possible that it represents the torii at Kaiko no Yashiro.

44. A willow stump will generate new sprouts and thus create a pleasing effect. A pine stump, however, will soon rot and become infested with termites and the like.

BIBLIOGRAPHY

Arnheim, Rudolf. *Art and Visual Perception: A Psychology of the Creative Eye.* Berkeley: University of California Press, 1954. Revised edition published as *Art and Visual Perception: The New Version*, 1974.

————. *Visual Thinking.* Berkeley: University of California Press, 1969.

Barr, Charles. "CinemaScope: Before and After." *Film Quarterly* 16:4–24 (Summer 1963).

Bauer, Wolfgang. *China and the Search for Happiness: Recurring Themes in Four Thousand Years of Chinese Cultural History.* Translated by Michael Shaw. New York: Seabury Press, 1976.

Bring, Mitchell, and Josse Wayembergh. *Japanese Gardens: Design and Meaning.* New York: McGraw-Hill, 1981.

Brower, Robert H., and Earl Miner. *Japanese Court Poetry.* Stanford: Stanford University Press, 1961.

Bunnell, Lafayette H. *Discovery of the Yosemite, and the Indian War of 1851.* Chicago: Fleming H. Revell, 1880.

Chatelet, Albert. *Impressionist Painting.* New York: McGraw-Hill, 1962.

Conder, Josiah. *Landscape Gardening in Japan.* 2nd rev. ed. Tokyo: Maruzen, 1912.

De Bary, Wm. Theodore; Wing-tsit Chan; and Burton Watson, comps. *Sources of Chinese Tradition.* New York: Columbia University Press, 1960.

Dewey, John. *Art as Experience.* New York: Capricorn Books, 1958. 7th printing.

Donnell-Kotrozo, Carol. *Critical Essays on Postimpressionism.* Philadelphia: The Art Alliance Press, 1983.

Duke-Elder, Stewart, ed. *The Foundations of Ophthalmology*, Vol. 7 of *System of Ophthalmology.* St. Louis: C. V. Mosby, 1962.

Dyas, Robert. "Landscape Design with Prairie Plants." In *Prairie: A Multiple View*, edited by Mohan K. Wali, pp. 411–16. Grand Forks: University of North Dakota Press, 1975.

Eaton, Leonard K. *Landscape Artist in America: The Life and Work of Jens Jensen.* Chicago: University of Chicago Press, 1964.

Egami, Yasushi, ed. "'Dōji kudensho tsuki Senzui narabi ni yagyō no zu' kōkan" (Text Collation of the Mediaeval Book of Landscape Gardening, *Senzui narabini Yagyō no Zu Accompanied by Dōji Kudensho [sic]*). *Bijutsu kenkyū* (Journal of art studies), 247 (July 1966): 32–41 and 250 (January 1967): 22–40.

Focal Encyclopedia of Film and Television Techniques, The. Edited by Raymond Spottiswoodie *et al.* New York: Hastings House, 1969.

Focal Encyclopedia of Photography, The. Edited by A. Kraszna-Krausz *et al.* Vol. 2. London: Focal Press, 1965.

Gibson, James J. *The Perception of the Visual World.* Boston: Houghton Mifflin, 1950.

Gion-kyō Senzui narabi ni yagyō no zu (The "Gion canons" Illustrations for designing mountain, water, and hillside field landscapes); interior title *Gion-kyō narabi ni Sakuteiki, ryōkan gassatsu* (The "Gion canons" and the *Sakuteiki* combined in one volume). Ms. dated Kanpō 2 (1742), Mudōji Library of Enryakuji in Shiga Prefecture.

Gion-kyō Senzui narabi ni yagyō no zu (The "Gion canons" Illustrations for designing mountain, water, and hillside field landscapes). Ms. in the Library of the Faculty of Agriculture of Kyoto University, n.d.

Hakeda, Yoshito S. *Kūkai: Major Works, Translated, with an Account of His Life and a Study of His Thought.* New York: Columbia University Press, 1972.

Hall, Edward T. *Beyond Culture.* Garden City, N.Y.: Anchor Press/Doubleday, 1976.

Hayakawa, Masao. *The Garden Art of Japan.* Translated by Richard L. Gage. Tokyo: Weatherhill/Heibonsha, 1973.

Higuchi, Tadahiko. *The Visual and Spatial Structure of Landscapes.* Translated by Charles S. Terry. Cambridge, Mass.: M.I.T. Press, 1983.

Hisatsune, Shūji. *Kyōto meien ki* (Records of renowned Kyoto gardens). 3 vols. Tokyo: Seibundō Shinkōsha, 1969.

Hobbs, Jack A. *Art in Context.* 3rd ed. New York: Harcourt Brace Jovanovich, 1980.

Hōjōki. In *Hōjōki, Tsurezuregusa* (An account of my ten-foot-square hut, Essays in idleness), edited by Minoru Nishio. Nihon Koten Bungaku Taikei (Compendium of classical Japanese literature), vol. 30. Tokyo: Iwanami Shoten, 1957.

Itoh, Teiji. *Space and Illusion in the Japanese Garden.* Translated and adapted by Ralph Friedrich and Masajiro Shimamura. Tokyo: Weatherhill/Tankosha, 1973.

————. *The Gardens of Japan.* Tokyo: Kodansha International, 1984.

Itten, Johannes. *The Art of Color: The Subjective Experience and Objective Rationale of Color.* Translated by Ernst van Haagen. New York: Reinhold Publishing, 1967. 4th printing.

Jensen, Jens. *Siftings: The Major Portion of "The Clearing" and Collected Writings.* Reprint. Chicago: Ralph Fletcher Seymour, 1956.

Jenyns, Soame. *Japanese Pottery.* London: Faber and Faber, 1971.

Kaoku zakkō (A miscellany of reflections on architecture). Compiled by Nadari Sawada. N.p., Tenpō 13 (1842).

Kuck, Loraine. *The World of the Japanese Garden: From Chinese Origins to Modern Landscape Art.* Tokyo: Walker/Weatherhill, 1968.

Kurosawa, Akira. *Something Like an Autobiography.* Translated by Audie E. Bock. New York: Alfred A. Knopf, 1982.

Lutgens, Frederick K., and Edward J. Tarbuck. *Essentials of Geology.* Columbus, Ohio: Charles E. Merrill, 1982.

McCullough, William H., and Helen Craig McCullough, trans. *A Tale of Flowering Fortunes: Annals of Japanese Aristocratic Life in the Heian Period.* 2 vols. Stanford: Stanford University Press, 1980.

Miyako meisho zue (Pictures of celebrated places in the capital). Compiled by Ritō Akisato. Reprint. Tokyo: Jinbutsu Ōrai Sha, 1967.

Mori, Osamu. *Heian jidai teien no kenkyū* (A Study of Heian-period gardens). Kyoto: Kuwana Bunseidō, 1945.

Morrison, Darrel G. "Utilization of Prairie Vegetation on Disturbed Sites." Unpublished article.

Murasaki Shikibu. *The Tale of Genji.* Translated by Arthur Waley. New York: Modern Library, 1960.

Nakane, Kinsaku. *Kyoto Gardens.* Translated by Money L. Hickman. Hoikusha Color Books, vol. 9. Osaka: Hoikusha, 1965.

———— (text) and Shigeo Okamoto (photographs). *Kyūtei no niwa, daimyō no niwa* (Imperial gardens, daimyo gardens). Vol. 5 of *Nihon no teien.* Tokyo: Kōdansha, 1981.

Newsom, Samuel. *Japanese Garden Construction.* Tokyo: Domoto, Kumagawa, and Perkins, 1939.

Olmsted, Frederick Law. "The Yosemite Valley and the Mariposa Big Trees: A Preliminary Report (1865)." Edited by Laura Wood Roper. *Landscape Architecture* 43 (October 1952):12–25.

Roper, Laura Wood. *FLO: A Biography of Frederick Law Olmsted.* Baltimore: Johns Hopkins University Press, 1973.

Rowley, George. *Principles of Chinese Painting.* Princeton, N.J.: Princeton University Press, 1959.

Saitō, Katsuo. *Nihon teien dentō no kiban* (The traditional foundations of Japanese gardens). Vol. 1 of *Saitō Katsuo sakutei gihō shūsei* (Saitō Katsuo's selection of works on the techniques of garden making). Tokyo: Kawade Shobō Shinsha, 1976.

————. *Zukai Sakuteiki* (The illustrated *Sakuteiki*). Tokyo: Gihōdō, 1979. 7th printing.

Sakuteiki (Notes on garden making). In *Kodai-Chūsei geijutsuron* (Art theories of the ancient and medieval periods), edited by Tatsusaburō Hayashiya. Nihon Shisō Taikei (Compendium of Japanese thought), vol. 23. Tokyo: Iwanami Shoten, 1975. 2nd printing.

Santayana, George. *The Sense of Beauty: Being the Outlines of Aesthetic Theory.* New York: Charles Scribner's Sons, 1936.

Saunders, E. Dale. *Mudra: A Study of Symbolic Gestures in Japanese Buddhist Sculpture.* Bollingen Series, vol. 58. New York: Pantheon Books, 1960.

Sawa, Takaaki. *Art in Japanese Esoteric Buddhism.* Translated by Richard L. Gage. Tokyo: Weatherhill/Heibonsha, 1972.

Senzui narabi ni yagyō no zu (Illustrations for designing mountain, water, and hillside field landscapes). Collotype reproduction of the Bunshō 1 (1466) Ms. in the Sonkeikaku Library, published in the Sonkeikaku Sōkan series. Tokyo: Ikutoku Zaidan, 1930.

[*Senzui narabi ni yagyō no zu*] (untitled). Ms. dated Jōō 3 (1654). Ōta Ms., after Professor Shōjirō Ōta, Historiographical Institute of Tokyo University.

Senzui narabi ni yagyō no zu. Ms. in the Nihon University Library in Tokyo, n.d.

Shigemori, Mirei. *Nihon teien shi zukan* (Historical album of Japanese gardens). 26 vols. Tokyo: Yūkōsha, 1936-39.

Shimizu, Yoshiaki, and Carolyn Wheelwright, eds. *Japanese Ink Paintings from American Collections: The Muromachi Period*. Princeton, N.J.: The Art Museum, Princeton University, 1976.

Shimoyama, Shigemaru, trans. *Sakuteiki: The Book of Garden*. Tokyo: Town and City Planners, 1976.

Shinchō kōki (The chronicle of Nobunaga). Edited by Takahiro Okuno and Yoshihiko Iwasawa. Kadokawa Bunko, vol. 2541. Tokyo: Kadokawa, 1970. 2nd printing.

Soothill, William Edward, and Lewis Hodous, comps. *A Dictionary of Chinese Buddhist Terms: With Sanskrit and English Equivalents and a Sanskrit-Pali Index*. Reprint of Kegan Paul edition. Taipei: Ch'eng Wen Publishing Company, 1975.

Treib, Marc, and Ron Herman. *A Guide to the Gardens of Kyoto*. Tokyo: Shufunotomo, 1980.

Tsunoda, Ryusaku; Wm. Theodore de Bary; and Donald Keene, comps. *Sources of Japanese Tradition*. New York: Columbia University Press, 1961. 5th printing.

Tyler, Stephen A., ed. *Cognitive Anthropology*. New York: Holt, Rinehart and Winston, 1969.

Uehara Keiji, ed. *Ishigumi sonoo no yaegaki den, kaisetsu* ("Teachings on rock compositions and a full complement of garden enclosures," with commentary). Tokyo: Kajima Shoten, 1971.

———, ed. *Kaisetsu Senzui narabi ni yagyō no zu, Sakuteiki* ("Illustrations for designing mountain, water, and hillside field landscapes" and "Notes on garden making," with commentary). Tokyo: Kajima Shoten, 1972.

Watson, Burton, trans. *Records of the Grand Historian of China, Translated from the Shih chi of Ssu-ma Ch'ien*. 2 vols. New York: Columbia University Press, 1961.

———, trans. and ed. *The Columbia Book of Chinese Poetry: From Early Times to the Thirteenth Century*. New York: Columbia University Press, 1984.

Williams, Christopher. *Origins of Form*. New York: Architectural Book Publishing Company, 1981.

Wyman's Gardening Encyclopedia. Edited by Donald Wyman. New York: Macmillan, 1972. 2nd printing.

Xenophon. *The Memorabilia and Apology, the Economist, the Symposium, and Hiero*. Translated by H. G. Dakyns. Vol. 3, pt. 1 of *The Works of Xenophon*. London: Macmillan, 1897.

Yokoi, Tokifuyu. *Nihon teien hattatsu shi* (The historical development of the Japanese garden). Tokyo: Sōgensha, 1940.

Yoshinaga, Yoshinobu, *Composition and Expression in Japanese Traditional Gardens* (*Nihon teien no kōsei to hyōgen*). Tokyo: Shōkokusha, 1962.

Zōen daijiten (Encyclopedia of landscape gardening). Edited by Keiji Uehara. Tokyo: Kajima Shoten, 1978.